THE INVISIBLE

FLÂNEUSE?

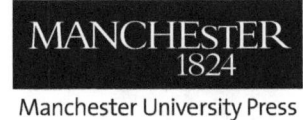

MANCHESTER
1824

Manchester University Press

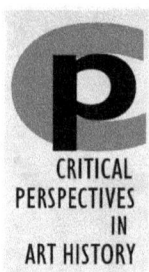

CRITICAL
PERSPECTIVES
IN
ART HISTORY

SERIES EDITORS
Tim Barringer, Marsha Meskimmon
and Shearer West

EDITORIAL CONSULTANTS
Nicola Bown, Robin Cormack, John House, John Onians,
Marcia Pointon, Alan Wallach and Evelyn Welch

The invisible *flâneuse?*

Gender, public space, and visual culture
in nineteenth-century Paris

EDITED BY ARUNA D'SOUZA
AND TOM MCDONOUGH

Manchester University Press

Published by Manchester University Press
Altrincham Street, Manchester M1 7JA
www.manchesteruniversitypress.co.uk

British Library Cataloguing-in-Publication Data is available

ISBN 978 0 7190 7942 9 paperback

First published by Manchester University Press in hardback 2006

This edition published 2008

Typeset by D R Bungay Associates, Burghfield, Berks

Contents

Illustrations

Contributors

Ting Chang is Assistant Professor of Art History at McGill University, Montreal. Her work has been published in the *Burlington Magazine* and the *Oxford Art Journal*. The present essay is a part of a book in progress on European collectors of Asian art in the late nineteenth century, a project supported by the Social Sciences and Humanities Research Council of Canada and the Getty Research Institute.

Aruna D'Souza is Assistant Professor of Art History at Binghamton University, State University of New York. She is the editor of *Self and History: A Tribute to Linda Nochlin* (2001), and is currently preparing a book entitled *Cézanne's Bathers, Biography, and the Erotics of Paint*, forthcoming from Penn State University Press.

Tom Gretton teaches in the History of Art department at University College London. He is finishing a monograph on the Mexican printmaker José Guadalupe Posada, and currently also publishing on the general-interest illustrated news magazines of Paris and London from c. 1850 to c. 1900. Forthcoming essays on this topic include "Signs for Labour-value in Printed Pictures After the Photomechanical Revolution: Main-stream Changes and Extreme Examples around 1900" (2005), and a discussion of the (rare) representation of "collateral damage" inflicted in colonial and imperial wars from the 1870s to around 1900.

Ruth E. Iskin is Assistant Professor in the Department of the Arts at Ben Gurion University. Her work has been supported by the Mellon at the Penn Humanities Forum, University of Pennsylvania, the Ahmanson-Getty at UCLA and the Killam at the University of British Columbia. Her Ph.D. is from UCLA, Department of Art History, and her essays have been published in the *Art Bulletin*, *Discourse*, and *Nineteenth-Century Contexts*. Her book, *Impressionisms, Parisian Consumer Culture and Modern Women* is forthcoming from Cambridge University Press.

Marni Kessler is Assistant Professor of nineteenth-century European Art in the Kress Foundation Department of Art History at the University of Kansas. She received her Ph.D. from Yale University. She is currently completing *Sheer Material Presence, or the Veil in Late Nineteenth-Century French Avant-Garde Painting*, a book that links the phenomenon of the veil to avant-garde art practice, medical theories, and architectural conditions in nineteenth-century Paris. She has published articles in the *Art Bulletin* and the *Woman's Art Journal* and has forthcoming essays in *Nineteenth-Century Contexts* and *Picturing Power: The New York Chamber of Commerce, Portraiture, and its Uses*, ed. Karl Kusserow (Columbia University Press).

Simon Leung teaches contemporary art history, critical theory and new genre in the Studio Art Department at the University of California, Irvine. His solo museum exhibition "Proposal for The Side of the Mountain," an opera/film/sculpture, was presented at the Santa Monica Museum of Art in 2002. His work has been shown at the Whitney Biennial (1993) and the Venice Biennale (2003); also at the Museum of Modern Art; PS1 Museum; NGBK (Berlin); the Art Institute of Chicago; Museum of Contemporary Art (LA MOCA); Generali Foundation (Vienna); MIT List Visual Arts Center (Cambridge, Mass.); Kunsthalle Fredericianum (Kassel); and the International Museum of Surfing (Huntington Beach). Leung's recently published writings appeared in *Surface Tension: Problematics of Site* (2003); *Negotiations in the Contact Zone* (2003); and *radiotemporaire* (2002). He is co-editor of the anthology *Theory in Contemporary Art Since 1985* (2004).

Tom McDonough is Assistant Professor of Art History at Binghamton University. He is the editor of *Guy Debord and the Situationist International: Texts and Documents* (2002), and has written extensively on urbanism and modern subjectivity. He is currently preparing a book on montage and French culture in 1968.

Linda Nochlin is the Lila Acheson Wallace Professor of Modern Art at the Institute of Fine Arts, New York University. In 2004, she was the Norton Professor at Harvard University, where she gave a series of lectures titled "Bathers, Bodies, Beauty: The Visceral Eye." She is currently co-curating an exhibition at the Brooklyn Museum of Art on "Neo-Feminism" with Maura Reilly.

Helen Scalway is an artist based in London, concerned with representations of the experience of negotiating the city. She studied at The London Institute and is currently a Research Associate in the Department of Cultural Geography, Royal Holloway College, London University. Among other city projects she has produced an artist's book, *Travelling Blind*, the result of loitering on the London Underground to ask Tube passengers to draw 'their' London Underground networks.

Greg M. Thomas is Associate Professor at the University of Hong Kong, where he teaches various aspects of Western art and cross-cultural interaction. A specialist in nineteenth-century France, he is the author of *Art and Ecology in Nineteenth-Century France: The Landscapes of Théodore Rousseau* (2000) and various essays on nineteenth-century art.

Janet Wolff is Professor of Arts at Columbia University. From 1991 to 2001 she was Director of the Program in Visual and Cultural Studies at the University of Rochester, after teaching for a number of years at the University of Leeds in England. She is the author of several books, including *The Social Production of Art* (1981), *Aesthetics and the Sociology of Art* (1983), *Feminine Sentences* (1990), *Resident Alien* (1995), and *AngloModern* (2003).

1

Introduction

Aruna D'Souza and Tom McDonough

The twelve essays assembled in this volume had their origin in a session of the 2001 annual conference of the College Art Association, in a panel for which we had asked participants to reconsider the assumption that women's experience of nineteenth-century modernity was severely circumscribed by social proscriptions regarding their occupation of the city's public spaces.[1] We sought, in other words, to extend and even question the dominant model within feminist art history that had been developed in the middle years of the 1980s by Janet Wolff and Griselda Pollock – a model that, however fruitful, had been undermined both by the discovery of significantly more complex spatial practices of women in this period, and by examinations of masculine anxieties embodied in the *flâneur* that had weakened claims of his confident appropriation of the urban realm. These challenges, arising largely outside the discipline of art history (in film studies, urban history, literary theory, and the like), had yet to be fully assimilated into our understanding of the roles played by gender and urban life in representations of women in the city that Walter Benjamin famously characterized as the "capital of the nineteenth century"; it is our hope that this book, like the panel from which it derived, will contribute to that assimilation and to the consolidation of a new model for understanding women's experience of public space during this crucial moment in the articulation of a culture of modernity.

These questions surrounding the paradigms of the *flâneur/flâneuse* have more than a mere historical interest. Indeed, the widespread contemporary fascination with nineteenth-century Paris as a crucible for modernity (that dialectical notion of modernity first adumbrated by Benjamin in his great essays of the 1930s) dates back only about a generation, that is to the later 1970s and early 1980s. This timing is by no means coincidental: it corresponds rather precisely to a moment of great restructuring in Western Europe and North America, a shift that has been variously characterized as that from Fordism to post-Fordism or, more generally, from modernity to post-modernity. The shift had its urban component as well, seen most clearly in Thatcherite England and, a little later, in Reagan-era America; it was marked by a displacement of an urban underclass and the reconquering – in the wake of the upheavals of the 1960s – of the city centers for a new segment of the middle class. This spatial restructuring was accompanied by a cultural celebration of urban "dynamism" in the work of many neo-expressionists or the avatars of graffiti art (although graffiti itself cannot by any means be considered simply a celebration). For critical historians, these diverse social and cultural phenomena appeared to find an echo in an earlier moment of fundamental transformation: the advent of modernity and its characteristic cultural modalities in the years around the mid-nineteenth century, a transformation experienced and registered most acutely in Paris.

Hence the historical study of this period was a choice of more than antiquarian interest; it seemed to open routes to a better understanding of our own era of reaction and retreat. Not least among the transformations was the paradoxical role of gender within this new dispensation: if the workforce was becoming increasingly feminized, with the massive expansion of a tertiary sector of service labor, the culturally dominant representations of women were decidedly domestic, with a return to idealized images of homemakers and mothers. The city was again coded as a site of (white, masculine) pleasure, and hence as a potential threat to bourgeois femininity – even as lived experience provided examples of a tremendous variety of spatial practices across different genders, classes, and ethnicities. Such contemporary dichotomies were the immediate motivation for the examination of the historical condition of cultural invisibility that Wolff termed the "*flâneuse*." We should not separate the problematic of the present-day conjunction of the terms "woman" and "the city" – with all the competing *and* complementary claims of ideology and social practice thereby entailed – from our studies of nineteenth-century discourses. Between these two very different moments runs the thread of connection Elizabeth Wilson has so perceptively described: women have continued to be "an irruption in the city, a symptom of disorder, and a problem."[2]

The appearance of these symptoms within the arts and, more generally, within the sphere of nineteenth-century visual culture, is the subject of the essays collected in this book. Drawing on a large interdisciplinary body of scholarship, the authors track the elusive *flâneuse* in and out of visibility across a variety of visual media, while also calling into question the fictive mastery of her male counterpart. The limitations of such bourgeois discursive constructs as the *flâneur/flâneuse* are examined, as they confront their class and racial others – whether in the cities of the "Orient" or within the depths of Paris itself. In this introduction, we wish to accomplish a more modest task: to provide a summary history of the debate around the "*flâneuse*" within art history and the ends to which this concept has been deployed, and to suggest the multiple directions taken by recent scholarship both within and outside the discipline – scholarship which, along with that presented here, promises to transform our understanding of that troubling couple, women and the city.

We might begin our history by noting that Wolff's 1985 essay on "The Invisible *Flâneuse*: Women and the Literature of Modernity" was something of a digression from her primary research concerns of that time. If her foremost interest in these years was directed to the operative role of culture in the relationship between class and gender in the nineteenth century – and particularly in the question of social and sexual segregation into "public" and "private" spheres[3] – the "*flâneuse*" article was somewhat anomalous: less a historical study than a salvo launched against a critical body of writings on modern urban life that she characterized as "the literature of modernity." Significantly, although it opened with a discussion of the implications of Max Weber's analysis of rational-legal society – with its emphasis on the separation of office from home – for our understanding of gender, Wolff asserted that ultimately she was uninterested in "the more orthodox sociological analyses of modernity."[4] Neither Weber, then, nor Norbert Elias were the authors of that "literature of modernity" she took as her subject; this consisted, rather, of

> the more impressionistic and essayistic contributions of those writers who locate the specifically "modern" in city life: in the fleeting, ephemeral, impersonal nature of encounters in the urban environment, and in the particular world-view which the city-dweller develops.[5]

These writers included sociologists Georg Simmel and Richard Sennett and, in their capacity as literary critics, authors Charles Baudelaire, Walter Benjamin, and Marshall Berman. Although selective in the extreme, the constitution of this corpus had a particular logic: it isolated two moments (Simmel and Benjamin on one hand, Sennett and Berman on the other) that bracketed the twentieth century's anxious concern to define modernity, both of which had looked back to Baudelaire for evidence and inspiration. Wolff's aim in "The Invisible *Flâneuse*" was, as she described it, to consider those accounts "from the point of view of gender divisions in 19th-century society."[6]

That the literature of modernity had remained largely silent on the subject of those divisions would be Wolff's contention, a conclusion surely influenced by her colleagues within British feminist sociology, who were contemporaneously critiquing the persistent absence of considerations of gender within their own discipline. In the early 1980s, Margaret Stacey had described two possible accounts of the division of labor, the first of which addressed its role in *production* and the social control of workers (i.e., the securing of the class order), and the second of which addressed its role in *reproduction* and the social control of women (i.e., the securing of the gender order).[7] From its origins in the nineteenth century, sociology had taken the former and its sites (the marketplace, the state apparatus) as its primary subject, neglecting the latter and its spatial locus (the home). The discipline at this formative moment consisted precisely of a group of male authors, writing for a male audience, attempting to explain and if possible control "the immense changes which were taking place in the public arena and which altered the previously understood social order in ways which many found profoundly worrying."[8]

Sociology, then, had traditionally concentrated on a public realm of social institutions and activities from which women had largely been excluded; these latter had been consigned and confined to the private realm of the family[9] – relegated, that is, to a condition of disciplinary invisibility, excluded a priori from its concerns. Feminist sociologists called for a critical examination of this dichotomy between public and private, an analysis that would constitute the gender order

> as integral to the concept of society, and as, potentially, primary. By addressing the most basic social division of patriarchy, male and female spheres, we begin to ask fundamental questions about the social patterning of gender.[10]

These scholars, in other words, noting the very clear line of demarcation between public and private that their discipline's founders had unwittingly helped to define, would conclude that social space was structured at some foundational level by gender difference.

Wolff would transpose the feminist critique of orthodox sociology on to her object, the hybrid literature of modernity. As she succinctly stated at the opening of her article, that literature "describes the experience of men. It is essentially a literature about transformations in the public world and in its associated consciousness."[11] Its authors – sociologists, social commentators of one sort or another – like their mainstream brethren consistently ignored the private realm, the domestic arena that was women's primary domain. Its protagonists, "invoked to epitomize the experience of modern life," were invariably male figures: the dandy, the stranger, the *flâneur*.[12] Within these academic essays, literary prose, and poetry, Wolff contended, women were largely absent; confined to the home, to "the invisible arena of the private," they fell outside the purview of the pseudo-sociological gaze of the literature of modernity. Such a literature excluded the possibility of feminine equivalents to its heroes of modern life: "the solitary and independent life of the *flâneur* was not open to women."[13] The sexual division of public from private in the nineteenth century prohibited women from strolling alone in the city – hence, a feminine version of the *flâneur*, Wolff flatly stated, did not exist.

However, as her title suggested, the critical question surrounding the *flâneuse* was not simply one of her absolute non-existence, but one of her occlusion from a patriarchal discourse on the modern city. Gender, that is, would need to be seen as mapped not only *on to* the divide between public and private, but also *across* it: this would be the challenge ultimately posed by Wolff in the "*flâneuse*" essay. Strictly speaking, there may have been no female equivalents of the *flâneur* (George Sand notwithstanding), but there were indeed women active in the public realm. In one sense, the literature of modernity may be understood as a controlling mechanism for regulating *the ways in which women became visible in public*. Hence when women did appear in these writings, they were clearly positioned within a conceptual hierarchy: "Women only appear . . . through their relationships with men in the public sphere, and via their illegitimate or eccentric routes into this male arena – that is, in the role of whore, widow or murder victim."[14] – as, in other words, subordinate or determined subjects in relation to a public realm of male concerns. Something similar was true for women at the other end of the social spectrum, for, that is, the *haute bourgeoises* whose careful attention to fashion was a public sign of their husbands' wealth and position. And among middle-class women "the establishment of the department store in the 1850s and 1860s," Wolff noted, "provided an important new arena for [their] legitimate public appearance."[15] The invisibility of these women revealed the necessity for a feminist literature of modernity, one that would undertake "the gradual opening up of areas of social life and experience which to date have been obscured by the partial perspective and particular bias of mainstream sociology."[16] This would entail a thoroughgoing theorization of gender in relation to modernity: on one hand, a critical examination of the "oversocialization" of the public realm, so that the complexity of "private" behaviors such as consumption might be recovered;[17] and on the other hand, a concomitant socialization of the private realm, so that the domestic arena of the home might be seen as fully embedded in the same processes of modernization that were affecting the "public" world beyond.

Wolff's 1985 text was above all else a critique of the academic gaze of her discipline, that of sociology *qua* "literature of modernity"; her self-proclaimed task was to signal its "partial perspective and particular bias" in the name of feminist revisionism.[18] Three years later Griselda Pollock, her colleague at Leeds, extended that task to the disciplinary gaze of art history in "Modernity and the Spaces of Femininity"[19] – specifically, to the social art-historical account of French Impressionism, a movement whose recent analysis by T. J. Clark had profoundly altered the disciplinary terrain.[20] In her response to what was seen by many feminist art historians to be at once a rich and productive examination of the period and an extremely partial one, Pollock took Clark to task for his problematic delineation of modernity: if he had replaced its superficial definition as simply being "of one's time" with a much more complicated picture of a set of social relations that took place within the new spaces of capitalism – the Second Empire's realms of "leisure, consumption, the spectacle, and money"[21] – his understanding of the role of gender and sexuality in those spaces (and in their representation, a central concern in Clark's chapters on Manet's *Olympia* and the *Bar at the Folies-Bergère*) remained lacking. Though Clark "nods in the direction of feminism by acknowledging that these paintings imply a masculine viewer/consumer," Pollock wrote, "the manner in which this is done ensures the normalcy of that position leaving it below the threshold of historical investigation and theoretical analysis."[22]

Clark, in other words, had failed to interrogate the masculine viewpoint of his "painting of modern life." That phrase was an adaptation, of course, from Baudelaire's famous 1863 essay on the draftsman Constantin Guys, "The Painter of Modern Life."[23] Art historians had long utilized this essay to align the artist and *flâneur*, extending Baudelaire's homage to Guys to Impressionism more broadly,[24] and for Wolff it was a founding moment of the literature of modernity in its celebration of the solitary male stroller.[25] Pollock would develop this insight further by analyzing the *flâneur*-artist's position within vision through a critical examination of his look. In her words:

The *flâneur* symbolizes the privilege or freedom to move about the public arenas of the city observing but never interacting, consuming the sights through a controlling but rarely-acknowledged gaze. . . . The *flâneur* embodies the gaze of modernity which is both covetous and erotic.[26]

The site of pleasurable looking, this look actively cast women as passive, erotic objects, subjecting them to a kind of voyeuristic control; it was in this sense that the visual purview of the bourgeois stroller – now the representative of middle-class masculinity in its entirety – became thoroughly implicated in issues of gender. In such terms, we should hear the echo of feminist accounts of vision and Lacanian psychoanalysis by scholars such as Laura Mulvey and Jacqueline Rose, published in the pages of *Screen* in the 1970s and early 1980s, and central to Pollock's understanding of a properly feminist critique of art history.[27] Hence Pollock located the power of the *flâneur* in the particular organization of the visual field, in other words in his claim to the male look – a visual stake that was both inscribed within and inscribing of the categories of sexual difference, the gender order. The *flâneur*-artist's subject position was predicated upon the availability of public space to his vision, such that sexual difference was "the product of a lived sense of social locatedness, mobility and visibility, in the social relations of seeing and being seen."[28]

One could not, in sum, simply map women on to the already existing and hith-erto unexamined categories of modernity, modernism, and sexuality; for Pollock the issue became one of vision and its limits, of the politics of representation in the nineteenth century. It was the organization of urban space according to the terms of the male look that made it impossible for women to operate as active participants in the public world: reduced to an erotic object of vision, rather than its subject, the bourgeois woman was excluded from a particular experience of modernity. But Pollock also disputed the notion, shared by Clark and Wolff, that the public, mascu-line arena could be straightforwardly identified with the "spaces of modernity." On the contrary, she argued that the spaces most characteristic of modern experience were not as clearly marked as the division of the bourgeois world (according to the model of the separation of spheres) into public/male and private/female would have it. Returning to those same images that Clark had treated in his account of modern-life painting in Second Empire Paris – works such as *Olympia* or *Bar at the Folies-Bergère*, or images of *cafés-concerts* and music halls by Manet, Degas, and others – Pollock discovered that modernity was not represented as taking place in exclusively masculine, because public, domains: rather, the spaces of modernity were in fact marginal spaces, those in which the city's "new subjective experiences of exhilaration and alienation, pleasure and fear, mobility and confinement, expan-siveness and fragmentation," were most intense.[29] These spaces of intersection happened to be sites in which bourgeois men came into contact with women who were sexually available (prostitutes), or at least imagined to be such (working-class women). They were places in which cross-gender, but also cross-class, encounters were negotiated in monetary terms – places in which the female body was reconceived as a commodity.

To recode the city according to this more complex spatial division was to reposition gender at the center of historical analysis, a criterion that Clark's account had failed to meet in his almost total privileging of class:

> The encounters pictured and imagined are those between men who have the freedom to take their pleasures in many urban spaces and women from a class subject to them who have to work in those spaces often selling their bodies to clients. . . . Undoubtedly these exchanges are structured by relations of class but these are thoroughly captured within gender and its power relations. Neither can be separated or ordered in a hierarchy. They are historical simultaneities and mutually inflecting.[30]

Bourgeois women precisely were excluded from these urban spaces. Drawing what she called a "mental map" of Paris, Pollock described a city divided into the domains of the fallen woman and the *femme honnête*, organized by the terms of a discourse about femininity that defined the respectability of bourgeois women according to those sites about which they had or did not have knowledge: the private spaces of the domestic sphere and the sites of consumption and display in the public realm on one hand, and those marginal, sexually fraught or at least ambiguous places on the other. It is no coincidence, then, that those examples Pollock provided of the ways in which this exclusion was effected in lived experience were themselves fully embedded in representation, that they functioned on the level of reputation and not on the level of a literal segregation:

> For bourgeois women, going into town mingling with crowds of mixed social composition was not only frightening because it became increasingly unfamiliar, but because it was *morally dangerous*. . . . The public space was officially the realm of and for men; for women to enter it entailed unforeseen risks. . . . For women, *the public spaces thus construed were where one risked losing one's virtue, dirtying oneself; going out in public and the idea of disgrace were closely allied*.[31]

Beyond its implications for an understanding of everyday life in nineteenth-century Paris, Pollock's argument had particular consequences for art historical analysis. Because the Impressionist artist's look, as constructed in his [*sic*] paintings, was coincident with that of the *flâneur*, the women artists associated with the movement – Pollock was particularly interested here in Berthe Morisot and Mary Cassatt – were in a notably disadvantaged position. As women of a certain social status, they were subject to the same types of dissuasions and exclusions in their daily lives as other members of their gender and class; as Impressionists, they were doubly segregated, for they could not admit to knowledge of those sites that constituted the "painting of modern life" on which the movement staked its artistic importance. Whether or not Cassatt and Morisot had ever been to the Folies-Bergère, the Moulin Rouge, or the *café-concert*, they could not represent those sites and maintain their status as respectable women; their roles as women and as artists

invariably contradicted each other according to the ideological constructions of
femininity at the time. The invisibility of the *flâneuse*, in other words, rendered the
position of the female artist if not invisible, then at least very difficult.

While accepting the basic premise of Wolff's argument – that the "historical asymmetry" between being a woman and being a man in Paris in the later nineteenth
century resulted in an unequal access to those experiences traditionally defined as
modern – Pollock employed a significantly different theoretical construct, one
which depended upon a particular deployment of the notion of ideology. Her argument developed a range of ideas regarding the "politics of representation" –
Marxist, psychoanalytic, semiotic – that had circulated around the journal *Screen*
in the 1970s and 1980s, most significantly the idea that images actively produce ideology, rather than being merely reflective or illustrative of it. Drawing upon the
work of Marxist philosopher Louis Althusser, these writers treated cultural practices as signifying or semiotic systems, "sites that produce meanings and positions
from which those meanings are consumed."[32] Not necessarily congruent with the
entire field of social existence, such signifying systems nonetheless determined the
way in which the subject understood the world of social relations. Their production and reproduction in culture ensured the production and reproduction of subjects in ideology.

According to this theoretical lens, the terms of the *bourgeoise*'s exclusion from
the sites of modernity were treated by Pollock as the very means by which she was
constructed as a (gendered) subject in later nineteenth-century French society: the
middle-class woman's spatial purview (or lack thereof) was one of the mechanisms
by which a definition of a class-specific femininity was secured. From this point of
view, it is logical that Pollock would have limited her "mental map" to the spaces
represented in Impressionism, and to the way in which such representation was
structured, rather than mapping practices both "representable" *and* "unrepresentable." (She did, however, concede that there was "nonetheless an overlap
between the purely ideological maps and the concrete organization of the social
sphere."[33]) Measuring these ideological constructions negatively against the actuality of lived experience, it was the very distance of this cosseted view of feminine
inaccessibility to urban space from the actuality of female participation in Parisian
street life (the bourgeois promenade, the department store, new spaces of recreation and leisure) that provided the measure of ideology's power to construct subjective experience.

The danger here, of course, is that ideology comes to seem a straitjacket, a closed
structure impervious to change or critical intervention. (Although it should be
noted that Pollock did claim that artists like Morisot and Cassatt had both worked
within and, at times, subverted the institutional and formal framework in which
they had made their art, so that "those protocols of painting defined as initiating
modernist art – articulation of space, repositioning of the viewer, selection of location, facture, and brushwork" could properly be identified as the means by which

these artists "invested [the private sphere] with meanings other than those ideolog-
ically produced to secure it as the site of femininity."[34]) This is by no means to deny
the particular social limitations placed on art's producers, and women generally, by
their specific gender and class identities at a given historical moment, but one may
still wish to note the problems involved in asserting the all-powerful ideology of the
separation of spheres even as women clearly did claim a status within public space
which was not that of the "fallen woman." As Elizabeth Wilson asks in an article
titled "The Invisible *Flâneur*" (1992), her response to Pollock and Wolff: "is it
appropriate to counter this interpretation of an ideology by recourse to empirical
fact?"[35]

The question is a crucial one, and her answer is no less apposite: "Ideology
thus becomes a rigid and monolithic monument of thought. By an inversion of
'reflectionist' theories of ideology, instead of ideology mirroring reality, reality
becomes but a pale shadow of ideology, or even bears no relation to it at all."[36] As
Wilson points out, such a vision of ideology is not only historically limiting, it is
also politically enervating, producing the image of a seamless structure of thought
arrayed against women, one that disallows in advance any reply, any transformation. Yet the nineteenth-century "separation of spheres" was no monolith, nor for
that matter was Impressionism. Both Wolff and Pollock accepted the concept –
developed in historical studies of the period – that society clearly had been organized into public and private lives, and that this organization was closely related to
gender difference; although this was posited by Wolff and Pollock as a social construction rather than a simplistic reflection of society itself, it had been nonetheless "extremely influential in the creation of a specifically middle-class way of life
and self-identity in this period."[37] Wilson counters this claim by pointing out that,
for all its coding as "feminine," the domestic sphere was as much a space of masculine dominance as the public world, and that the private realm of the home was
the site of female work (by domestic servants and bourgeois mothers). Similarly, if
one broadened one's view of the contested sites of modernity upon which
Impressionist practice concentrated and included the private spaces of the home
as an equally valid site for the constitution of the bourgeois world at the end of the
nineteenth century, Cassatt and Morisot might reassume their centrality in the art
history of the period.

For Wilson, the *flâneur* cannot be understood as a descriptive account of masculine experience of the city, but as "a mythological or allegorical figure who represented what was perhaps the most characteristic response of all to the wholly
new forms of life that seemed to be developing: ambivalence."[38] The *flâneur* was
not a figure of either/or exclusions (masculine or feminine, public or private),
but embodied precisely the undecided, the uncertain, in bourgeois experience of
the city. As such, he needs to be interrogated on the basis of the types of anxieties he assuages. Not least among such anxieties were those relating mutually to
sexuality and public space, terms whose meanings were undergoing fundamental
and troubling shifts during this period. Both, that is, were being subsumed into

the marketplace as commodities, goods whose control escaped the purview of the individual subject. This cleaving of sexuality and public space to the market would put masculine authority at risk precisely because it troubled the fiction of mastery and control embodied in the doctrine of the separation of spheres. The commodity mediated between public and private domains, clouding any clear boundary between the two; in fact, the so-called "public" life organized around the *flâneur* "was played out in a zone that was neither quite public nor quite private, yet which partook of both"[39]– a zone that included the cafés, department stores, arcades, and boulevards of the city, spaces in which the commodity had full sway. The metropolis must, then, be read not as the instrument or unproblematic site of masculine authority, but as the space which puts that desired authority at risk. The *flâneur*, then, is a compensation, a defense mechanism against the threats posed by his environment. As such, Wilson concludes that

> there could never be a female *flâneur*, for this reason: that the *flâneur* himself never really existed, being but an embodiment of the special blend of excitement, tedium and horror aroused by many in the new metropolis, and the disintegrative effect of this on the masculine identity. . . . He is a figure to be deconstructed, a shifting projection of angst rather than a solid embodiment of male bourgeois power. . . . He floats with no material base, living on his wits, and, lacking the patriarchal discourse that assured him of meaning, is compelled to invent a new one.[40]

Wilson's insistence on the *flâneur* as an anxious figure, rather than a representation of actual masculine experience, might prompt a revisiting of Pollock's essay, "Modernity and the Spaces of Femininity." For Pollock the *flâneur*, as bearer of the gaze, is an instantiation of patriarchal power, positioning women as the objects of an erotic and covetous look. Wilson's argument reminds us, despite its rather offhanded dismissal of the feminist rereading of Lacan which subtends Pollock's work,[41] that if the look is a way of taking the other as an object, it is actually in an effort to repair a fundamentally lacking self. In fact, rather than dismissing psychoanalysis as a useful tool for feminist critique as Wilson is wont to do, one might say that the problem lies in the fact that Pollock's use of the theory of the male look as elaborated by scholars such as Laura Mulvey is decidedly partial. In "Visual Pleasure and Narrative Cinema," Mulvey speaks of two modes of the look: one scopophilic, in that it supplies pleasurable looking by allowing the subject to take other people as objects by submitting them to a controlling gaze, the other narcissistic, in that it provides an ideal image of the subject that, in the mirror stage, substitutes for the otherwise insufficient, alienated self. While Pollock employs the notion of the look as a form of visual fetish, as an assertion of male authority over women on the city streets by recasting them as erotic objects, she leaves aside the narcissistic look, and thus is silent on the ways in which the *flâneur* was, like the notion of femininity itself, an ideological construction or representation that had as its purpose the making invisible of the instability at the heart of masculinity. In other words, we must accompany our critique of patriarchal constructions of modern femininity with a deconstruction of the myths of masculinity as well, and pay particular attention both to the ways in which a set of visual tropes (sites, subjects, viewpoints) elaborated the reassuring fantasy of control *and* to the moments within representation when that fantasy broke down.

The issue that remains for the contributors to this volume is as follows: how might art history or the history of visual culture absorb these critiques of Wolff and especially of Pollock into a new critical position that accepts their basic motivations while introducing a more subtle understanding of the ways in which social life was organized and represented in the French metropolis during the nineteenth century? How, in other words, does one retain the political impetus of Pollock's critique of art history, her attention to the place of the producer and the asymmetry of positions within art production (and within modernity more generally), while accounting for the actual and even symbolic presence of women on the streets of Paris? The essays gathered in this volume propose a variety of answers to these questions, echoing recent scholarship revisiting and revising the *flâneur/flâneuse* paradigm in other disciplines. Janet Wolff opens the dialogue by returning to the issues she first raised in her "Invisible *Flâneuse*" article, now considering the figure of the *flâneuse* in terms of three distinct but related issues: first, women's access to urban space in the early twentieth century; second, the ways in which the *language* of modernity introduces gender biases; and third, alternatives posed by feminist historians for rethinking the public/private divide in order to describe a modernity in which women would no longer be invisible. Finally, Wolff discusses recent architectural and urban theory that places an emphasis not on the rigidity of the built environment and of urban community, but on its *provisional* nature – a perspective that allows greater attention to the ways in which women have actually negotiated the city in everyday life, rather than on the ideological obstacles or exclusions that have been set up against them.

Both Wolff and Pollock, as we have described, made extensive use of the concept of the separation of spheres, a model that at its most simplistic followed a rather rigid view of the divisions between public and private life in the nineteenth century. That model has become increasingly problematic in light of subsequent work by feminist historians[42] and art historians, for example, Kathleen Adler's investigation of the suburban quarter of Passy in relation to Berthe Morisot's paintings, such as her *View of Paris from the Trocadéro* (1872). For Adler, these works point to the possibility of seeing certain liminal urban spaces as sites in which the ideology of separate spheres falters.[43] In this anthology the chapter by Greg Thomas, dealing with the parks of Paris in the nineteenth century, investigates such spaces as occupying a position straddling public and private in the contemporary imagination. It argues that the parks were a marginal urban space where women's authority might compete with, and sometimes even dominate, that of the *flâneur*. He examines both the role of the parks in the social topography of mid-century Paris and their representation in Impressionist painting; there, women were often shown actively exploring park space or consuming the modern pleasures on offer. If women artists such as

Morisot and Cassatt emphasized this *flâneuse*-like freedom, all the works show a marked ambiguity of vision, confounding any easy distinction between public and intimate space, or indeed between male and female gazes. For Thomas, the new parks offered spaces where women could at least evade some of the pressure of the *flâneur*'s gaze and take control of some of the habits and visual attitudes that were shaping modernity.

Even those most clearly coded symbolic spaces, the supposedly masculine realms of the boulevards, were troubled by the presence of women. As Marni Kessler's discussion of the veil worn by bourgeois women in Second Empire Paris demonstrates, even the most banal of fashion accessories could gain a particular currency as an emblem of the respectability of the woman who wore it. An emerging urban modernity recoded this item, advertising it as a shield against the unhealthy dust of a city undergoing massive renovation – and more subtly figuring it as a means for limiting the proper woman's view of that city. Women's fashion and the medico-hygienic discourses of femininity met in the veil, a conjunction whose meanings may be analyzed within both popular imagery (periodical illustrations, photographs) and more canonical works of art (Manet's *Concert in the Tuileries*).

Another significant avenue of investigation is the exploration of the limits of the *flâneur* paradigm: where did this canonical formulation collapse under the stress of external threat or internal contradiction? Ting Chang's paper, addressing the modes of disorientation that marked the extended tour of Asia by Théodore Duret and Emile Guimet in the 1870s, deals with the ways in which the identity of the nineteenth-century *flâneur* was radically threatened when confronted with the *terra incognita* of the non-western world. Duret, in many ways the quintessential connoisseur of urban spaces, was unable to maintain this pose of the confident *flâneur*, abandoning the spontaneous and improvised stroll in the face of the unknown realms of East Asia and their orientalized Others. For Chang, anxiety becomes a central term in the elaboration of a new historical model for understanding urban experience in light of gender and racial differences.

Another limit-case of the *flâneur* paradigm, this time linked not to race or gender but to class, is addressed by Tom McDonough, who examines the reports in the press of violent attacks and robberies throughout Paris in the winter of 1844–45. No one seemed immune, and every passer-by was suspected of harboring criminal designs toward his neighbors. Reflections of the panic are found in sources as diverse as diaries, police reports, and popular caricatures, yet the sources of this fear were ultimately revealed to be fictitious: the supposed crimes that sparked these anxieties around public space and the stranger were largely manufactured or were shown to be pure rumor. The effects of the panic were real enough, however: the State used middle-class fears to justify mass sweeps through working-class neighborhoods, extending its control over mobile populations that were increasingly restive in these years previous to the 1848 Revolution. In this complicated nexus of imagined crime and concrete subjugation, the networks of power that guaranteed the *flâneur*'s confident appropriation of the space of the city were exhibited at a particularly significant moment of their deployment.

While in these contributions, as in Wolff's and Pollock's texts, there is an interest in the ways in which *flânerie* is a lived, occupiable position available or unavailable to urban subjects based on their gender, class, or sexuality, Wilson's text hints at another avenue of investigation, one that has proven an especially fertile field of study: the idea that the *flâneur* himself is a purely social construction, a mythological figure, as it were, who exists only in discourse but never in the world of real social relations. Priscilla Parkhurst Ferguson's work is important in this regard: she asks us to recognize the ways in which, through the course of the nineteenth century, the *flâneur* was elaborated and existed across a range of texts whose audience was by no means exclusively masculine, or even exclusively urban.[44] By analyzing the ways in which nineteenth-century illustrated magazines translated the phenomenological effects of urban life into an array of texts and images, thus reproducing the spectacle of metropolitan culture in the experience of turning a page, Tom Gretton demonstrates that the position of the *flâneur* was one at least temporarily occupiable by anyone – male or female, urban or provincial, bourgeois or petty bourgeois. At the same time, as a discursive construct, the *flâneur*-position elaborated in these journals had real, lived effects, allowing the reader to by-pass those restrictions which constituted the definition of the *flâneur* – restrictions of gender and class – at the same time as, paradoxically, reinforcing such a restrictive identity for the figure, and thus for occupants of the public realm.

If two main strategies for rethinking gender and public space in nineteenth-century Paris involve, first, complicating our understanding of the ways in which public and private were organized and, consequently, gendered in social practice, and, second, questioning the authority that the *flâneur* construction seemed unproblematically to represent, a third avenue of investigation pursued by contributors to this volume involves research into ways in which female visibility and female looking were incorporated into city life. Turning her attention to advertising posters made in the *fin-de-siècle*, Ruth Iskin finds the possibility of a female mode of *flânerie*, one that is, not coincidentally, fully imbricated in the consumer's gaze. If the prohibitions against women venturing out into public space were loosened at the end of the century, it was under pressure from the needs of an ever-expanding marketplace: an ideology of confinement, in other words, was replaced with an ideology of consumption. The advertising posters, at the same time as they sold goods, were crucial in selling to women a new set of possibilities for their own experience of the city, one in which a range of activities – browsing bookstores, bicycling, sightseeing, and most important, window-shopping – were deemed respectable and even laudable.

Many of the theorists of the gender-urban space relationship in the nineteenth century specifically cited shopping – especially in the form of the department store – as being a potentially rewarding site for reconstructing moments of female *flânerie* in the period. (As mentioned above, Janet Wolff and Elizabeth Wilson were particularly interested in such investigations.) While recent scholarship on nineteenth century consumer practices, and on the centrality of women as consumers in the period, have focused on shopping as a potentially liberatory activity for women,[45] Aruna D'Souza's essay asks how the construction of shopping as a particularly *feminized* activity impacted its ability to become an object of the *flâneur's* gaze. In posing the question "Why did the Impressionists never paint the department store?," D'Souza investigates a momentary blind spot in what is often conceived as the *flâneur's* limitless visual appropriation of urban space: that an institution so crucial to the new spectacle culture of the late nineteenth century was entirely absent from the repertoire of the "painters of modern life" suggests that shopping was conceived as a kind of problem for the bourgeois man, possibly because of the new freedoms it putatively offered to women.

In all of these essays, the idea of *flânerie* has been discussed in terms of its various representations. As Linda Nochlin reminds us, however, there is an experiential component of the issues at stake that must be taken into account. Her text, part diaristic, part art historical, raises the issue of the complexity of the individual's perceptions and use of public space of the city, of the continual renegotiation of gender that not only takes place within space but is shaped by and actively shapes the city as well. Such is the logic of the inclusion of two texts by contemporary artists, Simon Leung and Helen Scalway. Leung's poetic investigation of the sites of anonymous male sex allows us to better understand the potentially multiple uses of public space as well as the fragility of that space as a normative category in bourgeois society. Scalway's account of her walks through contemporary London likewise reminds us of the very real stakes of these academic debates, returning us to the pavement of the city streets and our ever-contingent negotiations of their multiple obstacles, both physical and social. "The Contemporary *Flâneuse*" indicates both the lines of continuity and the ruptures between nineteenth-century discourses and our own.

The editors of this volume have, in the long course of its preparation, accumulated several debts that must be acknowledged. Our thanks are first extended to the original participants in the "Invisible *Flâneuse?*" conference panel and to the contributors to this anthology, who collectively have inspired our rethinking of questions of gender and representation in the space of the modern city. We would also like to thank Tim Barringer, one of the editors of the present series, and our editors at Manchester University Press, who skillfully and with great patience and forbearance guided us through to publication. Maya Lin and Jenny Holzer and their respective assistants were exceedingly generous in providing images for reproduction. And it is with deepest gratitude that we acknowledge our debt to three scholars whose contributions, in conversation and argument, continue to provide models for feminist art history in the twenty-first century: Rosalyn Deutsche, Linda Nochlin, and Janet Wolff.

Notes

1 "The Invisible Flâneuse?: Rethinking Women's Experience of Public Space in 19th-Century France," A. D'Souza and T. McDonough, co-chairs, College Art Association 89th Annual Conference, Chicago, February 28–March 3, 2001. The original participants in this panel were T. Chang, T. Gretton, M. Kessler, K. Smith, and G. M. Thomas, with L. Nochlin, respondent.

2 E. Wilson, *The Sphinx in the City: Urban Life, the Control of Disorder, and Women* (Berkeley and Los Angeles: University of California Press, 1991), p. 9.

3 See, for example, J. Wolff, "The Culture of Separate Spheres: The Role of Culture in 19th-Century Public and Private Life," in *The Culture of Capital: Art, Power and the Nineteenth-Century Middle Class*, eds J. Wolff and J. Seed (Manchester: Manchester University Press, 1988), pp. 117–134. Wolff at this time was director of a three-year project grant for the study of nineteenth-century middle-class culture, awarded by the British Economic and Social Research Council; other participants in this project included its research fellow, London-based social historian J. Seed and, notably, Wolff's colleague at the University of Leeds, G. Pollock.

4 J. Wolff, "The Invisible *Flâneuse*: Women and the Literature of Modernity," *Theory, Culture & Society* 2, no. 3 (1985), pp. 37–38.

5 J. Wolff, "The Invisible *Flâneuse*," p. 38. As her description of such "impressionistic and essayistic contributions" suggests, Wolff owed a particular debt in defining this literature of modernity to sociologist D. Frisby; see for example his *Sociological Impressionism: A Reassessment of Georg Simmel's Social Theory* (London: Heinemann, 1981).

6 J. Wolff, "The Invisible *Flâneuse*," p. 39.

7 M. Stacey, "The Division of Labour Revisited or, Overcoming the Two Adams," in *Practice and Progress: British Sociology, 1950–1980*, eds P. Abrams, R. Deem, J. Finch, and P. Rock (London: George Allen & Unwin, 1981), p. 172.

8 M. Stacey, "The Division of Labour Revisited," p. 175.

9 See E. Gamarnikow and J. Purvis, "Introduction," in *The Public and the Private*, eds E. Gamarnikow, M. Arnot, E. Bartels, V. Beechey, L. Birke, S. Himmelweit, D. Leonard, S. Ruehl, and M. A. Speakman (London: Heinemann, 1983).

10 E. Gamarnikow and J. Purvis, "Introduction," p. 3.

11 J. Wolff, "The Invisible *Flâneuse*," p. 37.

12 J. Wolff, "The Invisible *Flâneuse*," p. 41.

13 J. Wolff, "The Invisible *Flâneuse*," p. 44.

14 J. Wolff, "The Invisible *Flâneuse*," p. 44.

15 J. Wolff, "The Invisible *Flâneuse*," p. 44.

16 J. Wolff, "The Invisible *Flâneuse*," p. 45. Already in this description of the project, something of the complexity of the discourse around the *flâneuse* appears, for what is entailed is both an understanding of representation (of, that is, the constitution of "partial perspectives" and "particular biases") *and* a representation of society (of "areas of social life and experience" occupied by female subjects).

17 This, of course, has been the subject of much work since the time of Wolff's essay. See, notably, M. B. Miller, *The Bon Marché* (Princeton, N.J.: Princeton University Press, 1981) and, most recently, L. Tiersten, *Marianne in the Market: Envisioning Consumer Society in Fin-de-Siècle France* (Berkeley and Los Angeles: University of California Press, 2001).

18 J. Wolff, "The Invisible *Flâneuse*," p. 45.

19 G. Pollock, "Modernity and the Spaces of Femininity," in *Vision and Difference: Femininity, Feminism and the Histories of Art* (London and New York: Routledge, 1988), pp. 50–90. Her earlier work on representations of urban life should also be noted, particularly G. Pollock and C. Arscott (with J. Wolff), "The Partial View: The Visual Representation of the Early 19th-Century Industrial City," in *The Culture of Capital*, pp. 191–233. Like the later "Spaces of Femininity" essay, this text argued that such images must be read in the context of other discourses about the city, and that they were deeply enmeshed in the "real relations" of class and gender. This may also be an apposite moment to cite a related work by another Leeds scholar, responding to Wolff and Pollock: J. Tagg, "The Discontinuous City: Picturing and the Discursive Field" (1989), in *Grounds of Dispute: Art History, Cultural Politics and the Discursive Field* (Minneapolis: University of Minnesota Press, 1992), pp. 134–156.

20 T. J. Clark, *The Painting of Modern Life: Paris in the Art of Manet and his Followers* (Princeton, N.J.: Princeton University Press, 1984).

21 G. Pollock, "Spaces of Femininity," p. 52.

22 G. Pollock, "Spaces of Femininity," p. 53. R. Deutsche provides a more subtle, though no less damning, reading of Clark's position: "[his] repression of feminism is not . . . necessitated by his interest in the category of class. Instead, it is authorized by his image of the social as a complete entity in which a single set of social relations are privileged as determinate." See her *Evictions* (Cambridge, Mass. and London: The MIT Press, and Chicago: Graham Foundation for Advanced Studies in the Fine Arts, 1996), pp. 196–198.

23 See C. Baudelaire, "The Painter of Modern Life" (1863), in *The Painter of Modern Life and Other Essays*, trans. and ed. by J. Mayne (London: Phaidon Press, 1964).

24 This tradition is best summarized in R. L. Herbert, *Impressionism: Art, Leisure, and Parisian Society* (New Haven and London: Yale University Press, 1988), pp. 33–37.

25 See J. Wolff, "Invisible *Flâneuse*," p. 38.

26 G. Pollock, "Spaces of Femininity," p. 67.

27 See, for example, L. Mulvey, "Visual Pleasure and Narrative Cinema" (1975), in *Visual and Other Pleasures* (Bloomington and Indianapolis: Indiana University Press, 1989), pp. 14–28; and J. Rose, "Sexuality in the Field of Vision," in *Sexuality in the Field of Vision* (London: Verso, 1985). We might note in passing the misuse of the term "gaze" in much of this work, from Mulvey through Pollock. In Lacanian theory, the gaze is not possessed by the individual who looks, but by the Other; hence, upon the helpful suggestion of R. Deutsche, throughout this account we have replaced "the gaze" with the more appropriate term "the look."

28 G. Pollock, "Spaces of Femininity," p. 66.

29 J. Tagg, "The Discontinuous City," p. 136.

30 G. Pollock, "Spaces of Femininity," p. 54.

31 G. Pollock, "Spaces of Femininity," p. 69. Emphasis added. A related argument was made by feminist film theorist M. A. Doane, significantly utilizing the same R. Doisneau photograph ("Un regard oblique") referenced by Pollock; see M. A. Doane, "Film and the Masquerade" (1982), in her *Femmes Fatales* (New York and London: Routledge, 1991), pp. 17–32.

32 G. Pollock, "Feminist interventions in the histories of art: an introduction," in *Vision and Difference*, p. 6.

33 G. Pollock, "Spaces of Femininity," p. 68.

34 G. Pollock, "Spaces of Femininity," p. 87.

35 E. Wilson, "The Invisible *Flâneur*," *New Left Review* no. 191 (January–February 1992), p. 99.

36 E. Wilson, "The Invisible *Flâneur*," p. 100.

37 L. Davidoff and C. Hall, "The Architecture of Public and Private Life: English Middle-Class Society in a Provincial Town, 1780 to 1850," in *The Pursuit of Urban History*, eds D. Fraser and A. Sutcliffe (London: Edward Arnold, 1983), p. 327. The work of these historians was especially significant for Wolff and Pollock, both of whom cite the latter essay; see also C. Hall, "The Butcher, the Baker, the Candlestickmaker: The Shop and the Family in the Industrial Revolution," in *The Changing Experience of Women*, eds E. Whitelegg, M. Arnot, E. Bartels, V. Beechley, L. Birke, S. Himmelweit, D. Leonard, S. Reuhl, and M. A. Speakman. (Oxford: Martin Robertson, 1982), pp. 2–16.

38 E. Wilson, "The Invisible *Flâneur*," p. 93.

39 E. Wilson, "The Invisible *Flâneur*," p. 96.

40 E. Wilson, "The Invisible *Flâneur*," p. 109.

41 E. Wilson, "The Invisible *Flâneur*," p. 101–3. In Wilson's words, "We might have expected an emphasis on signifying practices and representations to result in a fluid universe of shifting meanings. . . . Instead, the opposite has happened, and thus in a curious way the Lacanian discourse replicates or reinforces the ideology it was meant to deconstruct" (p. 102).

42 See the helpful literature review by L. K. Kerber, "Separate Spheres, Female Worlds, Woman's Place: The Rhetoric of Women's History," *Journal of American History* 75, no. 1 (June 1988), pp. 9–39.

43 K. Adler, "The Suburban, the Modern, and 'une Dame de Passy'," *Oxford Art Journal* 12, no. 1 (1989), pp. 3–13.

44 P. Parkhurst Ferguson, "The *Flâneur*: The City and its Discontents," in *Paris as Revolution: Writing the 19th-century city* (Berkeley and London: University of California Press, 1994), pp. 114. For Ferguson, the *flâneur* was essentially a textual strategy which allowed writers to negotiate the increasingly complicated city over the course of the nineteenth century, and thus changed in response to changing urban conditions, and changing relationships between artists and the metropolis. "The practice of *flânerie* turned the artist's unique, and uniquely modern, relationship to that city into a spectacle, a projection of the imperative need to make sense of the city. Ultimately, *flâneur* was a strategy of representation' (p. 81).

45 See, for example, L. Tiersten, *Marianne in the Market*.

2

Gender and the haunting of cities (or, the retirement of the *flâneur*)

Janet Wolff

There has been a good deal of discussion in the past fifteen years on the topic of the *flâneuse* – the female version of modernity's urban stroller.[1] Was there such a person, or did the ideology of separate spheres, together with the architecture and organization of public space, render female *flânerie* impossible? Did the expansion of the public sphere, and the birth of new activities – shopping and cinema-going are usually cited here – create the conditions in the late nineteenth century for the *flâneuse* to make an appearance? Or – a different approach to the question – is the problem not so much women's lack of access to the street but rather the distortions of cultural theory and social history, which foreground certain (male) activities and render women invisible? I want to consider the figure of the *flâneuse* in terms of three separate but related issues: women's access to urban space in the early twentieth century; the ways in which the *language* of modernity introduces gender biases; and alternatives posed by feminist historians for rethinking the public/private divide, in order to describe a modernity in which women are no longer invisible. Although these are important matters to address, I also believe that new work in architectural and urban theory suggests a more profitable approach. Here, the emphasis is on the *provisional* nature of the built environment and of the urban community, a perspective which – instead of looking at obstacles and exclusions – allows us to consider the ways in which women actually negotiate the city in everyday life. In the end, after all the discussion about women's access to the practice of *flânerie*, we may sympathize with the rather rhetorical question asked by James Donald in a recent book, when he says "To put it bluntly, why on earth should any woman *want* to be a *flâneur*?"[2]

The *flâneur* (the French term is always used, in English as well as in German) is the person who strolls aimlessly in the modern city, observing people and events, perhaps (if the *flâneur* happens also to be a writer or an artist) with a view to recording these observations in word or image. Although this particular figure has a pre-history in eighteenth-century thought, it is generally agreed that its prominence in the literature of modernity dates from Baudelaire's mid-nineteenth-century essays on modern life, and particularly his 1859 essay, "The Painter of Modern Life." Here, the *flâneur* appears as the "modern hero" – the person whose experience epitomizes the fragmented and anonymous nature of life in the modern city, observing the fleeting and ephemeral aspects of urban existence (changing fashions, brief encounters). The theme was taken up half a century later by the German critic Walter Benjamin, for whom Baudelaire was the poet of modernity, and the arcades of Paris the essential space of *flânerie*.

> Strolling could hardly have assumed the importance it did without the arcades. . . . It is in this world that the *flâneur* is at home. . . . The arcades were a cross between a street and an *intérieur*. . . . The street becomes a dwelling for the *flâneur*; he is as much at home among the façades of houses as a citizen is in his four walls.[3]

The *flâneur* is not the only figure invoked as the epitome of the modern experience – Baudelaire and Benjamin also offer the dandy, the rag-picker (the *chiffonnier*) and the prostitute as emblematic modern urban types.[4] All of these have their origins in the radically new conjunction of the rise of commodity culture and the expansion of major metropolitan centers. This characterization of modernity has a good deal in common with descriptions offered by sociologists at the turn of the century, notably Georg Simmel, whose 1903 essay, "The Metropolis and Mental Life," explored the subjective aspects of urban existence, in particular its increased tempo, its greater impersonality and its cultivation of a detached (blasé) attitude. The typical urban dweller is accustomed to a state of anonymity unknown in the face-to-face communities of rural society, or even of small-city life. The *flâneur* emerges both as a possibility created by such conditions, and as the prime exponent of urban living.

The *flâneur*, however, is necessarily male. The privilege of passing unnoticed in the city, particularly in the period in which the *flâneur* flourished – that is, the mid-nineteenth century to the early twentieth century – was not accorded to women, whose presence on the streets would certainly be noticed. Not only that – as many historians of the period have pointed out, women in public, and particularly women apparently wandering without aim, immediately attract the negative stamp of the "non-respectable." It is no accident that the prostitute appears as the central female trope in the discourse of modernity. The problem for women was their automatic identification with this "streetwalker" whenever they walked in the street. Discussing London in the 1870s, Deborah Epstein Nord identifies the problem for middle-class women: "when they ventured onto the city streets under the conditions necessary to urban strolling and observation, they took on the persona of the fallen woman."[5] It emerges, then, that the *flâneur*, the central figure of modernity, was inherently gendered male. And the account of urban experience, now seen through the eyes of the *flâneur* and his cohorts, instantly renders women invisible or marginal. It is therefore not surprising that since the mid-1980s – at the very time that *flânerie* took center stage in the sociological discourse of modernity – feminist critics have challenged this way of conceptualizing modernity. It is not a matter of objecting to women's actual exclusion, but rather of suggesting that this exclusion is compounded by later twentieth-century approaches which gave priority to the street and the public arena in the very definition of modernity.

There have been a number of responses to the recognition of this privileging of male experience in the literature of modernity. Some writers have wanted to insist that women's absence from the public sphere has been overstated – that there have, indeed, always been women in the urban arena, and increasingly so towards the end of the nineteenth century. Such writers rightly object to any implication that women's place was solely in the private sphere of the home. For one thing, as Leonore Davidoff and Catherine Hall have shown in their comprehensive and important study of English middle-class life from 1780–1850, the public and private arenas have never been separate and discrete, but always intersected – through family networks and marriage ties in relation to economic structure, in women's contribution to enterprise, and in men's own relationship to the domestic scene.[6] Mica Nava has pointed out that "women's appropriation of public spaces, in both symbolic and material ways, was growing rapidly" in the late nineteenth and early twentieth centuries. This is confirmed by Peter Fritzsche in his study of Berlin in 1900, and by Judith Walkowitz's discussion of the new spaces available for women in a redefined public domain in London in the 1880s, and Kathy Peiss's study of working-class women's culture in turn-of-the-century New York.[7] Others have argued that not only *do* women appear in the urban landscape – they do so, in the later period, in the very role of *flâneuse*. Here, the emphasis has been on the two particular activities whose characteristics, it is argued, are those of *flânerie*, namely shopping and cinema-going. Anne Friedberg's well-known discussion of what she calls "les *flâneurs* du mal(l)," with its double reference – back to Baudelaire's *Les Fleurs du mal*, and forward to the newest type of shopping locale – focuses on these new opportunities for women in public: "As the department store supplanted the arcade, the mobilized gaze entered the service of consumption, and space opened for a female *flâneur* – a *flâneuse* – whose gendered gaze became a key element of consumer address."[8] Friedberg perceives the cinema as the contemporary, postmodern, culmination of this extension of the place of *flânerie*, situated as it often is within the shopping mall. In her case, the logic of extension is a dual one – first, having to do with the kind of public space the cinema occupies (one in which women can move freely and without suspicion), and second, depending on a historical connection between cinema and arcade (the original space of *flânerie*). As she sees it, "the cinema was born out of the social and psychic transformations that the arcades produced," via the earlier, protocinematic devices of the panorama and the diorama.[9] Here, the freedom to wander is no longer about the literal movement of bodies in space, but rather about the mobility of the gaze, confronted by the moving image. Similar arguments have been made by other film historians, substituting the virtual *flânerie* of movie-viewing for the physical wandering of the urban stroller. For example, Giuliana Bruno has proposed, in her study of film in Naples in the first decades of the twentieth century, that

> the cinematic situation made it possible for the female to experience a form of *flânerie*, as film, triggered by a desire for loitering, offered the joy of watching while traveling. The "spectatrix" could thus enter the world of the *flâneur* and derive its pleasure through filmic motions. We may see film spectatorship as providing access to the erotics of darkness and (urban) wandering denied to the female subject.[10]

Anke Gleber makes something of the same case in her discussion of film and *flânerie* in Weimar Germany, though the connection she wants to make between urban strolling and film-viewing is more in the nature of parallels and similarities than the stronger claim of cinema-going as itself the new *flânerie*.[11]

I am sympathetic, of course, to the desire to recover (and rediscover) women's place in modernity, and to counter those stories which render women quite invisible. It is important to emphasize women's continuing role in the public sphere – whether as shoppers, philanthropists or workers (professional, clerical, and working-class) – and the great value of much feminist history has been to examine and describe these activities.[12] But because it is equally important to keep in mind the actual constraints, exclusions, and dangers faced by women in the urban environment, I want to insist that the role of *flâneuse* remained impossible despite the expansion of women's public activities, and despite the newer activities of shopping and cinema-going. For central to the definition of the *flâneur* are both the *aimlessness* of the strolling, and the *reflectiveness* of the gaze. Benjamin himself believed that the decline of the Paris arcades, brought about by the Haussmannization of the city, signalled the end of *flânerie*, the department store itself epitomizing this transformation.[13] That experience which had once been neither public nor private (the arcade representing a kind of liminal space), and which had been fundamentally without aim, became instead both an activity removed from the street, and one with a very specific aim – namely shopping and consumption. As Priscilla Ferguson puts it:

> When *flânerie* moves into the private realm of the department store, feminization alters this urban practice almost beyond recognition. . . . By abolishing the distance between the individual and the commodity, the feminization of *flânerie* redefines it out of existence. The *flâneur*'s dispassionate gaze dissipates under pressure from the shoppers' passionate engagement in the world of things to be purchased and possessed. The *flâneur* ends up going shopping after all.[14]

The department store cannot be the scene of urban strolling, not only because it is an enclosed and circumscribed space, but, more importantly, because shopping is a pre-defined and purposeful activity. In the case of cinema-going, feminists have made much of both women's freedom to attend this semi-public place – a "legitimized public pleasure" for women, as Giuliana Bruno has called it[15] – and women's access to a new kind of looking, the gaze previously associated with the urban *flâneur*. Anke Gleber describes this activity of the female spectator:

The darkened space of the cinema removes her from the gaze of others, while at the same time allowing her own gaze unrestricted, extended access to all the shocks and impressions of modernity, approximating and even exceeding the experience of the street. This onset of the cinema finally gives women the right to indulge their scopic desires.[16]

But here too it seems to me that it is to stretch the meaning of the concept of the *flâneur* too far to describe the female cinema spectator as a *flâneuse*. Like the department store, the cinema (and particularly the cinema in the suburban mall, which is Anne Friedberg's focus) can hardly be understood as public space. Women's relatively unproblematic admission to the movie house was, in the early years of cinema, a long way from general access to urban life. In addition, there is something a little strange about considering the "mobilized gaze" of film specta-torship as on a par with the look of the urban stroller. The spectator sits quite still, faces forward, and confronts a pre-arranged sequence of moving images which, to be sure, she can interpret freely – even glancing away, scanning the screen, and so on – but which ultimately offer nothing in the way of self-determined direction of the gaze or, indeed, possibilities of reflective response to the parade of images. In general, I see no real advantage in these attempts to recuperate the discourse of *flânerie* for women by simple change of locale. For women in the city, negotiating the geography and architecture of public space in the early twentieth century, the role of *flâneuse* remained unavailable. Walter Benjamin's friend and colleague, Franz Hessel, published one of the first sustained discussions of urban strolling in 1929, in a book entitled *Spazieren in Berlin* (later, on republication, entitled *Ein Flaneur in Berlin*).[17] Rather surprisingly, the first essay in this book of short impressions is entitled "The Suspect" ("Der Verdächtige"), and Hessel here reveals that as *flâneur* in Berlin, he is always the subject of suspicious looks.[18] This does not accord with the "classical" notion of the *flâneur*, who is assumed to pass unchallenged and in virtual anonymity. For Benjamin, who reviewed the book in 1929, this only confirms his view that the conditions of urban strolling, present in the Paris of the arcades, are never really reproduced in other cities or in later periods.[19] Women, of course, were almost invariably regarded with suspicion as they traversed the streets of the modern city. It is only with the extended view of *flânerie* (one might call it the "non-classical" concept of the *flâneur* – like Hessel as Berlin wanderer) that we might be willing, in acknowledging the advent of "the new woman" and the expansion of women's public presence, to admit the exis-tence of the *flâneuse*.

The question is, though, why *should* we do this? Here, we might choose to address the question of women in the city from a different point of view. As has often been pointed out, the invisibility of women in the literature of modernity has nothing much to do with women's actual lives in the period. Rather it is a product of the *dis-course* of modernity itself. In deciding to focus on the public sphere – on the street and the urban space – and in privileging the figure of the *flâneur*, historians and sociologists have produced a quite biased view of modern life, one oriented to the roles and experiences of men at the expense of women.[20] As Rob Shields puts it:

> Without attention to gender there is a tendency to represent the city as a generally public space, that is to focus on its street life, leaving out the home life within the tenements, flats, dwellings and backyards in which family life takes place. . . . The domestic remains *invisible* in representations of the city as a public "space" which is thought of as merely the built analogue or architectural concretisation of the public "sphere."[21]

The point is that it was, for the most part, male sociologists and cultural critics who identified the features of modern city life in the early years of the last century, and this story has been taken up in the years since then by other male writers – sociologists, urban geographers, architectural historians. Until the 1970s and the advent of feminist critiques, the lives observed and described (and, perhaps, empathized with) were mainly those of men. Accordingly, we have inherited a very partial view of modernity and of urban life, one which marginalizes other experiences. The suggestion, then, has been that we reconceptualize "modernity," to take account of the intersections of public and private and of the particular experiences of women (and, for that matter, of other "invisible" denizens of the city – marginalized by class or by ethnicity). Very likely shopping would figure more prominently (though not in order to discover any possibility of female *flânerie*). Such a story of modernity from the point of view of women would be illuminating in other ways, too. Deborah Epstein Nord notes that in turn-of-the-century London, even though it was true that any woman stroller was seen as a prostitute, the divide between respectable and non-respectable was sometimes less clear for women themselves. Particularly in the case of middle-class women reformers, working with and on behalf of prostitutes to oppose the repressive Contagious Diseases Act, a certain "necessary if ambivalent identification with the woman of the streets" emerged.[22] The strict divide of "respectability," which was always in any case a product of male anxieties and the male psyche, though inevitably having real consequences for the lives of women, proves to be something rather different from the point of view of women "on the street."[23] In another context, Marsha Meskimmon has shown the striking difference in the visual arts between the portrayal of prostitutes by male artists in Weimar Germany (for example, the well-known paintings of Otto Dix and Georg Grosz) and paintings by women artists, whose representations of prostitutes "posed alternatives to the simplistic rendering of the 'bad' woman out in public and, indeed, to the 'mother/whore' binary."[24] Of such a work by the artist Gerta Overbeck, Meskimmon says this:

> In her sketch, the prostitute is shown as but one type of women worker. . . . In Overbeck's work, the banality of the daytime shop setting is in stark contrast to the more usual conventions of placing the prostitute on the street, in the brothel or the bedroom, to emphasise the seduction, decadence and desire. Overbeck's prostitute is not "seducing" the viewer and we are not placed as the empowered consumer,

choosing to "purchase" the goods. . . . We are located with the female figure, we enter into a relation of comparability with this figure through the banal specificity of the representation. We encounter the prostitute as an ordinary working woman . . . much in the way Overbeck herself encountered the sex workers in her locality.[25]

Such a reorientation of point of view produces quite a different conceptual framework for the exploration of modernity and its urban figures. This shift of focus, privileging instead the perspective of women in the city, brings into view experiences and connections generally obscured by the dominant tropes and theories of modern life. It is not so much a question of substituting one kind of subject-position for another, though, but rather opening up the possibility of seeing women's complex negotiations of city life, real obstacles and constraints, and ideological constructions which attempt to fix and constrain them.

It is not difficult, I think, to explain why theories of modernity have privileged the *flâneur*. For when we consider that a crucial aspect of this uniquely modern practice is the *reflectiveness* entailed in urban observation, it becomes clear that the critic, for whom this figure looms so large, identifies strongly with him. The *flâneur is*, in fact, the critic – the writer, artist, sociologist – whose detached observations might well be reported in literary or visual texts. For Baudelaire, the illustrator Constantin Guys was the archetypal *flâneur*. For Benjamin, Baudelaire himself was the *flâneur* of the nineteenth century. In general, in the literature on the topic, a crucial aspect of urban wandering is the "reading" of the urban environment and the production of texts – exactly the task of the social theorist and the urban ethnographer.[26] In other words, the importance of the *flâneur* is, amongst other things, the *self*-importance of the sociologist of modernity, for whom this poetic figure serves as prototype. He has proved to be an attractive and suggestive figure, and one giving us a certain grasp of the peculiar features of life in the metropolis – fragmentation, anonymity, speed, and so on. But I think it is safe to suggest that it will be no great loss to ask the *flâneur* to cede his position in the center of the stage, and to take up, instead, a place on the margins, as just one of the city's inhabitants. Certainly a newly feminized urban theory will achieve this displacement – without hard feelings, and with a lingering sympathy for the aimless stroller, who, after all, might not have had such an easy time of it himself, given the particular demands on masculine identity. Elizabeth Wilson has suggested that the masculinity of the *flâneur* is itself in question, in his failure to annihilate the threatening figure of woman with his gaze, and we could also observe that neither the aimless wandering nor the translation of observations of city life into literary and artistic texts accords well with the ideology of masculinity as purposive, focused and productive.[27] In these circumstances, we can now see, perhaps, why James Donald asks why any woman would even *want* to be a *flâneur*.

What I am suggesting, then, is that instead of either bemoaning women's lack of access to *flânerie* and to the public sphere more generally, or taking to task theories of modernity and the city which privilege the male experience, we adopt the rather different aim of exploring women's (and men's) actual lives in the modern city. This is Meskimmon's strategy, in her study of women artists in Weimar Germany, whose lives (and art) she discovers to be a complex negotiation of the structures and ideologies of gender in that period. Here, women move center stage in the modern metropolis, whether as prostitute, housewife, mother, "new woman," or androgyne (the "garçonne" of the 1920s and early 1930s). Seen anew in the context of their actual lives, and in their representation in paintings by women artists, these figures offer a striking contrast to their more familiar prototypes in the art of men and in the dominant ideologies of gender – ideologies of the "good" and "bad" woman (angel/whore, virgin/fallen woman). This strategy, of by-passing those ideologies and their narratives of women's place, allows us to consider the "multidimensional and contradictory manifestations" of the modern[28] which have always given space to women who, as Elizabeth Wilson has put it, "have survived and flourished in the interstices of the city, negotiating the contradictions of the city in their own partic- ular way."[29] It is a strategy already well known in another context, not usually asso- ciated with gender and modernity, namely the influential work of Michel de Certeau, and in particular the essays in his book, *The Practice of Everyday Life*, a study, as he puts it in the introduction to the book, of "the ways in which users . . . operate."[30] The much-quoted essay, "Walking in the city," draws a distinction between, on the one hand, what de Certeau calls the "concept-city" of urban dis- course and, on the other hand, the specific spatial practices of city inhabitants. The former – the imaginary totalization of urban planners and social theorists – cannot account for, or even perceive, the actual movements in the streets – the "pedestrian speech acts" of urban dwellers. What he calls "the rhetoric of walking" describes the ways in which walking in practice manipulates the formal codes of city space, both using them and transgressing them in ways disallowed (that is, rendered invis- ible) by the concept-city. De Certeau's interest is in the trajectories of everyday life – the ways in which people negotiate the street, the city, and, indeed, the social world in general. The linguistic metaphor employed – the concept-city as the formal rules of language, and the urban practices as individual speech acts – offers a way of understanding the relationship between structures and actions which is useful, too, in looking at women in the modern city. Without denying or ignoring the dominant physical and institutional structures of urban life (buildings, streets, officially sanctioned practices) and the gender ideologies in play (of men's and women's "proper" place), we can at the same time switch from the bird's-eye view to ground level (the image is de Certeau's) and observe the "rhetorics of everyday life" for women in the early twentieth-century metropolis.

But by now, the city itself seems to have evaporated – its structure and organiza- tion exposed as a fiction, even its physical attributes seen as quite secondary to the practices and discourses in which they are made visible. In James Donald's radical expression of this perspective, the city is "an imagined environment."[31] Indeed, the title of his recent book is *Imagining the Modern City*, and its central purpose is to investigate the discourses of the modern city, resisting throughout any notion of some underlying "real" city, unmediated by the languages of planning, literature, cinema, and other forms of representation. Although, as he once claimed "there is no such thing as the city,"[32] Donald is careful in his formulation of the city-as-text:

> Of course, cities are not only mental constructs. Of course, there are real cities. . . . But why reduce the reality of cities to their thinginess, or their thinginess to a question of bricks and mortar? States of mind have material consequences. They make things happen. . . . [W]hat particularly interests me is the power of *the city* as a category of thought. *The city* is an abstraction, which claims to identify what, if anything, is common to all cities. . . . The city we do experience – the city as state of mind – is always already symbolised and metaphorised.[33]

This is not quite de Certeau's point (though Donald cites him frequently) – we have somewhat shifted focus away from those rhetorics of walking (and other everyday practices) which traverse, negotiate and transgress the official structures and ideologies of the social world, and towards a conception of the city as an imagined environment – that is, a real physical environment always perceived through the prevailing discourses *about* the city. In one case, our attention is drawn to the contingencies of mundane urban life, which do not always accord with the official narratives about the city. In the other, the emphasis is on the operation of those narratives themselves, and the ways in which they constitute "the city." But in both cases, we can see the possibility of a new feminist urban theory, no longer constrained by assumptions of unwelcoming streets, multiple exclusions, and rigid patriarchal structures. Instead, those urban practices of negotiating public space (and gender ideology) become visible, including, of course, the lives and peregrinations of women in the city. None of this is to ignore the actual existence either of cities or of specific urban facts (architecture, physical layout, dangers for women in public). But the recognition of both the discursive and the provisional nature of those facts – seeing them as ultimately the product of past and present social interactions – enables the construction of *other* urban discourses, and here particularly discourses of the feminine (and of woman) in public space.

I want to conclude by talking about ghosts and the haunting of cities. In 1927, Virginia Woolf wrote an essay entitled "Street Haunting," a light-hearted fantasy about a woman's walk through London, ostensibly on a mission to buy a new pencil.[34] It is an essay often invoked by feminist critics, delighted to discover evidence of women's passage in the streets of the metropolis. For the same reason, attention is also paid to Woolf's Mrs Dalloway, who spends a good deal of time walking in London to buy flowers for her party.[35] Like the images produced by the German women artists discussed by Marsha Meskimmon, Virginia Woolf's heroines provide that rare thing – access to women's experience of the public in the early twentieth century. From this point of entry, we can undertake the task of rewriting the modern city. For Woolf, the notion of "haunting" has no particular connotations of ghosts or spirits; it merely carries its secondary definition of "frequenting."[36] But I am struck by the recurrent use of the language of ghosts and haunting in recent literature about the city and urban space. James Donald refers to "the haunted spaces of the city."[37] Rob Shields talks about "the dark silences of urban constructions"; and Rosalyn Deutsche has suggested the value of the concept of *prosopopoeia* (that is, giving voice to the dead) for urban theory.[38] And in her recent study of architecture and modernity, Hilde Heynen has proposed Daniel Libeskind's Berlin Jewish Museum as the ideal design for the necessary rewriting of modernity in the arena of architectural design, its voids and spaces invoking the absent and the dead in a manner she considers appropriate to our late-modern times.[39] Heynen's argument is that architecture must confront the failures and contradictions of modernity, and not offer a false celebration of harmony. Invoking Freud's notion of the uncanny, she explains that "architecture is capable of making us feel something of that which is repressed, that which exists beyond the normal and expected."[40] The uncanny is also identified by James Donald, as the "darkened spaces" which return "to haunt the City of Light."[41]

This apparently supernatural turn in urban and architectural theory is in fact something quite different: part of a critical strategy determined to show how our discourses and narratives illuminate, but also create, the object of study (the city, the public sphere), and also how those same discourses and narratives render invisible (make ghosts of) those practices and figures not given a name. For the same reason, the sociologist Avery Gordon has insisted that haunting is essential to the sociological imagination. As she puts it:

> Haunting is a constituent element of modern social life. It is neither pre-modern superstition nor individual psychosis; it is a generalizable social phenomenon of great import. To study social life one must confront the ghostly aspects of it. . . . The ghost is not simply a dead or a missing person, but a social figure, and investigating it can lead to that dense site where history and subjectivity make social life. The ghost or the apparition is one form by which something lost, or barely visible, or seemingly not there to our supposedly well-trained eye, makes itself known or apparent to us, in its own way, of course.[42]

This exploration of the uncanny, the repressed and the ghostly need not (though it can) be undertaken in psychoanalytic terms.[43] At the level of discourse, and at its simplest, it reminds us that narratives exclude and obscure at the same time as they define and highlight. The lives of women in the modern city – in private as well as in public (for the sociology of modernity has paid little attention to the domestic sphere) – are thus, as Gordon puts it, "barely visible, or seemingly not there." As a result, they haunt the discourse and the city itself – uncanny because not admitted to language and thought. Both James Donald and Rosalyn Deutsche are making a more radical point about discourse, however, and one which will prove useful in rethinking women's place in the early twentieth-century city. For these writers, the very vocabulary of urban history and urban theory constrains our understanding of the problems and possibilities of city life. As Deutsche explains (and her own interest is in the politics of the contemporary city), an approach which begins by complaining about which groups do not have access to the public arena (women, minorities, working-class people) makes the mistake of simply accepting "the public" as given. Rather, she says, the term "public" is itself a political term, one which defines its opposite ("the private"), and thereby already locates men and women in particular places. She insists instead on rejecting a vision of a unified public sphere in favor of acknowledging "the openness and indeterminacy of the democratic public."[44] This means recognizing the fundamental instability and provisionality of social categories, as well as the role of representation in producing entities like "the public." Similarly, James Donald advocates a "negotiative approach" to the city, one which can incorporate within its view moments of contradiction and confrontation.[45] This reconceptualization of the modern city thus allows us to abandon the kind of corrective analytic which notes women's absence from the city streets, and leaps at any opportunity to find women who do actually traverse the public arena – shoppers, workers, cinema-goers. Instead, it becomes possible – indeed essential – to explore the micro-practices of urban living, and the very specific ways in which women negotiate the modern city.

Of course there *is* a city, and there *are* public and private spaces. And of course in the modern city of the early twentieth century these spaces were in many ways gendered. But what I have been suggesting is that if we take "the city" or "the public sphere" as already given, clearly identifiable social facts, we are doomed to the depressing (and ultimately rather boring) point of view which perceives only exclusions and absences. If, instead, we understand "the city" as itself a discursive construct, and "the public" (and "private") as a narrative device, we may begin to entertain counter-narratives – to confront the "shadows and obscurities,"[46] the dark silences, and the ghosts. For these are not sinister and threatening presences, but only the figures obscured by narratives of fixity. I have already suggested that we relegate the *flâneur* to a position of less importance, and this demotion is reinforced by the disarticulation of the "public" – that is, of the natural habitat of the *flâneur*.[47] In the process, the question of female *flânerie* loses all importance and, at the same time, women become entirely visible in their own particular practices and experiences in the modern city.

Notes

1   Editors' Note: Reprinted from Janet Wolff, *Anglo-Modern: Painting and Modernity in Britain and the United States.* Copyright © 2003 by Cornell University. Reprinted by permission of the publisher, Cornell University Press.

2   J. Donald, *Imagining the Modern City* (Minneapolis: University of Minnesota Press, 1999), p. 112.

3   W. Benjamin, *Charles Baudelaire: A Lyric Poet in the Era of High Capitalism* (London: New Left Books, 1973), pp. 36–37.

4   D. Parsons suggests that the rag-picker is a more appropriate metaphor than the *flâneur* to characterize the fragmentary, commodity-driven city of modernity and one which,

according to her, allows women their place in the modern city. "*Flâneur* or *flâneuse?* Mythologies of Modernity," *New Formations* no. 38 (Summer 1999).

5 D. E. Nord, "The Urban Peripatetic: Spectator, Streetwalker, Woman Writer," *19th-Century Literature* 46, no. 3 (1991), p. 365.

6 L. Davidoff and C. Hall, *Family Fortunes: Men and Women of the English Middle Class, 1780–1850* (Chicago: The University of Chicago Press, 1987).

7 M. Nava, "Modernity's Disavowal: Women, the City and the Department Store," in *Modern Times: Reflections on a Century of English Modernity*, eds M. Nava and A. O'Shea (London: Routledge, 1996), p. 40; P. Fritzsche, *Reading Berlin 1900* (Cambridge, Mass.: Harvard University Press, 1996), pp. 63–66; J. Walkowitz, *City of Dreadful Delight: Narratives of Sexual Danger in Late-Victorian London* (Chicago: University of Chicago Press, 1992), p. 9; K. Peiss, *Cheap Amusements: Working Women and Leisure in Turn-of-the-Century New York* (Philadelphia: Temple University Press, 1986).

8 A. Friedberg, "*Les Flâneurs du Mal(l)*: Cinema and the Postmodern Condition," *Publications of the Modern Language Association of America* 106, no. 3 (1991), p. 420. See also her book, *Window Shopping: Cinema and the Postmodern* (Berkeley: University of California Press, 1993).

9 A. Friedberg, "*Les Flâneurs du Mal(l)*," p. 423.

10 G. Bruno, *Streetwalking on a Ruined Map: Cultural Theory and the City Films of Elvira Notari* (Princeton, N.J.: Princeton University Press, 1993), p. 51.

11 "The cinema releases the female spectator from her exclusion from the world, and also her reduction to a passive image. The sites of female *flânerie* have been inscribed into the filmic medium from its earliest times." A. Gleber, *The Art of Taking a Walk: Flânerie, Literature, and Film in Weimar Culture* (Princeton, N.J.: Princeton University Press, 1999), p. 186. The logical extension of this translation of *flânerie* from the streets to the cinema can be found in M. Featherstone's discussion of the "virtual *flâneur*" who engages with computer, hypertext, and the Internet: "The *Flâneur*, the City and Virtual Public Life," *Urban Studies* 35, nos. 5–6 (1998). M. Hartmann has also introduced the notion of the "cyber*flâneur/se*": cited by G. Gilloch, "'The Return of the *Flâneur*': The Afterlife of an Allegory," *New Formations* no. 38 (Summer 1999), pp. 106–107.

12 D. E. Nord, amongst others, has discussed women's public role as philanthropists and social investigators. *Walking the Victorian Streets: Women, Representation, and the City* (Ithaca, N.Y.: Cornell University Press, 1995), Part Three, "New Women."

13 "If the arcade is the classical form of the *intérieur*, which is how the *flâneur* sees the street, the department store is the form of the *intérieur*'s decay. The bazaar is the last hangout of the *flâneur*." W. Benjamin, *Charles Baudelaire*, p. 54.

14 P. P. Ferguson, "The *Flâneur* On and Off the Streets of Paris," in *The Flâneur*, ed. K. Tester (London: Routledge, 1994), pp. 23 and 35.

15 G. Bruno, *Streetwalking on a Ruined Map*, p. 51.

16 A. Gleber, *The Art of Taking a Walk*, p. 187. M. Hansen also discusses the mobilization of the active female gaze in cinema: *Babel and Babylon: Spectatorship in American Silent Film* (Cambridge, Mass.: Harvard University Press: 1991), p. 122.

17 F. Hessel, *Spazieren in Berlin* (Munich: Rogner & Bernhard, 1968 [1929]). For a detailed discussion of Hessel, and his importance to Benjamin, see A. Gleber, *The Art of Taking a Walk*, Chapter 4.

18 "Ich bekomme immer mißtrauische Blicke ab, wenn ich versuche, zwischen den Geschäftigen zu flanieren." F. Hessel, *Spazieren in Berlin*, p. 9.

19 W. Benjamin, "The Return of the *Flâneur* (1929)," *Selected Writings*, vol. 2 (Cambridge, Mass.: Harvard University Press, 1999), p. 265.

20 This point is made by E. Wilson, "The Invisible *Flâneur*," *New Left Review* no. 191 (January–February 1992), and *The Sphinx in the City: Urban Life, the Control of Disorder, and Women* (Berkeley: University of California Press, 1991); by M. Nava, "Modernity's Disavowal"; by G. Pollock, 'Modernity and the Spaces of Femininity," in *Vision and Difference: Femininity, Feminism and the Histories of Art* (London: Routledge, 1988); and in an earlier article of mine, "The Invisible *Flâneuse*: Women and the Literature of Modernity," *Theory, Culture & Society* 2, no. 3 (1985).

21 R. Shields, "A Guide to Urban Representation and What To Do About It: Alternative Traditions of Urban Theory," in *Re-Presenting the City: Ethnicity, Capital and Culture in the 21st-Century Metropolis*, ed. A. D. King (New York: New York University Press, 1996), p. 236.

22 D. E. Nord, "The Urban Peripatetic," p. 364. Nord bases her comments on the work of J. Walkowitz, *City of Dreadful Delight*, and L. Nead, *Myths of Sexuality: Representations of Women in Victorian Britain* (Oxford: Blackwell, 1988).

23 P. Petro has put this very well, in the context of her study of Weimar Germany: "The presence of women in places they had never been before (notably, in industry and in the cinema) explains the perceived threat of woman registered in various discourses during the Weimar years. And while it would be a mistake to assume that either the workplace or the cinema was entirely liberating for women, it would also be wrong to confuse male perceptions of woman with women's perception, for to do so would be to mistake male desire for female subjectivity." *Joyless Streets: Women and Melodramatic Representation in Weimar Germany* (Princeton, N.J.: Princeton University Press, 1989), p. 71.

24 M. Meskimmon, *We Weren't Modern Enough: Women Artists and the Limits of German Modernism* (Berkeley: University of California Press, 1999), p. 42. She discusses the work of the artists G. Overbeck, E. Haensgen-Dingkuhn and E. Lohse-Wächtler, amongst others.

25 M. Meskimmon, *We Weren't Modern Enough*, pp. 24–25.

26 See D. Frisby, "The *Flâneur* in Social Theory," and B. Mazlish, "The *Flâneur*: From Spectator to Representation," both in *The Flâneur*.

27 E. Wilson, "The Invisible *Flâneur*," p. 109.

28 R. Felski, *The Gender of Modernity* (Cambridge, Mass.: Harvard University Press, 1995), p. 211.

29 E. Wilson, *The Sphinx in the City*, p. 8.

30 M. de Certeau, *The Practice of Everyday Life*, trans. S. Rendall (Berkeley: University of California Press, 1984), p. xi.

31 J. Donald, *Imagining the Modern City*, p. 8.

32 J. Donald, "Metropolis: The City as Text," in *Social and Cultural Forms of Modernity*, eds R. Bocock and K. Thompson (Cambridge, UK: Polity Press/Open University, 1992), p. 442. See also J. Wolff, "The Real City, the Discursive City, the Disappearing City: Postmodernism and Urban Sociology," *Theory and Society* 21, no. 4 (1992).

33 J. Donald, *Imagining the Modern City*, pp. 8 and 17.

34 V. Woolf, "Street Haunting: A London Adventure," in *The Essays of Virginia Woolf*, vol. 4 (London: The Hogarth Press, 1994).

35 V. Woolf, *Mrs Dalloway* (New York: Harcourt Brace Jovanovich, 1925). See, for example, R. Bowlby, "Walking, Women and Writing: Virginia Woolf as *Flâneuse*," in *Still Crazy After All These Years* (London: Routledge, 1992). See also D. E. Nord, "The Urban Peripatetic," pp. 374–375.

36 At least, in *The American Heritage Dictionary* this is given as the secondary meaning of "haunt," the first being "to visit or appear to as a ghost or spirit."

37 J. Donald, *Imagining the Modern City*, p. 24.

38 R. Shields, "A Guide to Urban Representation," p. 231; R. Deutsche, "Reasonable Urbanism," in *Giving Ground: The Politics of Propinquity*, eds J. Copjec and M. Sorkin (London: Verso, 1999), p. 183.

39 H. Heynen, *Architecture and Modernity: A Critique* (Cambridge, Mass.: MIT Press, 1999), pp. 200–208, 222.

40 H. Heynen, *Architecture and Modernity*, p. 223. See also A. Vidler, *The Architectural Uncanny: Essays in the Modern Unhomely* (Cambridge, Mass.: MIT Press, 1992).

41 J. Donald, *Imagining the Modern City*, p. 73. See also A. Vidler, *The Architectural Uncanny*.

42 A. F. Gordon, *Ghostly Matters: Haunting and the Sociological Imagination* (Minneapolis: University of Minnesota Press, 1997), pp. 7–8.

43 For a brilliant analysis of the uncanny in modernity, which combines socio-historical and psychoanalytic methods, see P. Stallybrass and A. White, *The Politics and Poetics of Transgression* (London: Methuen, 1986).

44 R. Deutsche, "Agoraphobia," in *Evictions: Art and Spatial Politics* (Cambridge, Mass.: MIT Press, 1996), p. 325. On this basis, the discourse of ghosts is reversed, as Deutsche, to some extent following B. Robbins' lead, identifies "the public sphere" itself as the phantom – that is, as being imaginary. See *The Phantom Public Sphere*, ed. B. Robbins (Minneapolis: University of Minnesota Press, 1993).

45 J. Donald, *Imagining the Modern City*, pp. 144, 167.

46 J. Donald, *Imagining the Modern City*, p. 96.

47 The insistent presence of the *flâneur* in the literature on gender and modernity is itself perceived as a kind of ghost story by J. Donald, who asks "why does the spectral presence of the *flâneuse* haunt the discussion" of public space? J. Donald. *Imagining the Modern City*, p. 112.

3

Women in public: the display of femininity in the parks of Paris

Greg M. Thomas

Introduction

The classical model of the *flâneur* is encapsulated in many ways by Edouard Manet's *Street Singer* and Mary Cassatt's *Five O'Clock Tea*.[1] *Street Singer*, painted in 1862, is a quintessential embodiment of the *flâneur*'s gaze, inspired by Manet's chance encounter with a singer while strolling outdoors with his friend and fellow artist Antonin Proust in a section of Paris being destroyed and rebuilt by Haussmann. Proust cited the picture as a prime example of Manet's identity as a *flâneur*, and it is a virtual map of Baudelaire's notion of *flânerie* as a casual, urban, and sexually interested roaming about.[2] The 1880 *Five O'Clock Tea*, by contrast, epitomizes the opposite, embodying an inverse experience of modernity, with bourgeois women – Cassatt's own friends and relations – confined to the home, their movement constricted, their gaze deflected by the compressed interior spaces that defined their role in modern Parisian society. This is how Griselda Pollock has interpreted the picture, and her argument is based in part on Janet Wolff's account of the separation of spheres in nineteenth-century England: that is, the physical and symbolic division of society and culture into public space, dominated by men, and private space, the zone of women and family.[3] These two works thus represent two focal points in the gender economy of modernity in Paris in the later nineteenth century: men roaming the public sphere, women sequestered in the private sphere. Two sides of the same coin, both reinforce the classical notion of the *flâneur*. Neither picture suggests that women had access to the active gaze and scopic power of the *flâneur*. Wolff raised the theoretical possibility of the "*flâneuse*" as a counterpart to the *flâneur*, but only to emphasize its impossibility.

Two other paintings by these artists, however, take a more ambiguous view of flânerie. Cassatt's *Woman and Child Driving* of 1881 depicts a woman out in public, actively roaming the shady avenues of the newly renovated Bois de Boulogne (Figure 1). Though appearing stiff and alert to the presence of other gazes, this woman is also independent and in control of her movement, driving her companions unescorted.

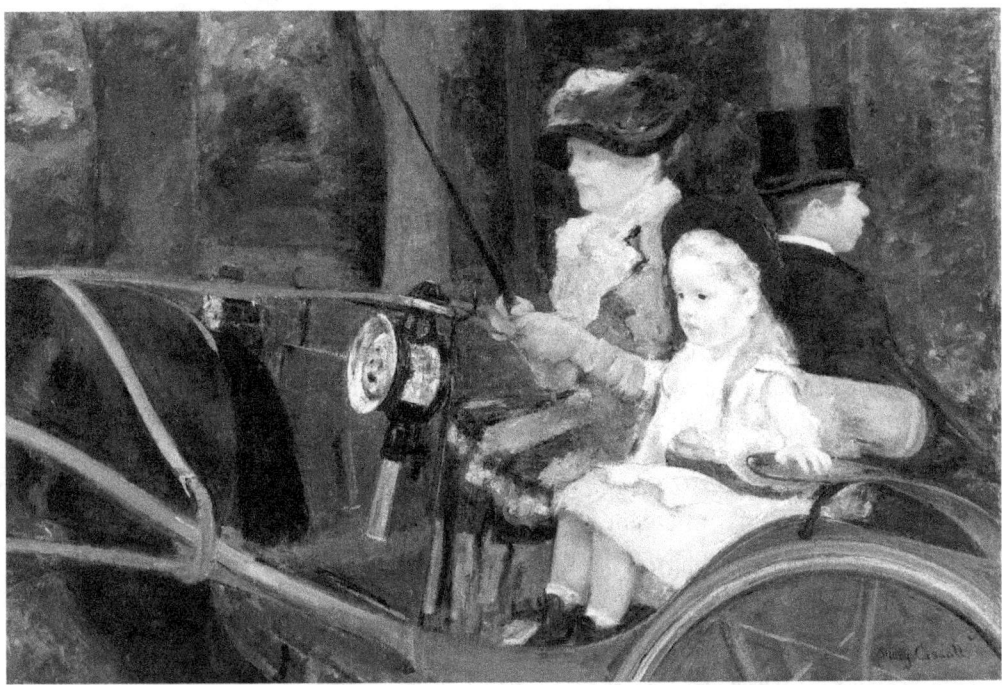

1 Mary Cassatt, *Woman and Child Driving*, 1881

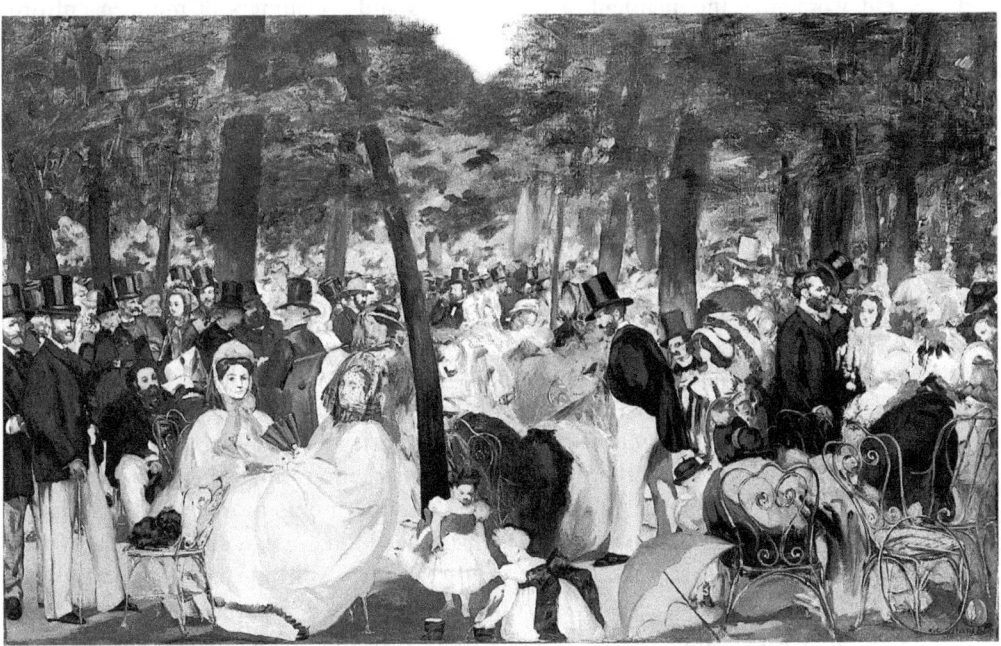

2 Edouard Manet, *Concert in the Tuileries*, 1862

Manet's *Concert in the Tuileries* of 1862 likewise blurs the *Street Singer*'s neat distinction between male subject and female object of the gaze (Figure 2). Men are roaming
the crowd and consuming the visual spectacle, which includes above all the elegantly
dressed women, but these bourgeois women take their own view of things, confidently returning and deflecting the viewer's gaze in the same way as Manet, standing
at the left edge. In both *Driving* and *Concert*, then, women take on some of the characteristics commonly attributed to men in public space, while the viewer's gender is left
more ambiguous.

While similar in complicating the gender economy of the Parisian visual order,
these two paintings also share a common setting, for both are staged in Parisian
parks. And it is on this relationship between ambiguous *flânerie* and park settings
that I will concentrate in what follows. Pollock identified parks and theater halls as
liminal spaces of modernity, urban sites caught between or outside the public and
private spheres, where women could be seen without being categorized as fallen
and sexualized, where they could inscribe alternate interpretations of femininity.[4] I
want to carry that argument further, charting the way parks allowed alternate views
of femininity and modernity to be staged in Paris. My argument will have two main
steps. Historically, I will show, parks were indeed key segments of public space to
which women laid equal claim as men; more specifically, parks staged family life
and feminine culture as positive and essential elements of the modern urban public
sphere, counterbalancing the dominance of masculine *flânerie*. Artistically, I will
further argue, they enabled painters such as Cassatt and Berthe Morisot to represent women as independent, active creators and consumers of modern culture,
diminishing the experiential constraints described by Pollock. While parks did not
quite convert bourgeois women into *flâneuses*, they did enable an alternate coding
of public space that undermines the model of the *flâneur*.

Whether such images actually represent a "*flâneuse*" or not depends on which
notion of *flânerie* one uses. Baudelaire conceived of the *flâneur* in very strict terms,
not just as a man, but as a male poet or artist endowed with a special capacity of
metropolitan and sexually charged vision.[5] Viewed this way, a *flâneuse* would have
to be a female poet or artist with a sexually cognizant gaze, and Elizabeth Wilson
has consequently suggested prostitutes as the closest approximation in Paris.[6] Yet
equating the prostitute with a Baudelaire or Manet would contradict the fundamental relation of power and visual domination that is really the heart of the idea of
the *flâneur*. Walter Benjamin extended the idea somewhat, applying it to the specific spatial experience of nineteenth-century Parisian boulevards, accompanied by
commercial culture and the male privilege of free movement in the city.[7] Recent
scholars, however, have interpreted the notion much more broadly. Priscilla
Ferguson defines *flânerie* in nineteenth-century Paris as a general mode of narrating the new urban text and fixing the modern, shifting, unknown city.[8] And
Anke Gleber uses *flânerie* as a trope representing a general practice of urban
roaming with a roaming gaze; she consequently posits the emergence of the *flâneuse*
in the literature and film of early twentieth-century Berlin.[9]

Did women, like men, roam Paris narrating the urban text? Apparently they did, on the evidence of photographic records (e.g. Figure 3) and paintings such as Morisot's *View of Paris from the Trocadéro* of c. 1871–72. But this overly broad interpretation of *flânerie* misses the main point, I think, which is to refine our measurement of how tightly women were constrained by the public/private spatial order of modern Paris and to what degree art reinforced or undermined the dominant power of the male *flâneur*'s gaze in the public realm. To gauge these qualities of modern culture, we have to identify not so much pictures that seem to take the *flâneuse* as a motif, but pictures whose viewpoint challenges the *flâneur*'s domination or grants female viewers an equivalent kind of scopic power. In judging Cassatt's now famous *At the Opera* of 1878, for example, the key question is not whether the man or the woman in the picture has the upper hand in their visual dual, but whether the viewer can be imagined to be a man or a woman who might view the entire scene as the personal object of his/her own privileged, casual glance. If ever there was a suitable candidate to be a *flâneuse*, it was Cassatt, who had the requisite class, freedom, and poetic genius.[10] And yet in the end, I do not think she fashioned a *flâneuse*'s point of view any more than Manet did. In a number of paintings set in parks, however, she, Manet, and Morisot represented women as equals to the *flâneur* in terms of defining and dominating the public sphere.

Parks and public spectacle

The parks of Paris were, first and foremost, an extension of boulevard culture, important segments of the public sphere intended to fulfill the same aims underlying the renovation of the urban center: to make Paris utterly modern in both form and function; to bring visual and social order to the city and its classes; to help solidify the emperor's power; to enhance health and hygiene; to spur investment and raise land values; to offer new forms of entertainment (the racetrack rather than the opera); and to create new modes of display for the bourgeoisie to naturalize its modern rites and forms of identity. For Napoleon III and his director of renovations, Baron Haussmann, Paris was to be the very definition of modernity, and parks were an absolutely integral element of the new order.

The process of park improvements has been well studied.[11] Hired by Napoleon III in 1853, Haussmann, along with his chief engineer for the parks, Adolphe Alphand, transformed the Bois de Boulogne between then and 1856. In 1859–60, Paris annexed surrounding land, nearly doubling the size of the city and encompassing both Boulogne, to the west, and the Bois de Vincennes, to the east. Vincennes was then acquired by the city and renovated between 1860 and 1863. Within Paris, Haussmann created innumerable pockets of greenery, along with several large new parks strategically placed to serve different neighborhoods: the Parc Monceau was acquired in 1860 and completed in 1861, the Buttes-Chaumont was installed between 1864 and 1867, and the Parc Montsouris was acquired in 1867 but completed only in 1878. The grandest and most important

interior parks, however, were the old royal gardens of the Luxembourg and
Tuileries palaces. Gracing the Left Bank, the Luxembourg Gardens were renovated, despite public protest, in the 1860s.[12] The Tuileries were not altered,
except by the destruction of the Tuileries Palace in 1871. Just as the neighboring
Rue de Rivoli served as a model for Haussmann's new boulevards, the Tuileries
were a model for the new parks. Except for a corner of the Tuileries reserved for
the imperial family, all these parks were open to the public, and indeed one of their
primary functions was to realize a physical public sphere. The continuous and
highly elaborate development of the parks throughout the emperor's reign testifies
to their central role in his conception of modern Paris. And although Haussmann
and Alphand met some fierce criticism, the parks for the most part succeeded
spectacularly; tourists and Parisians alike flocked to them and they were widely
heralded as shining emblems of modernization.

Interpretations and usage of the parks, however, varied considerably. In print
and visual culture of the time, representations of the parks ranged from images of
highly formalized ritual, reinforcing Haussmann's ideal public order, to images of
highly informal behavior and private experience. Across this spectrum, women and
families are prominent as both real users and implied viewers of the parks, suggesting that parks offered women the opportunity to play a more active role in the
public sphere, engaging modernity not only as objects of spectacle but also as subjects of it, consuming the pleasures on offer and helping define the experiences,
habits, and appearance of modernity in the public sphere.

The more formal mode of representation conforms to Haussmann's official
vision of Paris, and the most official example of all is the lavish two-volume book
called *The Promenades of Paris* produced between 1867 and 1873 by Alphand.[13] Its
official state function is clear from the opening list of people given copies of the
book, beginning with "the Emperor of France" and including European kings,
nobles, architects, engineers, and libraries. The book is largely an engineering trea-
tise, dominated by diagrams of benches, planters, plumbing, and so on, a lavish section on trees and bushes, and long technical explanations of every facet of the
renovations. Sections on individual parks are also peppered with wood engravings
showing the parks in action, and in these we learn how comportment and vision
were being engineered. Like diagrams of spectacle, the pictures typically show
mostly bourgeois Parisians strolling or riding along ample avenues while surveying
the artificial, picturesque sites and enjoying various kinds of commercial entertainment. Men, women, children, and family groups are all depicted, but all in very
formal ways. Play rarely appears among these promenades, and never the casual
merriment of, say, Renoir's *Luncheon of the Boating Party*. These are normative
images of official, neatly ordered bourgeois spectacle.

Whereas Impressionist paintings, furthermore, tend to reproduce the casual
glimpse of the *flâneur* himself, Alphand's prints tend to reproduce the elevated,
picturesque touristic gaze typical of guidebooks of the time. In Paris guides written
by the famous Adolphe-Laurent Joanne, for example, prints similarly depict

women, couples, and families, as well as individual men, promenading and partaking of entertainment in various parks, while the text emphasizes history, renovations, and picturesque effects.[14] In effect, Joanne and others thematized modern bourgeois spectacle as a key tourist attraction, even explicitly recommending that tourists visit the Bois de Boulogne in the late afternoon to watch the daily parade of fine fashion and fancy carriages.

To some extent, reality seems to have mirrored the official program. Photographs of the 1870s and 1880s reveal Parisians conforming to the park's ritual structures of pleasure and vision. One shows people promenading about the Tuileries fountain, striking the same poses as in Joanne's earlier prints. Another photograph shows carriages filing out of the Bois de Boulogne, confirming the synchronized ritual display described by numerous commentators. These same photographs, however, reveal other, less officially sanctioned modes of behavior and vision. Some show children playing, for example, and many show women out on their own, promenading with their children, with other women, or even alone. The Luxembourg Gardens in particular clearly offered a public space in which mothers, nannies, and children were relatively free to engage in the kind of play, childcare, and woman-to-woman exchange usually associated with the private sphere (Figure 3). In this case, the public and private spheres overlap and femininity plays a prominent role in defining modern public life.

Images from popular visual culture confirm this mixed identity of the parks. An 1887 painting by the Finnish artist Albert Edelfelt, for example, zooms in on the domestic subculture at Luxembourg.[15] No men are present, and the viewpoint has little suggestion of *flânerie*. Most of the women wear the distinctive costumes of nursemaids and nannies, suggesting the children are from bourgeois families, but two or three mothers are included as well. The park is cast as a public space overtaken by domestic life and dominated by the work, leisure, and gaze of women.

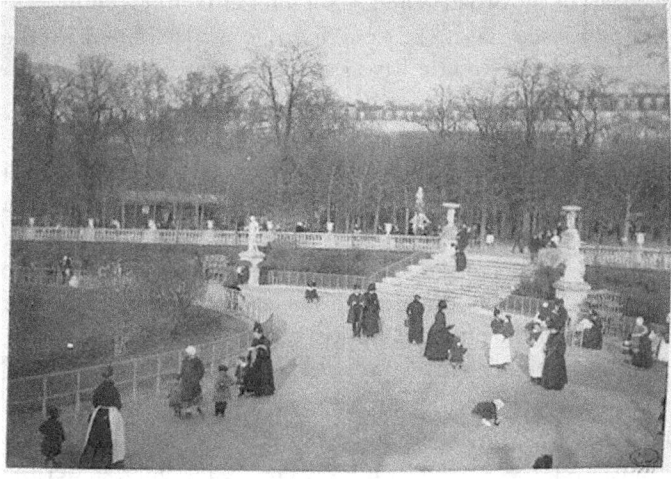

3 H. Blancard, photograph of the Luxembourg Gardens, 1887–89

Another, popular painting of the Luxembourg gives women a still more active role, not only showing children, mothers, and nannies, but also showing young women promenading in groups and actively conversing with young men of the Latin Quarter.[16] Both these examples contrast sharply with John Singer Sargent's 1879 painting of the park, which echoes Haussmann's vision of modernity by concentrating attention on one promenading bourgeois couple set against the garden's spare formal geometry.[17]

Such images indicate that in terms of both actual usage and representations in the visual and literary discourse of modernity, parks had a split personality. On the one hand, they functioned and were interpreted as extensions of the boulevard, staging spectacle based on the dominance of the *flâneur* and the view of women as objects of beauty, fashion, and family. On the other hand, they opened a space within the public sphere where women had more power to influence people's behavior and the interpretation of the modernized city. This power derived in large part from the fact that the ideal bourgeois family was a key token of what was modern and successful in the life of bourgeois men; the public display of wives, mothers, and private family life thus became important to the identity of men. But women's influence also derived from their freedom to use the parks, write about them, and paint in them.

Manet in the Tuileries

As the above analysis implies, when the Impressionists painted Haussmann's parks, they treated a subject carrying a complex mix of possible meanings, ranging across the public and the private, from the spectacle of women on display for the male *flâneur* to the ideal of the bourgeois nuclear family to the independence of women dominating a public space essential to modernity. Typical of his oeuvre, Manet evoked such complexities in his *Concert in the Tuileries* of 1862 (Figure 2).[18] Situated at the symbolic heart of the urban center, the Tuileries Gardens connected the Louvre to the Champs-Elysées and Arc de Triomphe while framed by the Seine along the south edge and the Rue de Rivoli along the north. The gardens were laid out by Le Nôtre in 1665, including the grand central alley with trees planted in quincunx patterns on both sides, terraces around the park's edges, scattered statues, and the octagonal fountain at the western end next to the Place de la Concorde. Minor alterations were made in the late eighteenth and early nineteenth centuries, and Napoleon III added the Orangerie in 1853 and Jeu de Paume (the royal family tennis courts) in 1861, both at the western edge. The gardens were apparently open to the public daily from morning to sunset, except for a section in the south-east corner reserved for the imperial family.[19]

Manet's painting probably depicts a grove of regularly planted chestnut trees in the south-western quadrant of the gardens. Joanne's 1876 guidebook identifies this as the location of daily concerts: "During summers, a music performance by the Paris garrison can be heard everyday except Sunday, from 5:00 to 6:00, under the chestnut trees that spread between the allée des Orangers and the grand alley in the middle."[20] Sundays were workers' holidays, and as we shall see with the Bois de Boulogne, the summer custom for the bourgeoisie was to promenade in the parks Monday through Saturday – not Sunday, as many writers assume – between about five o'clock and seven. By indicating that his scene includes one of these concerts, Manet thus specified a particular moment in a particular public ritual of the bourgeoisie. The precise location was also a significant marker of class identity; the Allée des Orangers was said to be "especially beloved by young and elegant mothers," whereas just across the grand central alley, the north-western quadrant, called Petite-Provence, was frequented by "old people, invalids, and kids."[21] This crowd, along with workers, is displayed in all its inelegance in an 1867 painting by Adolph von Menzel that is clearly set in Petite-Provence, with the central alley and palace off to the right. For his first major image of contemporary bourgeois public life, then, Manet treated one of the city's major spectacles – a key performance of class and gender – set in the imperial center of Haussmann's new imperial city.

As suggested by Robert Herbert and others, the painting certainly epitomizes *flânerie*, both by showing male artists and poets working the crowd and by reproducing the studied disarray and casual spontaneity of a *flâneur*'s vision.[22] At the same time, however, the picture also makes the family central to public identity and suggests women's multiple roles as fashion icons, active spectators, consumers of culture, and mothers. Manet's own figure at the far left acts as an explicit hinge between the worlds of the viewer and the viewed, thematizing *flânerie* and helping propel the viewer's reading from left to right across the frieze-like composition. Immediately right of him sit the picture's most prominent and clearly defined figures, two women who seem to play the part of *flâneuse* to Manet's *flâneur*. They, like Manet himself, return the viewer's gaze with inscrutable self-possession; like Manet, they consume the spectacle around them, including the concert that we assume is taking place behind the viewer; and their similar dresses, bonnets, and poses suggest something of a feminine equivalent to the men's *habit noir* – the replication of a standardized bourgeois type of fashionable costume and comportment. Manet's top hat is met by the bonnet and veil of the woman on the right. Where his gloved hand holds a cane, hers holds a fan. His black and grey is complemented by her blue and cream. Point for point, the women act as feminine equivalents to the *flâneur*.

The center of the picture, on the other hand, introduces a different kind of feminine identity. A pair of girls echoes the pair of women, suggesting that these near *flâneuses* may also be mothers.[23] By displaying their sand-play so prominently, Manet emphasizes the presence of casual family life in public parks, reinforced by the tangle of women and children stuffing the center of the space. Motherhood and childhood also dominate the right-hand side of the composition. To the right of the umbrella we see the back of a woman in a chair, her head and face obscured under a large black bonnet with ribbon and flower in red. Rarely if ever mentioned in analyses of the painting, this figure is bent forward, her left arm and billowy sleeve reaching out to hold the shoulder of a child – apparently a boy – wearing a propeller hat. Much of the child's face is carefully blotted out by a large white patch of paint. Though inconclusive, this white blotch most resembles a handkerchief pressed by the woman's right hand against the child's apparently runny nose. An unusually casual and intimate detail to include in the foreground of such an important image of formal promenading, it acts as a counterweight to the formal, frontal, and erect women at the left. This suggestion of play and family life is again reinforced by the presence of a second mother seated at the far right who similarly faces inward and holds a small girl on her lap; by the child's hoop resting against the empty chair; and by the ball carefully perched above Manet's signature. Messy, active, and difficult to discern, this entire vignette contrasts sharply with its mirror vignette on the left – the clear, colorful, and restrained group of Manet and the two seated women.

In *Concert*, private family life becomes an integral component of public spectacle, and the more official and touristic vision of order and promenading contends with a highly informal vision of chaotic play and family bustle. This is clearly the bourgeoisie at its most distilled and self-conscious; but it is a bourgeoisie in which feminine identity is complex, inconclusive. The men hover around the edges looking at the women, but the women they watch take on a range of identities, dominating the action and undermining the simple binary of subject and object implied by the concept of *flânerie*.

Other imagery of the period reveals similar complexities in the meaning or identity of the Tuileries. Compared to the formal spaces and promenades shown in the prints of Alphand and Joanne, Menzel's painting of the Tuileries introduces an array of contradictions. The palace is merely glimpsed in the background, the geometry of the trees is less apparent, and the space – on a Sunday, no doubt – is packed with wailing children, running dogs, and a wide variety of classes, ages, and ethnic types. A popular watercolor by Eugen von Guérard showing the same section of the park on a Sunday retains the clarity of the palace, the plantings, and the Rue de Rivoli, but only as a comical foil to the chaotic rumble of wild children in the foreground.[24] And a number of children's park guides could be cited that represent the Tuileries and other parks as vast playgrounds devoted wholly to children's pleasures, with monuments reduced to token signifiers of the site and adults virtually expunged from view.[25] Set against such a range of images, Manet's painting strikes a tentative balance between the powers of the public sphere and the private, between formality and informality, between the *flâneur* and the family.

Cassatt and Morisot in the Bois de Boulogne

In Haussmann's grand configuration of Paris, the central axis of modern spectacle that began at the Tuileries ended in the Bois de Boulogne. The Bois became widely recognized as the most important site of public spectacle in Paris. Already in 1856, the guidebook writer Adolph Joanne lavished praise on the recent renovations, especially modern amenities such as the artificial lake system, steam-powered rail

access, and new racetracks.[26] Fending off critics who regretted the transformation
of the Bois from forest to park, he writes: "It grows more beautiful every day and
before long, it will become one of Europe's most magnificent promenades."[27] This
claim was confirmed a decade later, in a guide to the city written by a constellation
of French writers and published at the time of the 1867 Exposition Universelle. In
a chapter devoted to the Bois, novelist Amédée Achard claims outright that "the
Bois de Boulogne is the promenade of Europe," greater and more universal than
any other park.[28] With repeated references to the spectacle of crowds and carriages,
Achard goes on to chart the regular daily and seasonal rhythms of the park: in the
summer, mornings are a quiet time for equestrians and lovers, while afternoons see
grand processions of carriages entering from the Champs-Elysées and circling the
lake from 5:00 to 7:00 p.m.; in winter, the processions peak between 2:00 and 4:00
p.m., with ice-skating offering another opportunity for grand spectacle.[29] Whereas
the Champs-Elysées used to be the "grande promenade" of Parisians, he sums up,
"today, it is no more than a grandiose and charming passage leading to the Bois de
Boulogne."[30]

While Joanne and Achard thus characterize the park as extending and supplanting the boulevard as the center of public urban spectacle, more detailed texts
introduce a more complex range of functions and meanings. Edouard Gourdon's
lengthy 1861 guide to Boulogne reiterates the observations of Joanne and Achard,
but augments it with discussions of the working classes, public holidays, and the
many attractions for children.[31] Still less official in tone is the *Guide to the Bois de
Boulogne* by Mary Osborne, an unknown writer, published to coincide with the
Exposition Universelle of 1878. Echoing Achard, this 126-page text opens with a
declaration of the park's international importance: "Every great capital of Europe
possesses, like Paris, its special promenade which, on certain days at certain times,
becomes the general meeting place of the cosmopolitan and fashionable circle."[32]
But she goes on to say that Boulogne is not only for the wealthy, for it offers
everyone "the absolute freedom to follow his/her tastes" – from young to old, from
"the high-class woman who skirts the banks of the Grand Lake to the enraptured
mother, urging on her child's first hesitant steps."[33] She praises the beauty, calm,
and solitude to be found in the park (features mentioned only briefly by Achard),
and talks at length about it being a balm to anyone's emotional suffering.

In the pictures and main body of her text, Osborne dutifully maps the tokens of
modern bourgeois spectacle: the high cost of Alphand's renovations; the modern
modes of reaching the park by carriage, train, and boat; the picturesque artificial
lakes; the good restaurants; the new racetrack, photography studio, and ice rink;
and so on. But at the same time, she dwells on some of the special experiences
available to women and children. She emphasizes the fun children have feeding the
swans on the lake, for example, and the longest chapter of the guide is devoted to
the children's garden, detailing all the animals, amusements, and performances to
be found in the garden's zoo, botanical garden, and playground.[34] Significantly, the
second longest chapter covers Longchamp, but most of this text recounts the

history of the site, with only a few pages at the end discussing the track and no description of the races themselves.[35] Osborne does hint at the track's importance as a place for women's display of bourgeois fashion, but considering the attention lavished on the children's garden, it seems Osborne located the modernity of Boulogne as much in the informal pleasures targeting women and children of various classes as in the ritualized elite entertainment of the racetrack. The fact that Osborne was (presumably) a woman makes the text doubly important, revealing the ability of women to participate directly in the construction of the discourse surrounding modernity and the public sphere.[36]

Paintings of the Bois similarly show a range of attitudes towards the park's identity. For Manet and Degas, the preferred motif was the track, and while their pictures of horse racing at Longchamp and elsewhere tend to portray women as fashionable fixtures of this modern diversion, they also reveal an interesting reversal of *flânerie*. For the women lining the edge of the track are also active spectators watching performances by men, making the races in this perimeter park something of an inverse of the theater and *café-concert* in the urban center. Renoir's major painting of the Bois focuses on its main winter spectacle, ice-skating;[37] men, women, and children are all present, playing many roles in the economy of entertainment and display, while the high vantage point and even distribution of dabbed figures work to reinforce an official, touristic vision of picturesque harmony.

Cassatt and Morisot took quite a different approach to Boulogne, emphasizing private, individual experience in the park and the relative freedom of women to enjoy this roomy segment of the public sphere. Cassatt's lone Boulogne scene is *Woman and Child Driving* of 1881, a large and elaborately worked out painting, but one that she apparently never exhibited in public (Figure 1). It focuses on one intimate anecdote within the Bois, showing Cassatt's sister Lydia driving the family's small carriage with their groom at back and Degas's niece, Odile Fèvre, riding along.[38] Again, the time is likely a weekday afternoon, not a Sunday as often assumed. In contrast to Renoir's earlier picture of a similar motif – *The Morning Ride* of 1873 – the space in Cassatt's work is highly compressed, a trait Griselda Pollock sees as essential to Cassatt's indexing of women's social and spatial restriction. Lydia and the girl are also stiff and restrained, implying they are conscious of the ubiquitous gaze of the *flâneur* policing the park's avenues and perhaps riding past in the viewer's position. On the other hand, the painting is quite exceptional in showing a woman active and in control. Lydia drives herself, and the firm structure of the harnessing apparatus emphasizes her power and skill. Renoir's image is only superficially similar in this regard; it uses the Bois unabashedly as a setting for official display of a high society portrait.

Owning such a carriage was a key signifier of bourgeois status in the parks, and the mobility of horseback riding and carriage driving helped separate the rich from the poor. In 1856, Joanne wrote that because the park is far from the city, "one must be idle and rich to be able to go promenading there often; because unless one lives in a nearby village, one must get there by carriage."[39] There were other means of access, including buses, a train, and carriage rentals, and the park filled with the poorer classes on Sundays, but the rest of the week it remained the reserve of the wealthy. According to Joanne, furthermore, the daily carriage promenade from four to five o'clock was highly self-conscious "theatre": "This is the best time to watch the costumes, carriages, horses, manners, vices, the absurdities of all those characters of different kinds – high world or the entire world, low world or *demi-monde* – who meet here to show off to one another, envy one another, and criticize one another."[40] Zola detailed this ritual of display in the opening scene of his 1872 *La Curée*, and Gourdon even claimed that the display of carriages in the Bois was more important for women than the display of fashion and jewels.[41]

Cassatt herself regularly went horseback riding in the Bois, and *Woman and Child Driving* clearly situates her well-established family within the culture of bourgeois display.[42] Yet the picture's bold cropping complicates that reading by blocking our view of the entire horse and carriage and excluding any sign of the crowds that figure so prominently in Manet's and Degas's works, the parade of carriages so lauded in guidebook descriptions of the Bois, and the formal landscaping, modern accoutrements, and commercial establishments that marked the modernity of Alphand's park design. Other promenaders may be near – what else but a passing carriage would give the viewer this close-up view? – but Cassatt does not acknowledge their presence and leaves their identity unclear. She casts the site as a dense wood pierced by the road on which Lydia drives and deserted side alleys like the one clearly receding in the upper left, just the sort commonly described by writers as offering a secretive hideaway for lovers and a quiet refuge from public crowds.

This effect of a fleeting moment caught between the public and the private is reinforced by the profoundly enigmatic expressions of the figures. The woman and girl are as rigid and self-conscious as their servant, all three equally under surveillance, equally constrained by the invisible social structure of the public sphere. At the same time, however, Lydia appears determined and powerful; she wears the anonymous reserve of a *flâneur*, with a sense of controlled energy emanating from her clenched right hand at the picture's center. And by pairing what initially appear to be a mother and daughter or aunt and niece, Cassatt emphasizes the social formation of the girl through family relations, with the active Lydia serving as a feminine model of modern public behavior. Thus the picture uses the park as a site of uncommon public assertiveness, where a woman, although on formal display, is able to enter public space and public culture as an active consumer of modern life and an active agent of social formation.

Morisot's imagery depicts the Bois de Boulogne in yet another way, based in part on her special relationship to the site; strolling and sketching in the Bois was part of Morisot's own daily routine, in the company of other women or with her daughter and nanny. Morisot and her family lived in neighboring Passy from 1852 to 1895, and as argued in depth by Kathleen Adler, Passy was a new and highly exclusive suburb isolated from the city, where bourgeois women's daily rituals structured social life, creating an alternate form of modern public space distinct from the urban center.[43] In painting various facets of women's public life in this feminine enclave, Adler says, Morisot created an alternate form of modern culture distinct from the Baudelairean celebration of the boulevards. Her paintings of the Bois were an extension of this, representing the park as a continuation of the suburb, a sort of personal backyard that appears quiet, relatively empty, and dominated by the incidental lives of bourgeois women – with all signs of modern spectacle excluded.

In casting the park in such personal and feminine terms, Morisot, like Cassatt, challenged *flânerie* as the dominant mode of viewing modernity. The resulting tensions are particularly evident in *A Summer's Day*, painted in 1879 and exhibited in the 1880 Impressionist exhibition as *The Lake in the Bois de Boulogne* (Figure 4).[44] The two women are apparently boating on the Grand Lake, possibly riding the ferry to the Swiss-style restaurant on the picturesque couplet of islands. Photographs and prints from the era clarify the configuration of the site and the expected forms of behavior; a poor but informative wood engraving from Gourdon's 1861 book, for example, focuses on the social grouping of the bourgeois family, male promenader, and jaunty boatmen for hire, along with the picturesque grouping of boats, swans, artificial lake, bridge, and châlet (Figure 5). While the trip was a centerpiece of Boulogne's modern entertainments, Morisot's painting subverts the formal, touristic view of the park by excluding the obvious signs of modern pleasure. The boat itself is barely visible, the boatman is excluded, and the restaurant and bridge are left out of view to the right, while one catches only a

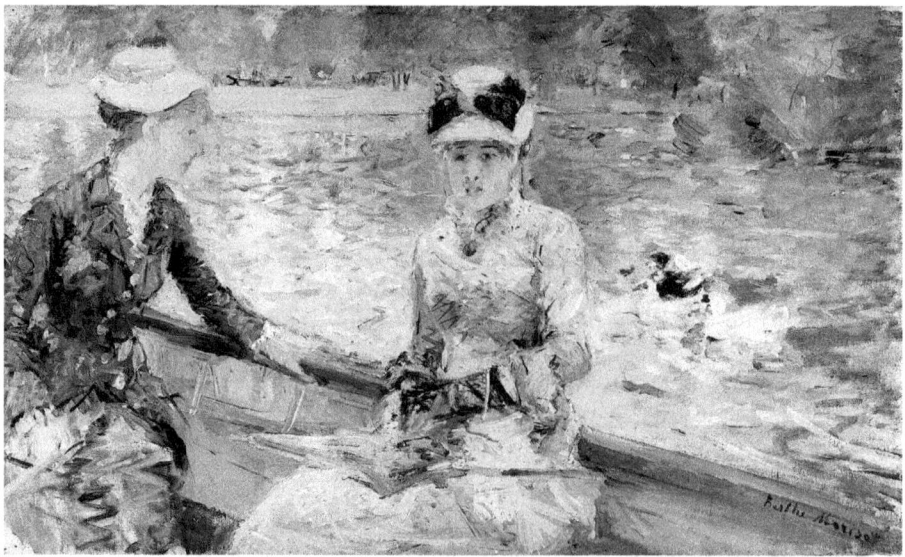

4 Berthe Morisot, *A Summer's Day*, 1879

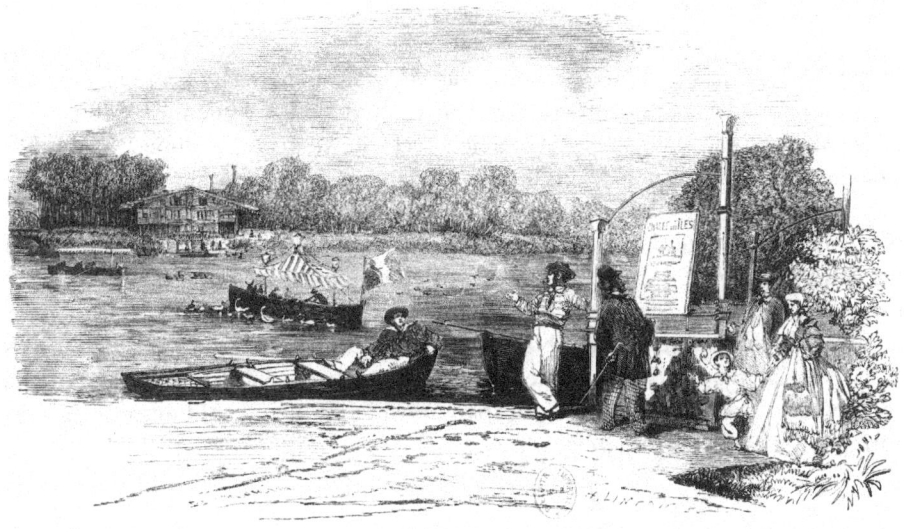

La rivière et le chalet des îles.

5 *The River and the Island Chalet*, 1861

glimpse of a passing carriage on the far bank. Attention is focused on the two
women, the water, and the ducks or swans – the only token of pleasure shown and
one that Osborne associated clearly with children and families.

Touristic appreciation of the scene is even more deeply undermined by
Morisot's open brushwork, which frays the dresses that could otherwise denote
high fashion and blurs the potentially picturesque delineation of water, space, and
wood. Tamar Garb has explained how this kind of technique was perceived at the
time as a feminized mode of vision,[45] making it easy for nineteenth-century viewers
to assume the viewpoint is that of a woman. The arrangement and expression of
figures reinforces this effect. With the foreground shallow and the horizon line
established only slightly above the two women's eye level, the picture posits a
viewer sitting in the boat, close to the woman in the center. Her return gaze – conscious but informal – seems to fix on someone she knows, while her pose is similarly
relaxed, as informal as can be expected in a public setting. Turning to gaze at the
water, the second woman seems equally at ease. All this suggests that the viewer is
another woman, engaged in an intimate gathering with friends. Squeezed together
and pressed into the left foreground, the three women appear restricted by the
same social and spatial constraints as the women and viewer in Cassatt's *Five
O'Clock Tea*, but with one major difference; here, this intimate, feminine world is
brought into the open, in a most public space at a most important site of modern
public spectacle. Again, the secluded, feminine sphere of Passy intersects the
public, spectacular sphere of Paris, and feminine experience is cast as an important
element of modern public life.

Conclusion

In the park pictures of Manet, Cassatt, and Morisot, then, the model of *flânerie* and the separation of spheres breaks down to some degree. Women are depicted as active viewers and consumers of public spectacle; some are grouped with other women, enjoying alternate forms of social engagement; and motherhood is brought into public view, emphasizing its importance to public bourgeois identity. The pictures also destabilize the identity of the viewer by confounding the dominance of the *flâneur*'s gaze as an interpretive trope. While not quite constructing an alternate trope of the *flâneuse*, they do represent women as competing equally with men for domination and definition of public space. Hausmann's parks were essential to this kind of social imagination; as zones of interchange between the private and public spheres, they opened a hybrid social space in which women could imagine participating on equal terms in public culture.

Notes

1 I am grateful to Valérie Munch and Noel Mak for their research assistance, and to colleagues at the University of Hong Kong who commented on one version of this essay. I also received financial assistance from the University of Hong Kong's University Research Committee.

2 A. Proust (1913), quoted in *Manet: A Retrospective*, ed. T. A. Gronberg (New York: Hugh Lauter Levin Associates, 1988), pp. 49–50. R. Herbert similarly uses it to define *flânerie* in his *Impressionism: Art, Leisure, and Parisian Society* (New Haven and London: Yale University Press, 1988), pp. 33–37; and the picture embodies many of the complexities of T. J. Clark's account of bourgeois spectacle, *The Painting of Modern Life: Paris in the Art of Manet and his Followers* (Princeton, N.J.: Princeton University Press, 1984).

3 G. Pollock, "Modernity and the Spaces of Femininity," in *Vision and Difference: Femininity, Feminism and the Histories of Art* (London and New York: Routledge, 1988), pp. 50–90; J. Wolff, *Feminine Sentences: Essays on Women and Culture* (Cambridge, Mass.: Polity Press, 1990).

4 G. Pollock, "Spaces of Femininity," pp. 79–85.

5 See K. Tester, "Introduction," in *The Flâneur*, ed. K. Tester (London and New York: Routledge, 1994), pp. 1–21.

6 E. Wilson, *The Sphinx in the City: Urban Life, the Control of Disorder, and Women* (Berkeley: University of California Press, 1991), pp. 47–64.

7 W. Benjamin, "Paris, Capital of the 19th century," *Reflections: Essays, Aphorisms, Autobiographical Writings*, trans. E. Jephcott (New York: Schocken Books, 1986), pp. 146–162.

8 P. Parkhurst Ferguson, *Paris as Revolution: Writing the 19th-Century City* (Berkeley: University of California Press, 1994).

9 A. Gleber, *The Art of Taking a Walk: Flânerie, Literature, and Film in Weimar Culture* (Princeton, N.J.: Princeton University Press, 1999).

10 G. Pollock, *Mary Cassatt: Painter of Modern Women* (London: Thames and Hudson, 1998), pp. 121–155.

11 See especially H. Massey Schenker, "Parks and Politics during the Second Empire in Paris," *Landscape Journal* 14, no. 2 (Fall 1995), pp. 201–219; F. Choay, "Haussmann et le système des espaces verts parisiens," *Revue de l'art* 29 (1975), pp. 83–99; R. Herbert, *Impressionism*, pp. 141–152; T. J. Clark, *The Painting of Modern Life*, Chapter 1.

12 H. Massey Schenker, "Parks and Politics," p. 201; A.-L. Joanne, *Paris illustré en 1870 et 1876: guide de l'étranger et du Parisien* (Paris: Hachette, 1876), p. 198.

13 A. Alphand, *Les Promenades de Paris . . .* (2 vols, Paris: J. Rothschild, 1867–73).

14 A.-L. Joanne, *Paris illustré en 1870: guide de l'étranger et du Parisien*, 3rd edn (Paris: Hachette, n.d.); also A.-L. Joanne, *Paris illustré en 1870 et 1876 . . .*

15 A. Edelfelt, *In the Luxembourg Gardens*, 1887. On nanny customs and costumes, see F. Faÿ-Sallois, *Les Nourrices à Paris au XIXe siècle* (Paris: Payot, 1980).

16 A painting apparently by E. Gluck, of unclear date, reproduced in M. Gaillard, *Paris au XIXe siècle* (Marseilles: AGEP, 1991), p. 128.

17 J. S. Sargent, *In the Luxembourg Gardens*, 1879.

18 This is no. 51 in D. Rouart and D. Wildenstein, *Edouard Manet: catalogue raisonné* (Lausanne: Bibliothèque des arts, 1975), vol. 1. It is discussed at length in N. G. Sandblad, *Manet: Three Studies in Artistic Conception* (Lund: C. W. K. Gleerup, 1954), which I have not been able to consult.

19 All this information is from A.-L. Joanne, *Paris illustré en 1870 et 1876 . . .*, pp. 191–196. The private reserve was opened to the public in summer, when the emperor was away; see Petit, *Promenades parisiennes* (Paris: A. Johanneau, n.d.), p. 261.

20 A.-L. Joanne, *Paris illustré en 1870 et 1876 . . .*, p. 196. All translations, unless otherwise noted, by the author. The same information appears in the 1885 edition: A. Joanne, *Paris illustré* (Paris: Hachette, 1885), p. 169. The catalogue of the 1983 Manet exhibition states that concerts were held twice a week, based on information from Duret's 1902 *Histoire d'Edouard Manet*; F. Cachin and C. Moffett, *Manet, 1832–1883* (New York: Metropolitan Museum of Art and Harry N. Abrams, 1983), p. 122 and n. 1.

21 A.-L. Joanne, *Paris illustré en 1870 et 1876 . . .*, p. 196.

22 See especially R. Herbert, *Impressionism*, pp. 37–38.

23 It is not certain that these two children are girls, since toddler boys commonly dressed like girls. But the propeller hat on the boy at right seems a deliberate demarcation of the sexes.

24 Undated, reproduced in M. Gaillard, *Paris au XIXe siècle*, p. 156.

25 Examples include: *Les Environs de Paris: récréations champêtres du petit monde parisien* (Paris and Pont-à-Mousson: Haguenthal, 1850); *Les Jardins de Paris* (Epinal: Pellerin, 1875); and P. Bonhomme, *Les Bébés des jardins de Paris* (Paris: A. Quantin, 1885).

26 A. Joanne, *Les Environs de Paris illustrés* (Paris: Hachette, 1856), pp. 3–26.

27 A. Joanne, *Les Environs de Paris illustrés*, p. 14.

28 *Paris-Guide par les principaux écrivains et artistes de la France*, vol. 2 (Paris: Librairie internationale, 1867), p. 1228.

29 *Paris-Guide*, pp. 1242–1244.

30 *Paris-Guide*, p. 1245.

31 E. Gourdon, *Le Bois de Boulogne* (Paris: A. Bourdilliat, 1861).

32 M. Osborne, *Guide au bois de Boulogne* (Paris: Auguste Ghio, 1878), p. 1.

33 M. Osborne, *Guide au bois de Boulogne*, pp. 2–3.

34 M. Osborne, *Guide au bois de Boulogne*, Chapter 8, "Jardin d'Acclimatation," pp. 27–42.

35 M. Osborne, *Guide au bois de Boulogne*, Chapter 14, "Longchamp," pp. 71–85.

36 The only further information I have found about Osborne is that she published one
    other book, *Légendes d'Etretat* (Paris: Lahure, 1875), about the renowned coastal vil-
    lage, addressed directly to children and emphasizing the healthful importance of vaca-
    tions in the countryside.

37 *Skaters in the Bois de Boulogne*, 1868. On skating in the Bois, see E. Gourdon, *Le Bois de
    Boulogne*, pp. 279–284.

38 Identification of the figures is widely agreed upon, based on an 1879 letter from
    Cassatt's mother to Cassatt's nephew R. Cassatt; the letter is quoted in A. Effeny,
    Cassatt (London: Studio Editions, 1991), p. 58. For other information about the
    painting, see especially A. D. Breeskin, *Mary Cassatt: A Catalogue Raisonné of the Oils,
    Pastels, Watercolors, and Drawings* (Washington, D.C.: Smithsonian Institution Press,
    1970), no. 69, and J. A. Barter, *Mary Cassatt: Modern Woman* (Chicago and New York:
    The Art Institute of Chicago and Harry N. Abrams, 1998), cat. no. 34.

39 A. Joanne, *Les Environs de Paris illustrés*, p. 14. Details about transportation, schedules,
    and prices appear on pp. 4–8.

40 A. Joanne, *Les Environs de Paris illustrés*, p. 14.

41 E. Gourdon, *Le Bois de Boulogne*, pp. 158–169.

42 On Cassatt's family and lifestyle, see especially N. M. Mathews, *Mary Cassatt, A Life*
    (New Haven and London: Yale University Press, 1994). Her habit of riding in the Bois
    is pointed out in M. Shennan, *Berthe Morisot: The First Lady of Impressionism*
    (Thrupp, Stroud, Gloucestershire: Sutton Publishing, 1996), p. 239.

43 K. Adler, "The suburban, the modern and 'une dame de Passy'," *Oxford Art Journal*
    12, no. 1 (1989), pp. 3–13. See also K. Adler and T. Garb, *Berthe Morisot* (Oxford:
    Phaidon Press, 1987), pp. 105–124.

44 This according to C. S. Moffett, *The New Painting: Impressionism 1874–1886* (San
    Francisco: The Fine Arts Museum of San Francisco, 1986), pp. 300–312.

45 T. Garb, "Berthe Morisot and the feminizing of Impressionism," in *Perspectives on
    Morisot*, ed. T. J. Edelstein (New York: Hudson Hills Press, 1990), pp. 57–66.

4

Dusting the surface, or the *bourgeoise*, the veil, and Haussmann's Paris

Marni Kessler

The foreground of a photograph taken c. 1850 during construction around the Palais Royal is filled with rubble and dust (Figure 6).[1] This picture documents a particular moment in Paris's pathology, a moment characterized by cultural chaos, disorder and change. Almost one half of this image contains the fragments of what had been there before. Forming a mosaic of the past, the rubble lingers at the physical surface of the photograph in abstract patterns. Simultaneously indexical and dead, and always a measure of change, this debris represents the metamorphosis of the physical city, and it also charts changes in late nineteenth-century social ideologies. At this time in France, dust became a trope for contemporary social anxieties over a perceived breakdown in class structure and moral behavior. While dust had always proliferated in Paris, the transformation of large sections of the city between 1852 and 1870 by Napoleon III and Baron Haussmann raised even more. On a literal level, a perceptible veil of dust settled over Paris as buildings were demolished and constructed, but what I want to show is that this dust was actually directly related to limiting bourgeois women's engagement with aspects of urban life and culture.[2] For Haussmann's dust generated the need for women to be veiled, which, in turn, affected how women saw and were seen in the spectacular new city.

Dust and the actual veil its presence inspired in French fashion are the historical remnants that allow us to trace shifts in ideology that inflected the position of bourgeois women in Paris during the second half of the nineteenth century. For the veil that was ostensibly a means of protecting the face from the filth of the construction also controlled how women experienced the city. And although there were at least three types of urban maskings in Haussmann's Paris – the unifying fabric of the new buildings, the dust of the destruction and construction which fell over the city, and the subsequent veiling of the female face – my focus here will be on the latter two and how they fit together to produce a framework for reading the conditions determining life for women in modern Paris. In fact, I will argue that the veil's popularity was actually a visual manifestation of the *bourgeoise*'s particularly vexing status in the city.

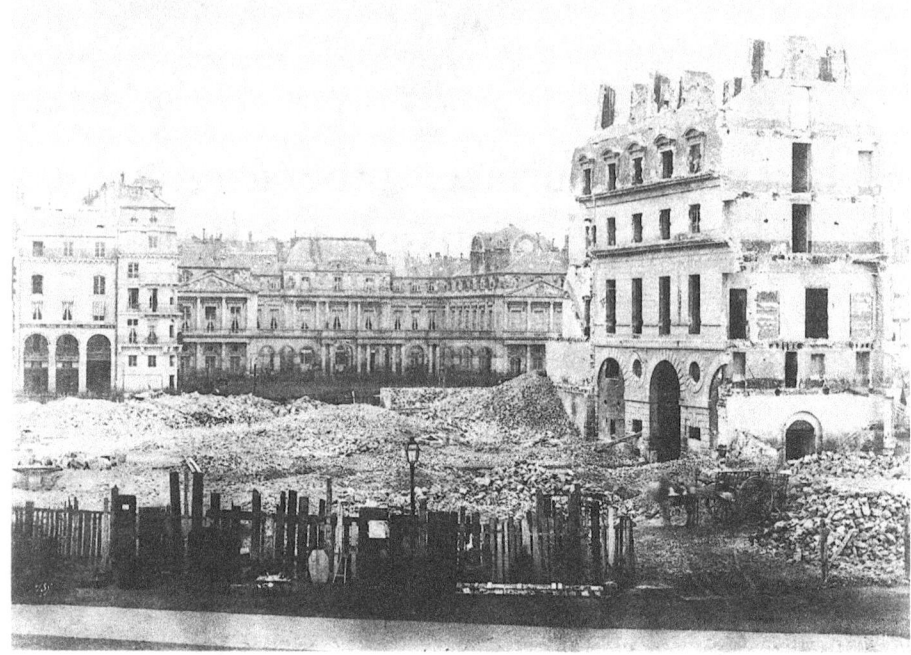

6 Charles Marville, *Palais Royal*, c. 1850

To be sure, the veil was only one of the devices that shaped women's lives in Second Empire Paris. As the old city was erased by its own dust and by Haussmann's buildings and boulevards, cultural imperatives increasingly erased proper women from parts of public life, for women who wanted to maintain their respectability were actively discouraged from visiting certain areas of the new city. Although not a transparent representation of social reality, an excerpt from Jules Michelet's *La Femme* of 1859 epitomizes a strain of the dominant ideology that endeavored to restrict proper women's activity:

> She [the *bourgeoise* alone] can hardly ever go out in the evening; she would be taken for a prostitute. There are a thousand places where only men are to be seen, and if she needs to go there for some reason, the men are amazed and laugh like fools. For example, should she find herself delayed and hungry at the other end of Paris, she will not dare to enter a restaurant. She would be an event, she would be a spectacle. All eyes would constantly be fixed on her.[3]

Women walking about the city without an escort were, according to Michelet, subject to inaccurate evaluations of their status. Mingling with the masses became, for a woman of respectable standing, increasingly unfamiliar and somewhat dangerous. The newly articulated geography of Paris and the moral risks associated with unaccompanied travel clearly affected respectable women's circulation within the modern city. In effect, as sidewalks made strolling in the city less messy and more enjoyable, the proper woman was limited from completely free use of them. As the renovations redefined and further codified zones of public and private, masculine and feminine, working class and bourgeois, the city progressively came to signify the world of labor, politics, and education, commonly perceived as the realm of men.[4] Public parks and uniform building façades were constructed in an effort to rejuvenate the health of the city and its inhabitants, to create the illusion of social equality, and to mask some of Paris's conflicts. The body of the city, or rather the face of the city, was literally and figuratively effaced by dust, veils, and façades, its signs of difference and politics smoothed over in order for it to appear, at least on the surface, coherent and unmarked by friction.

At the same time, the Parisian fashion industry began to erase the individual identities of particular women. The development of mass-produced clothing blurred lines of distinguishability previously established by *couturières*.[5] And the popular veil also obfuscated some signs of personal uniqueness. In an 1863 issue of *Le Journal des demoiselles*, one writer noticed the ways in which veils created the appearance of uniformity: "in the midst of these white dresses and all these veiled faces, even a woman's mother would have difficulty recognizing her."[6] While it did not obliterate the presence of the woman beneath it, the veil complicated the individualized features of the face.

While women were beginning to look somewhat homogeneous, so were the buildings being constructed around them. Indeed, one of the intentions of Haussmann's work was to produce a city of congruous surfaces and pleasing spaces. Paris benefitted from Haussmann's buildings, parks, and boulevards that enabled traffic, air, and water to circulate more easily. However, the program involved the displacement of parts of the population – primarily the poor, working classes, prostitutes, and bourgeois families – by shifting them to other areas of the city and its suburbs. The grand boulevards further standardized the surface of Paris, opening out sections that had been narrow, expanding and standardizing the field of vision.

At the very same time that broad fields of vision were facilitated by Haussmann's vistas, fashionable veils functioned dialectically to restrict the respectable woman's view. The veil, then, was integrated with the very structure of the new city, since one of its functions was to protect the proper woman from the dust, the ubiquitous traces of the old Paris. Yet, while it screened out some dust, the veil also filtered the *bourgeoise*'s view. This need for the manipulation of vision is linked to the fear that direct visual contact with the now more conspicuous prostitute would contaminate the respectable woman's character. By mid-century, especially after the construction of wide boulevards and the destruction of areas that were previously locales for brothels, prostitutes were even more noticeable in Paris. Additionally, the prohibitive rents in the Haussmannized districts of the city forced many prostitutes on to the streets, making them appear to be more numerous than before. Even though the prostitute was regarded as a necessary evil of bourgeois society, she nonetheless had to remain undetectable in public. In fact, one of the main goals of the regulationist movement spearheaded by Alexandre Parent-Duchâtelet in the 1830s was to ensure the invisibility of the venal woman.[7] His work was both symptomatic of and an instigation for spreading fears of social contagion.

Contemporary accounts promoted a panic as they warned of the abundance of prostitutes in the city. For example, in his guide to Paris of 1869, James D. McCabe, Jr. noted the prominence of the *demi-monde*:

> You cannot go into any public place in Paris without meeting one or more women that you will recognize at a glance as belonging to the class known in French society and fiction as the Demi-Monde. You find them at the theatres, in the concert halls, in the Cafés, on the Boulevards, in the Champs Elysées, and at Longchamp they have almost driven respectable women from the ground. Before you have been in the city a week, you will be convinced that these women are very numerous.[8]

What seemed to be an escalation of prostitution increased pre-existing concerns over class mixing. This, coupled with the growing popularity of mass-produced clothing that made it economically feasible to disguise conspicuous signs of class difference, catalyzed the need for a means of both differentiating the respectable woman from the prostitute and keeping the *bourgeoise* from directly seeing the prostitute.

Octave Uzanne, a cultural critic invested in maintaining this ideology, generated worries about class mixing in the new city. He wrote about the Second Empire: "The new ease of life produced almost immediately a general abandon of the line of demarcation that delimited the existence of a sedentary aristocracy. All social classes found themselves mixing little by little... "[9] The broadening of Parisian streets, a by-product of which was the increased visibility of the people upon them, also further solidified the perceived need for more firmly established class divisions. The veil, I would argue, became a device of discrimination within this visual crisis, since its presence or absence would indicate a woman's status. Despite the fact that any woman could conceivably wear a veil, contemporaries believed that the manner in which she wore it, in concert with its design and her posture, would signal her class. Further measures were taken by government officials to facilitate the readability of a venal woman's class. In addition to restrictions on their behavior and the times of day during which they solicited clients, prostitutes were subjected to strict clothing guidelines.[10] They were required to wear understated clothes, regulation-sized or no hats, and were prohibited from adorning themselves with accessories that called attention to their appearance.[11] Therefore, the veil, an accessory which contemporaries believed called attention to the woman wearing it, was codified as bourgeois and aristocratic, partly to enable this taxonomy of the social order.

The medicalization of dust

I want here to suggest that the popularity of veils in Haussmann's Paris was only tenuously linked to fashion. Rather, its increased usage was more specifically connected to fears of class confusion, the dust emitted by the razing of parts of Paris, and to the coincident, if not resultant, rise of scientific and medical discourses at the time. The renovations of the city generated dust, which in turn led public officials to study its effects and to warn of the dangers of inhaling that dust. As an actual presence and as a concept, dust conflated fears of physical contamination and moral degeneracy. In Parent-Duchâtelet's studies of the 1830s, the discourse of dirt provided a vehicle with which to link sewers, filth, and putrefaction to prostitution, and by extension, prostitution to the potential contamination and destruction of bourgeois society. Given the fact that dirt was regarded as dangerous to public health at the time, the dust emitted by Haussmann's renovations must have induced considerable alarm, worsening already significant anxieties over the health of the city's inhabitants. Zola's description of construction in *The Ladies' Paradise* is a fictional indication of a contemporary's reaction to the dust:

> At the slightest gust of wind, clouds of plaster flew about and covered the neighbouring roofs like a fall of snow. The Baudus in despair looked on at this implacable dust penetrating everywhere – getting through the closest woodwork, soiling the goods in their shop, even gliding into their beds; and the idea that they must continue to breathe it – that it would finish by killing them – empoisoned their existence.[12]

The Baudus own a shop on a street where a department store has been built, and for them the dust symbolizes the end of the small business and the beginning of the more competitive market created by the *grands magasins*. Both metaphorically and literally, the Baudus perceive that the dust has the ability to poison and kill, not just their financial livelihood, but their physical bodies as well.

In addition to the actual fear induced by the dust of construction, Paris after 1850 faced even more problems caused by other kinds of pollution. The city was more directly affected than it had been before by industry, which had, prior to that year, taken place mostly outside of the city.[13] The razing of entire parts of Paris, in combination with the acceleration of industrialization, resulted in an increase in air pollution which, in turn, necessitated the study of its effects upon the health of the population.

While an organized French national health movement began under the Bourbon Restoration, it was not until the Second Empire that more serious inroads were made in Paris itself. As industrialization flourished between 1850 and 1870, air and water pollution, identified as problems earlier in the century by Lavoisier, Boussingault, and Cloquet, increased as well. The overcrowding of workspaces, in conjunction with an awareness of the impurities emitted by steam engines and bitumen and rubber factories, caused concern, and by the middle of the century the bourgeoisie was obsessed with filth, degeneration, and infection.[14]

Beginning in the 1860s, public hygiene and urban hygiene became part of the discourse of medicine, requiring that doctors consider health in broader, more urban terms.[15] Louis Pasteur, a leading proponent of contagionism, connected the minuscule to larger questions when in 1862 he analyzed the composition of dust and organisms in the air and related his findings to public health. Perhaps the most telling example of this obsession with air and its effect upon Parisians was the practice by the 1850s of taking air samples from active parts of the city like the Opéra, the Place de la Concorde, and the Jardin du Luxembourg at varying times of day, and studying their dust content.[16]

The rhetoric of urban hygiene grew out of long-standing fears that the architectural changes of Paris simply exacerbated. The very formation and success of urban hygiene, a field so engaged with the problems of the new metropolis, illustrates the depth of these anxieties over disease that the transformation of Paris brought closer to the surface. Whereas the stagnant pools of water and constricted streets of the old Paris posed certain health risks, the elimination of those same urban challenges raised others. In 1848 the Comité Consultif d'Hygiène Publique was established in order to advise the government on issues pertaining to public health, and the Organisation de Médecine Publique was developed to address the quality of the air and its effect upon the health of Parisians.

"Many epidemic diseases are contagious, and these contagions may travel in air currents, wind, and clothes"[17] claimed Benoist de la Grandière, articulating the previously unsubstantiated, yet commonly held, fear that disease spread through the air. In 1882, Robert Koch identified the tubercle bacillus, the micro-organism responsible for the spread of tuberculosis, discrediting Pidoux and the others who opposed theories of contagionism by arguing that the disease was inherited.[18] Koch's work represented a shift in what David S. Barnes has called the "historiography of medicine," for it authenticated the validity of the hitherto controversial germ theory.[19] Adding further to the inroads of Koch, Dr Jules Rochard, an influential hygienist whose *Traité d'hygiène sociale* and *Encyclopédie d'hygiène et de médecine publique* were owned and consulted by many French families, reiterated that dust carried the lethal tubercle bacillus.[20]

Ironically, while I have argued that Haussmann's architectural changes were partly to blame for increasing dust and fear of disease, the structures of his buildings themselves disclose an even longer-standing concern about infection through physical proximity between people and the dirt on the street. In an effort to lessen the possibility of human contact with dust and the diseases that it harbored, many of Haussmann's buildings were equipped with balconies. These balconies were intended, in part, as protected extensions of the bourgeois interior into the city.[21] High enough above the masses of people and germs, the balcony enabled the bourgeoisie to witness life below without necessarily being contaminated by it.

Gustave Caillebotte's *View Through a Balcony Grill* (1880) (Figure 7) becomes, within this context, an illustration of the ways in which the balcony could separate the public from the private, the filthy from the sanitary. A view through the balcony of Caillebotte's home on the boulevard Haussmann, this painting takes as its subject the iron grill that physically and visually isolates the man who sweeps the macadam-covered street below from the family inside. It differentiates the space of contagion from the less threatening interior of the bourgeois home.[22] The interstices of the grill work are filled with the bright flickers of a passing carriage, a street

7 Gustave Caillebotte, *View Through a Balcony Grill*, 1880

cleaner, kiosks, lamp-posts, and the street, collapsing *matière*, that which it represents, and the surface of the canvas. Caillebotte's choice to paint the screen between the dusty street and the pristine interior of his home may be seen as a visual exegesis of the bourgeois fears and ideologies that science and medicine fueled through their elaborate public warnings. Indeed, Caillebotte would have known that scientists had been studying the effects of dry ground sweeping since the late 1850s, as much was made of its ill effects in contemporary periodicals, and he certainly would have understood the importance of a clean home, as this was widely publicized as well.[23] A scientifically based causal connection between dust and health simultaneously forged a tropic connection between dirt and morality. In other words, an apparently clean and healthy home became a measure of moral goodness, while a dusty and dirty home or street was equated with degradation and disease.

By the middle of the century, the growing field of medicine was promoting its beliefs through a propagandistic blend of scientific knowledge, politics, and ethics.[24] Bourgeois women in particular were targeted by the medical community and encouraged to protect themselves from any kind of contamination, mainly because they were thought to be more susceptible to disease and because they were considered responsible for maintaining the physical and moral health of present and future generations. In a popular journal of family health, this fusion of science, women, morality, and the good of the country is apparent in Maurice Barenne's words: "Woman is the fervent soul of the family. . . . The health and happiness of women, is the health and happiness of all people."[25] Women's health, and by extension, the health of the family, was clearly of great concern to late nineteenth-century doctors, some of whom worked with government officials to institute what they considered to be appropriate rules of behavior for respectable women in the new city.[26]

When Robin and Pouchet examined dust particles during the cholera epidemic of the late 1840s and discovered that dust contained choleric material,[27] contemporaries were given the scientific substantiation they needed for advocating that respectable women protect themselves by veiling their faces. Dr Emile Beaugrand's *L'Hygiène ou l'art de conserver la santé* of 1855, a popular household health guide, claimed: "[T]he white or colored veil . . . protects the face from cold during the winter, and, during the summer, keeps the eyes safe from dust and the too-strong rays of the sun."[28] Since no studies seem to have been conducted on the veil's ability to inhibit the passage of airborne contaminated particles, I would suggest that the veil – and its medical materialist justification – served simply to curb the escalating social anxiety over germs and disease.

Obviously dust fell upon everyone – men, women, and children of all classes. Yet, the medical community's directives were pitched at bourgeois women.[29] Although working-class women, especially laundresses, were most affected by the tuberculosis and cholera epidemics, it was still bourgeois women who were invited by etiquette books, fashion journals, and the medical community to use veils. Since concerns over germs and disease were two of the motivating factors behind the bourgeoisie's desire to mark out clearer class distinctions, it makes sense that the veil would have been an active agent in helping to maintain those divisions.

Ironically, this "classing of the veil" denied its use to those who most needed the protection it offered from inhaling dust. While it was an imperfect means for filtering out impure particles, it was effective in keeping some contaminants out. Sartory and Langlais blamed poor ventilation and the fact that laundresses handled dust-embedded clothing for their high rate of tuberculosis and cholera. Yet the visual and textual evidence suggests that laundresses did not actually cover their mouths to limit their inhalation of tainted particles. In his article published in the *Revue des cours scientifiques de la France et de l'étranger* in 1870, John Tyndall quoted J. B. Dancer who suggested that people whose work involves the production of excessive amounts of dust wear "*pareils respirateurs*."[30] Surprisingly, despite both the hazards associated with the profession and the admonitions of scientists and doctors, images of laundresses and ironers depict them with uncovered faces, which implies that few did wear "*pareils respirateurs*."[31] In addition to the apparent disregard for the health of laundry workers whether through their own ignorance or volition, clothing from contaminated homes was not disinfected, further increasing the possibility of infection both for the laundresses themselves and for the families to whom the clothes belonged.[32] The brushing, banging, and hanging of micro-organism-laden clothes linked the bourgeoisie and the working class in a way far more dangerous than casual contact on the streets. The site of cleansing and purification was, ironically, the space that actually generated disease.

While the medical community was alarmed by the staggering death rate among laundry workers, little effort was made to improve their working conditions or to educate them in the proper handling of infected garments. Edgar Degas's *Ironers* of 1884–86 depicts the kind of cramped and bleak spaces in which these women worked. Even the scumbled background of the painting, the masterful result of oil paint on unprimed, thickly woven canvas, becomes the visual equivalent of the dusty and murky atmosphere in which the laundresses perform their jobs. The picture captures two women —one is hard at work over a shirt sleeve, while the other yawns so widely that her mouth opens into an oval. This kind of behavior, the absent-minded breathing-in of large quantities of dusty air, would have increased one's chances of contracting an airborne disease. And although Degas's images are anything but fixed or reportorial, they certainly function across scientific, medical, and artistic discussions. As long as the inhabitants of the most poorly ventilated spaces of the city remained uninformed of the consequences of their unhealthy work environments, modern medicine would prove ineffective in combating the spread of epidemic disease in the spectacular new city.

Seeing through the veil

The veil shielded those women literate enough to understand the directives that warned of dust's unhealthy composition and wealthy enough to be able to afford the family health books, etiquette manuals, and fashion journals that glamorized this accessory. A fashion journal of 1860 boasted: "This new type of veil offers advantages with regard to its charm and the useful service it renders in protecting the face entirely from wind and dust."[33] This is an overstatement of the veil's ability to protect the face, yet it is part of the symbolic discourse of the veil that circulated widely and magnified its actual usefulness. While women were encouraged to adopt veils to shield themselves from sun, dust, and wind, those same veils did more than simply protect; they also affected the way respectable women were seen in the city. The veil's facility in altering appearance is well documented by contemporary observers. In 1852, one fashion journal writer remarked: "[T]heir bonnets are more elaborate than ever; their little faces are lost in layers of lace and little ribbons."[34]

An image from *La Mode illustrée* of 1860 is an example of the kind of veil this author describes (Figure 8). Made of tulle, lace, and a *soutache* of silk, the complex weave of this garment, the *voile à barbes*, all but disguises the appearance of the woman who wears it. This is the veil that protects "the face entirely from wind and dust," according to the description that accompanies it. The writer does not mention that this particular veil also alters the topography of the face beneath it. Its intricate web almost obliterates the mouth and nose, each caught behind the decorative lower half. Yet the eyes remain vaguely there, punctuated by broad arches meant to represent eyebrows. While mute and unable to smell, this woman could see, albeit in a compromised way. The absence of all facial features but the eyes calls attention to the ways in which the veil jeopardizes vision on both sides. The densely woven veil, then, could mark out a system of power for the woman behind it. She could be both seer and not seen. Her identity could be concealed at the same time that her veil would reveal her status as *bourgeoise*.

While the veil disallowed easy visual access to the woman behind it, it also encouraged the concentration of the gaze of the viewer who looked at her. The very constitution of the veil itself, really an elaborate system of densely or loosely woven threads, sometimes flecked with dots, as in an image from *La Mode illustrée* of 1864, surely declares that its function is not necessarily only that of protecting the woman from the gaze and the elements (Figure 9). A graph of irregularly organized loops of thread, this veil brands the face so that skin and fabric read as one plane. It does not mask the face behind it, but rather it causes us, and of course the woman, to look through it. Forced to look even more closely to synthesize all of the parts of the woman's scotomized face, the outside viewer could become enmeshed in the viewing system. So, while the veil could, in varying degrees, perform the work of concealing, an outside viewer could decrease that success by looking more carefully to sharpen the blurred face on the other side.

Although some veils undercut the pleasure of the viewer, allowing the wearer to resist absolute surveillance, the crucial issue remains: the veiled woman's vision

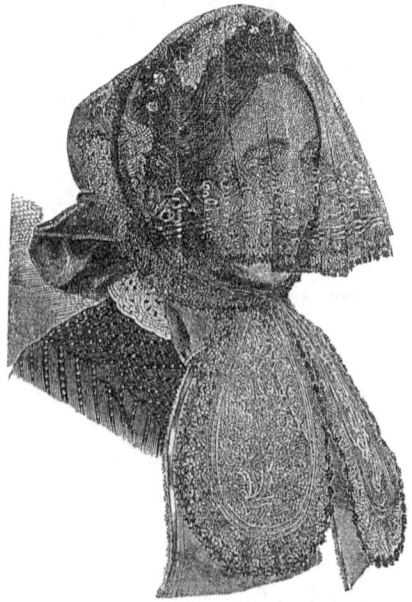
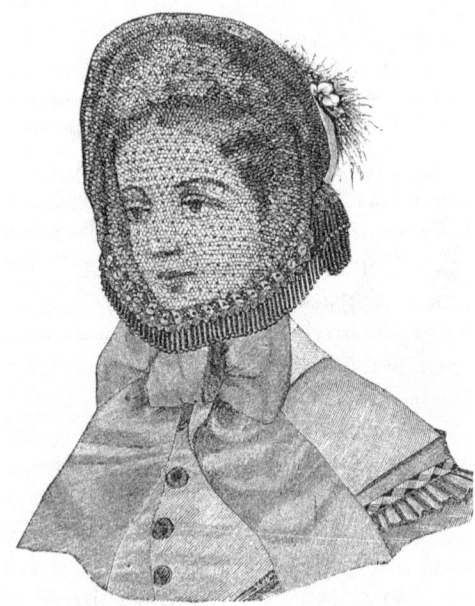

8 *La Mode illustrée, journal de la famille*, 1 April 1860   9 *La Mode illustré, journal de la famille*, 22 May 1864

was impeded. How did the woman behind the veil see? What did the five veiled women in Edouard Manet's *Concert in the Tuileries* of 1862 see when they left the gardens through the west exit and faced the broad expanse of the Place de la Concorde (see Figure 2)? They must have seen it through a shifting and changing grid, sometimes punctuated by black dots, as in the case of Madame Loubens in the foreground of the painting.

The veil of the Second Empire was the filter through which the *bourgeoise*'s view was siphoned. While fashion journals, etiquette books, and the medical community encouraged the use of veils by bourgeois women between the 1850s and 1880s, by 1890, doctors concluded that it obstructed vision. In an article entitled, "Contre les voilettes," which appeared in *La Fronde*, the writer acknowledged the work of a doctor who "began to declare war against the voilette. He affirmed that it is deadly to the eyesight . . . dotted veils being the most dangerous."[35] Doctors were not alone in recognizing that the veil could be harmful to vision. In her etiquette book of 1893, Baronne Staffe exclaimed that "Veils, and certainly dotted veils, are injurious to the eyesight."[36] The fashionable dotted veil had interfered with respectable women's vision long before social and medical authorities deplored its use. During the Second Empire, however, and for the first twenty years of the Third Republic, there is little evidence that veils were anything but miraculous protection from dust, sun, and wind, not to mention their ability to diminish signs of ageing. And while other varieties of veils were worn prior to Haussmannization, those veils were more loosely constructed and worn mainly at the beach.

French fashion journals of the 1850s, 1860s, and 1870s, the comprehensive analysis of which allows an insight into social trends, demonstrate the popularity of the veil at the beach and in the countryside where air is presumably healthy. But more importantly for my argument, these same periodicals chronicle an explosion of the wearing of veils in the city where air is less healthy. Unlike earlier veils, the Second Empire veil was enmeshed with the city structure itself. Not only did its form mimic the radiating grid that translated a circuitous, medieval city into a more modern one, but it also screened the face from the remnants of the old Paris. The veil of the Second Empire is never simply a fashion accessory, but is, rather, bound to the discourse of the new city, functioning as a visual and physical filter between the woman who wore it and modern Paris.

Since knowledge of the spectacle of the modern city could threaten the proper woman's position in society and lead to her downfall, it makes sense that the *bourgeoise* was actively encouraged to veil herself when in the city. As Anthea Callen has pointed out in relation to the late nineteenth century: "knowledge, temptation and containment were all equated with the visual: the eye was the organ both of revelation and of control. . . . Looking was, therefore, an activity to be discouraged in women —whose submission to an assertive male gaze/sexuality was its guarantee of meaning, and thus power."[37] The veiling of the respectable woman, indeed the deliberate discouragement of her looking, was a means of controlling her exposure to the city, the male gaze, and even her sexuality.

The *flâneur*, or Baudelaire's paradigmatic man about town, had the privilege of observing the city through the anonymous and less obstructed gaze, while the *bourgeoise* had a veiled view. This hierarchy of vision was not enforced through strict dichotomies, but rather through the proper woman's weakened vision. Not blinded by the veil, she was nevertheless held back, protected, and shielded from modern life. Since a proscribed vision of modern Paris was symbolically equated with a controlled exposure to modernity, the respectable woman's vision had to be somewhat obfuscated. Her access to Paris already restricted by institutional structures, the proper woman was further detached from public life by the physical barrier of the veil.

Considered within this discourse of late nineteenth-century visuality, Manet's picture of fashionable Parisians enjoying a concert in the Jardin du Tuileries may be read as tracing these levels of vision for *bourgeoises*. This is to say that the five most obvious veils in this painting chart five intensities of seeing in Haussmann's city. The two thinnest veils, worn by the women behind the blue and yellow bonnet-clad figures in the foreground, would disrupt vision less than the black veil of the woman (Manet's mother) in front of the top-hatted gentleman (Manet's brother) to the right of center. She is so encased in her veils – we see only a swatch of black hair and the vague indication of an eye – that her presence is read only through that which visually liquidates it. In other words, her identity has been obscured by the very veil that actually defines her space in the painting.

Still, no one is more elaborately veiled, and no one's vision is more highly filtered, than that of Madame Loubens in the foreground. A fabrication of heavy black netting and dots, her veil brands a relatively small part of the surface of the canvas. Yet, Manet heightens its effect by performing the clever ocular trick of practically twinning her with her pictorial counterpart, Madame Lejosne. Besides the difference of the veil, both are dressed in almost identical yellow capes and bonnets with blue bows. The visual comparison between the two most conspicuous figures in an excessively populated painting only magnifies the impact of Madame Loubens' veil both upon her and upon the viewer. It infiltrates her visual field, reminding her of her position within the social hierarchy by continually calling attention to the ways in which her view of the Tuileries is caught within the netting of her veil. For us, Loubens' veil formally screens her face, simultaneously distinguishing her from Madame Lejosne and providing a paradigm for reading the painting as a whole. For it is here, in this small passage that layers of paint become metaphors for levels of engagement with the city. If we understand the veil as a trope for the complexities of modern life, then Madame Loubens' veil in the foreground works as a blueprint for the picture as a whole, enabling us to see displaced veils and veiling practices throughout. The complicated play of patterns on the surface of *Concert in the Tuileries* causes wrought-iron chair backs, umbrellas, hats, playing children, and trees to function like filters through which we unravel the threads of the painting, really a microcosm of the intricate pattern of modern Parisian bourgeois society. Even the structure of the composition itself performs the work of a veil, simultaneously dispersing and forcing the proliferation of random particles into some semblance of clarification. And like a cloud of dust, the picture perpetually renews itself, shifting some things into focus, others into obscurity, and then back again. As a modern reader, I find myself trapped in an elaborate nexus of black suits and dresses, top hats, and trees that operate not unlike the weave of the veil. I have to labor through this tangle in order to decipher the veiled women in the painting. Not considering the potential of the women whose backs are turned to the viewer, there are five, as I count them, but they at once evade the gaze and are captured by it.

Even the faces of some of the unveiled women are veiled by the thick layers of paint that constitute them. For example, the surface of Madame Lejosne's face is alternately impastoed and thinned. At once *matière* and skin, the paint and the weave of the canvas become the veil through which we read her likeness. Unlike the more crisply delineated details of the faces of the men at the edges of the left side of the canvas (Manet and his brother), Madame Lejosne's face is blurred by dabs of fleshy pigment. She is closer to us than the figures to her left, yet we see her through more actively applied brushstrokes. Like her counterpart, Madame Loubens, Madame Lejosne is veiled, at least in formal terms.

The respectable woman's engagement with modern Paris was inscribed upon a grid which both empowered her, for she could be somewhat hidden, and occluded her vision. And while crowds and uniform streets filtered life for all inhabitants of Paris, it was specifically women's vision that was further held in by veils. *Bourgeoises* were prevented from fully experiencing the spectacle of the new city, and what opportunity they did have was limited. If only on a subtle level, the veil was a means of redirecting the female gaze, of lessening the visual contact a woman had with the city so that her public respectability could be preserved.

Gustave Flaubert recognized this division in accessibility to urban life when he wrote in *Madame Bovary*:

> A man at least, is free; he may travel over passions and over countries, overcome obstacles, taste of the most far-away pleasures. But a woman is always hampered. At once inert and flexible, she has against her the weakness of the flesh and legal depen- dence. Her will, like the veil of her bonnet, held by a string, flutters in every wind; there is always some desire that draws her, some conventionality that restrains.[38]

Flaubert uses the veil as a metaphor for women's position in 1850s France. The woman's will, and as I read it, her freedom, which is likened to a veil, is always both in process and inhibited. This passage enacts a dichotomy between male and female, free and not free, unveiled and veiled. And even if this may be too strong an interpretation of the situation, Flaubert's words lead me to believe, his text, like the veil to which it refers, still serves as a filter through which to view the position of the respectable woman at this time. She was certainly distanced from Paris through restrictions against her entry into specific parts of the city. However, I hope that I have shown that one of the most profound means of inhibiting the *bourgeoise's* experience of modern Paris was through her veil which functioned not simply, and probably only minimally, to protect her from dust, wind, and germs. Rather, the veil affected how the *bourgeoise* was seen, and, more importantly, it inflected what she saw.

Notes

1 I would like to thank A. D'Souza and T. McDonough for inviting me to contribute to this anthology and for their keen editorial comments. I am also extremely grateful to P. Gordon who gave me expert feedback on this essay. Other friends and colleagues have read this at various stages, offering insight along the way: L. Nochlin, A. Solomon-Godeau, J. Heinrichs, M. Berger, and C. Jewers. I thank also the University of Kansas for awarding me a New Faculty Research Grant that helped fund some of the research and revising of this essay.

2 W. Benjamin privileged dust as both an active force in the production of history and as a container of history. See W. Benjamin, *The Arcades Project*, trans. H. Eiland and K. McLaughlin (Cambridge, Mass.: Belknap Press of Harvard University Press, 1999), pp. 102–103; and S. Buck-Morss, *The Dialectics of Seeing: Walter Benjamin and the Arcades Project* (Cambridge, Mass.: MIT Press, 1989), pp. 95–96.

3 J. Michelet, *La Femme*, in *Oeuvres completes de Michelet*, vol. XVIII (1858–60) (Paris: Flammarion, 1985), p. 413. All quoted translations are mine.

4 G. Pollock was one of the first to chart the ways in which the new city was segregated according to gender and class lines. See G. Pollock, "Modernity and the Spaces of Femininity," in *Vision and Difference: Femininity, Feminism, and the Histories of Art* (New York: Routledge, 1988), pp. 50–90. However, more recent scholarship has pointed out that there was more fluidity between public and private in the second half of the nineteenth century. See S. Marcus, *Apartment Stories: City and Home in Nineteenth-Century Paris and London* (Berkeley: University of California Press, 1999) and S. P. Johnson, *Boundaries of Acceptability: Flaubert, Maupassant, Cézanne, and Cassatt* (New York: Peter Lang, 2000).

5 The Bon Marché, Paris's first department store, opened in 1852, pioneering the sale of ready-made clothing, the availability of which aided the transgression of class borders through dress, which had previously been a more dependable visual measure of class.

6 *Le Journal des demoiselles* 4 (April 1863), p. 124.

7 Parent-Duchâtelet's flawed system of regulating prostitutes, based upon his own personal analysis of the women, their clientele, and their living conditions, categorized and registered prostitutes, assigning them to supervised brothels, or *maisons de tolérance*, in order to prevent the proliferation of the moral and physical degradation that he associated with prostitution.

8 J. D. McCabe, Jr, *Paris by Sunlight and Gaslight: A Work Descriptive of the Mysteries and Miseries, The Virtues, The Vices, The Splendors, and the Crimes of the City of Paris* (Philadelphia: National Publishing Co., 1869), p. 714.

9 O. Uzanne, *La Femme et la mode: métamorphoses de la Parisienne de 1792 à 1892* (Paris: Ancienne Maison Quantin, 1893), p. 194.

10 See H. Clayson, *Painted Love: Prostitution in French Art of the Impressionist Era* (New Haven: Yale University Press, 1991), p. 56; A. Corbin, *Women for Hire: Prostitution and*

Sexuality in France After 1852, trans. A. Sheridan (Cambridge, Mass.: Harvard University Press, 1990), p. 85. Corbin writes that municipal by-laws prohibited *filles en carte* from circulating while wearing a hat and Clayson cites police records that stipulated that hats on registered prostitutes had to be of a certain size. And while official proscription did not necessarily match social reality, the fact that the rules existed indicates a widespread anxiety over confusing the proper woman for a prostitute.

11 *Filles en cartes* could be arrested for violating any of the regulations upon their behavior and dress. However, due to the difficulty of distinguishing the *fille en carte* from the unregistered prostitute and even from the *bourgeoise*, public authorities were ineffectual in their efforts at enforcing these guidelines.

12 Emile Zola, *The Ladies' Paradise*, intro. and trans. Kristin Ross (Berkeley: University of California Press, 1992), p. 193.

13 See A. F. La Berge, *Mission and Method: The Early Nineteenth-Century French Public Health Movement* (Cambridge: Cambridge University Press, 1992), p. 3.

14 See A. Corbin, *Women for Hire*, p. 133.

15 R. Nye discusses the link between urban health and morality in his *Crime, Madness, and Politics in Modern France: The Medical Concept of National Decline* (Princeton, N.J.: Princeton University Press, 1984), p. 39.

16 See A. Sartory and M. Langlais, *Poussière et microbes de l'air* (Paris: A. Poinat, 1912), p. 41.

17 A. Benoist de la Grandière, *Notions d'hygiène a l'usage des instituteurs et des élèves des écoles normales primaires* (Paris: V. Adrien Delahaye, 1877), p. 31–32.

18 D. S. Barnes, in *The Making of a Social Disease: Tuberculosis in Nineteenth-Century France* (Berkeley: University of California Press, 1995), points out that prior to Koch's work, explanations for the spread of tuberculosis were essentialist.

19 I thank Dr S. Nuland of the Yale University Medical School for explaining to me the importance of the germ theory in instituting a change in medical models of tuberculosis in the 1880s. When proponents of the germ theory convinced its opponents that it was not the dust per se, but rather the contents of the dust that were hazardous, a more accurate understanding of contagion was established.

20 See Dr J. Rochard, *Encyclopédie d'hygiène et de médecine publique* (Paris: Bataille, 1895), p. 685.

21 For an overview of Haussmann's architectural changes see D. Van Zanten, *Building Paris: Architectural Institutions and the Transformation of the French Capital, 1830–1870* (Cambridge: Cambridge University Press, 1994).

22 Dust also symbolized potential contamination in the private realm as well, for household dust was thought to breed disease too. Young women who attended school, mainly of the bourgeoisie and upper classes, were educated in the importance of keeping a sanitary home and of regularly cleaning clothing. In fact, the Société de Médecine Publique et d'Hygiène Professionelle de Paris distributed books and pamphlets which strongly suggested that all clothes be brushed and shaken every day.

23 See *Revue d'hygiène et de police sanitaire de médecine* 1 (January 15, 1879), pp. 43–59, for a discussion of sweeping methods.

24 See R. Nye, *Crime, Madness and Politics*, p. 39 and A. La Berge, *Mission and Method*, p. 4; Jack Ellis, *The Physician-Legislators of France: Medicine and Politics in the Early Third Republic, 1870–1914* (Cambridge: Cambridge University Press, 1990), p. 1, also addresses what he calls the "interplay between medicine and politics."

25 Maurice Barenne, *L'Hygiène: Journal des familles* 1 (March 10, 1886), p. 2.

26 In fact, the Société de Médecine Publique et d'Hygiène Professionnelle de Paris, established in 1877, played an important role not only in the journals of public hygiene and medicine, but also in political and social journals.

27 A. Sartory and M. Langlais, *Poussière et microbes de l'air*, pp. 9–10.

28 Dr E. Beaugrand, *L'Hygiène ou l'art de conserver la santé* (Paris: Hachette, 1855), p. 123.

29 Information regarding health and the spread of contagious disease was published in books, journals, and periodicals intended for a bourgeois audience with expendable income. Additionally, most working-class women at this time were not literate.

30 J. B. Dancer quoted in J. Tyndall, "Poussières et maladies," *Revue des cours scientifiques de la France et de l'étranger* 15 (March 12, 1870), p. 239.

31 This argument assumes that visual culture is not only an active participant in the construction of social systems, but that it is also inflected by those systems it helps to produce.

32 This negligence lasted at least until 1906. See S. Bernheim and A. Roblot, "Tuberculose et blanchisseries," *L'Hygiène familiale* (February 1906), pp. 54–57. E. Lipton also points out in *Looking into Degas: Uneasy Images of Women and Modern Life* (Berkeley: University of California Press, 1986), pp. 130–131, that some ironers prepared food, ate, and slept in the very rooms in which they sorted dirty laundry.

33 *La Mode illustrée, journal de la famille* 14 (April 1, 1860), p. 106.

34 *Les Modes Parisiennes illustrées* 479 (March 20, 1852), p. 135.

35 "Contre les voilettes," *La Fronde* n.d. [Bibliothèque Marguerite Durand, DOS 391 MOD: Mode 1872–1911].

36 Baronne Staffe, *Le Cabinet de toilette* (Paris: Victor-Havard, 1893), p. 151.

37 A. Callen, *The Spectacular Body: Science, Method and Meaning in the Work of Degas* (New Haven and London: Yale University Press, 1995), p. 89.

38 Gustave Flaubert, *Madame Bovary*, trans. Eleanor Marx Aveling (New York: Random House, 1938), p. 103. [First published 1857.]

5

Disorienting Orient: Duret and Guimet, anxious *flâneurs* in Asia

Ting Chang

"Disorientation is the loss of the east. Ask any navigator," or so writes Salman Rushdie in his recent novel, *The Ground Beneath Her Feet*.[1]

> The east is what you sail by. Lose the east and you lose your bearings, your certainties, your knowledge of what is and what may be, perhaps even your life. Where was that star you followed to that manger? That's right. The east orients. That's the official version. The language says so, and you should never argue with the language.[2]

But at this point, Rushdie does precisely what he tells his readers to avoid; he shifts direction, changes track, and challenges the language of orientation:

> But let's just suppose. What if the whole deal – orientation, knowledge of where you are, and so on – what if it's all a scam? What if all of it – home, kinship, the whole enchilada – is just the biggest, most truly global, and centuries-oldest piece of brain-washing? Suppose that it's only when you dare to let go that your real life begins. . . . Suppose that you've got to go through the feeling of being lost . . . of losing your moorings, the vertiginous terror of the horizon spinning round and round like the edge of a coin tossed in the air.[3]

In one sense, Rushdie's gloss on disorientation can be read as a description of *flânerie* at its most radical: in allowing the act of wandering to impose its own logic, the *flâneur* enters spaces where the familiar becomes strange, where the maps are abandoned and the guides discarded. Yet there is also a counter-movement in *flânerie*, a constant pull out of the disordered web towards the poles of knowledge, control, and orientation. More often than not, the nineteenth-century male *flâneur* poses as a connoisseur, a skillful observer who dominates the spaces through which he moves with poise and detachment. As Rushdie observes, the more radical choice of disorientation is almost invariably avoided: "You won't do it. Most of you won't do it. The world's head laundry is pretty good at washing brains. Don't jump off that cliff, don't walk through that door . . . don't take that chance, don't step across that line."

This essay examines a striking instance of the *flâneur*'s desire and fear of crossing that line in the 1870s, a tension heightened by the geopolitics of the world system. Confronted by the complexity of the non-west, Théodore Duret and Henri Cernuschi, followed by Emile Guimet and Félix Régamey, refused to wander. Instead, each fell back on the reassurance of maps and guides.

Recent art historical and literary scholarship largely presents the *flâneur* as the quintessential figure of male authority, commanding through vision and knowledge the urban spaces in which he moves.[4] But one of the earliest and most suggestive theorists of *flânerie*, Walter Benjamin, had a different conception. In Benjamin's eyes, if the *flâneur* is a master, it is in a paradoxical sense: he is a master of the art of getting lost. The *flâneur* enters the labyrinth of the city in such a way that the familiar becomes strange and unsettling. Although he holds on to Ariadne's thread of knowledge, the *flâneur* does so in an oblique and indirect fashion.[5]

Edouard Manet painted Duret as a *flâneur* in the more conventional sense in his portrait of 1868 (Figure 10). Although the young critic is placed in an

10 Edouard Manet,
*Portrait of Théodore
Duret*, 1868

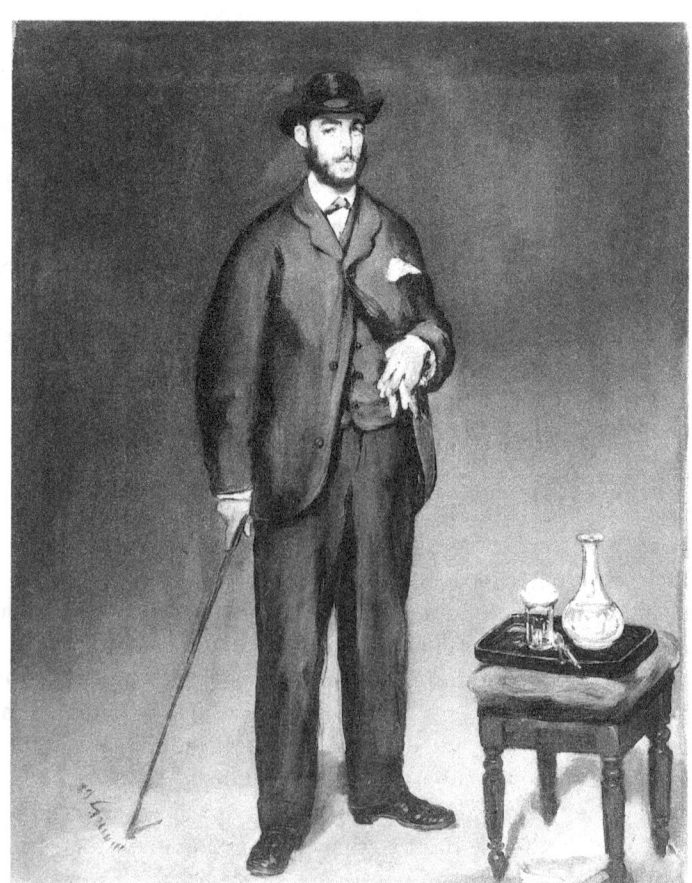

indeterminate, interior setting, his attributes of gloves, hat and walking stick, as well as his assured and knowing air, imply a connoisseur of metropolitan spaces. When Duret departed with a friend, Henri Cernuschi, on an extended tour of the Far East in 1871, however, the critic was unable to maintain his pose of confidence. In the published account of the journey, *Voyage en Asie*, Duret exhibited repeated symptoms of anxiety in his experience abroad. Very rarely does the reader find descriptions of improvised strolls through those unknown realms. Instead, Duret's itinerary is mapped out in a programmatic manner that is unthinkable for the *flâneur* in Paris. The adherence to a planned trajectory is one of the modes of *disorientation* that marked the travels of Duret and Cernuschi, and later, Guimet and Régamey. It is a sign that the identity of the *flâneur* became radically threatened by the *terra incognita* of the non-west. The immediate presence, rather than the loss, of the east made the east a space of disorientation; in its domain, Duret and his colleagues began to doubt the very ground beneath their feet. To reaffirm the threatened self, to regain composure and to collect themselves, the European visitors turned to the collecting of Japanese prints, bronze statues, porcelains, photographs, and divers *objets d'art* in Asia.

Priscilla Ferguson has proposed that after the Revolution of 1848 and the later disruption of urban renewal in the Second Empire, the *flâneur* underwent a major transformation in Paris, his home base. The *flâneur* in the second half of the nineteenth century became an emblem of loss within a larger "discourse of displacement."[6] "*Flânerie*," Ferguson writes,

> ceased to signify freedom and autonomy; it implied instead estrangement and alienation. An urban spectacle that dazed more than it dazzled, a revolution that seemed never to end, converted the *flâneur* into a figure of exile. The stroller able to quit the city streets at will turned into a drifter.[7]

Accordingly, this figure of exile replaced the more integrated, ambulatory philosopher of the July Monarchy as found in Balzac's novels, and as pictured by Monnier and Gavarni in *Les Français peints par eux-mêmes* of 1842.

After the demise of the Second Empire, the collapse at mid-century between *flânerie* and exile delineated by Ferguson was arguably complete. The idea of leaving Paris behind was more than attractive to Duret and Cernuschi in 1871. Their primary motivation for an extended tour of Asia was to go far away from the capital, to lose themselves in vast distances. The long siege by the Prussians and the bloody civil war in Paris propelled the two men outward. As Duret remarked at the end of May 1871 in a letter to Camille Pissarro, "the feeling of terror and menace is still everywhere in Paris. I myself have lost a close friend . . . shot at Sainte Pélagie by the prosecutor of the Commune. I have only one wish, to leave, to flee Paris for a few months."[8]

By September, Duret and Cernuschi had set out for Asia, first crossing the English Channel, then the Atlantic and Pacific oceans. Six weeks after they last saw Paris, the two Europeans arrived in Japan in October 1871.

In his *Discourse on the Origin and Foundations of Inequality Among Men* of 1755, Rousseau envisioned a philosopher traveller ("a Plato, a Thales, a Pythagoras") to report on different societies in the world.[9] Rousseau indeed called for exactly a pair of idealized predecessors to Duret and Cernuschi:

> two closely united men – rich, one in money and the other in genius, both loving glory and aspiring to immortality – one of whom would sacrifice twenty thousand crowns of his wealth and the other ten years of his life to a celebrated voyage around the world, in order to study, not always stones and plants, but for once men and morals.[10]

Rousseau's call for a quasi-scientific form of travel was reiterated by Diderot in the *Encyclopédie*: travel elevated the mind, among other benefits, and curtailed national prejudices.[11]

Duret and Cernuschi certainly engaged their travels as the exercise and discipline of European knowledge envisioned earlier by Rousseau and Diderot, but they were further driven by the urge to leave home, "to flee Paris." In their travels the Far East was at times insufficiently alien. It was, at times, all too ordinary.

When Duret and Cernuschi first arrived in Japan they were disappointed. Instead of wondrous differences and absolute alterity, they found too much of the familiar in Yokohama: too many European clubs, horse races and newspapers, too much French wine, and too much English beer.[12] "If I accept the least dinner invitation – and local hospitality is prodigious – I must put on my *habit noir* and white tie. Not only has Europe become closer to Japan, Europe has become entrenched," Duret protested.[13]

In pursuit of what he called the real Japan, Duret and Cernuschi traveled further inland, away from the port cities most exposed to European influence. They proceeded to Edo where the two men fully expected to be "en plein Japon."[14] Standing before a Buddhist temple in Edo, Duret explained, "we confronted an absolutely new architecture that owed nothing to the Greek and the Gothic. We felt at last in Asia."[15] To his relief, Duret finally experienced the radical "*dépaysement*" that he traveled so far to pursue.

It is striking that both to ease the disappointment of a cheerless Europeanization and later to regain control in the encounter of disorienting difference, Duret and Cernuschi turned to collecting. The fantasmatical Japan that they initially could not find and the "real Japan" that they located at length in Edo led the pair of travelers to the same operation. "I must say that as soon as we disembarked at Yokohama we began to buy bibelots," Duret recounted. "We started like everyone else, without fixed plans, without preferences, proceeding a bit haphazardly."[16] This apparent spontaneity was at first a means of buying the elusive Japan. Disoriented by their very *lack* of disorientation, the visitors proceeded to collect the Japan that evaded their grasp. Subsequently, in the face of that much-anticipated otherness, collecting functioned as a way to regain control. The experience of a profound *dépaysement* was then inverted by a longing for familiar parameters, and for that, Duret and Cernuschi turned to the order of classifications. "In Edo we systematize our acquisitions," Duret recalled.

> We had brought with us from Yokohama a Japanese who has long served as interme-
> diary to European merchants. He escorted us to a certain *Yaki*, a sort of Japanese auc-
> tioneer. Word of our purchases spread and the *Yaki*'s home became the meeting place
> of all the merchants, courtiers, and middlemen of Edo.[17]

The crucial assistance of local guides and merchants in the retreat to systematicity
suggests that the Japanese themselves were collaborating in the role of the exotic,
collectable other.

The vacillation, observable in the two travelers, between a search for and a flight
from the radical loss of their bearings is characteristic of the dialectical nature of the
flâneur, who is at once part of the crowd and aloof from the throng, a discreet and
unremarkable pedestrian in the metropolis who arrogantly resists incorporation
into his environment.[18] This very oscillation was repeatedly noted by Benjamin in
the *Arcades Project*. In one passage the author observed:

> Dialectic of *flânerie*: on one side, the man who feels himself viewed by all and sundry
> as a true suspect and, on the other side, the man who is utterly undiscoverable, the
> hidden man. Presumably, it is this dialectic that is developed in "The Man of the
> Crowd."[19]

This invisible man of the crowd, Benjamin further noted, troubled the French
police in 1798. In those turbulent times, the danger of the *flâneur* was precisely his
ability to evade surveillance and observation.[20]

Duret and Cernuschi, however, could hardly have disappeared into a Japanese
street. They had no desire to go native, for they needed to maintain their privileged
status as recognized foreign visitors, sometimes even dignitaries, and they were also
prevented from doing so by the authorities. Upon their request to go to Kyoto, for
instance, the two Europeans found themselves escorted by Japanese customs officials, armed guards, translators, and baggage carriers whose number swelled at one
point to forty-eight men. In Coryama, near Osaka, a sword-bearing policeman was
assigned to escort the visitors through the streets of the city. Clearly it was impossible
for Duret and Cernuschi under such circumstances to meander spontaneously.

But Duret's travel account nonetheless revealed some of the fleeting encounters
and fortuitous glimpses of *flânerie*. In spite of the programmed circuits and activities, and eluding even Duret's own authorial control, the *flâneur* at times broke free.
In a passage on domestic architecture in Edo, Duret recounted the invitation to
visit a Japanese home:

> We enter a house, and straight away a woman pours hot water in a teapot and offers us,
> as a sign of welcome, a few sips of lightly infused tea. What is most striking in the
> Japanese home are the small dimensions of everything. . . . All that surrounds the
> Japanese is of modest dimensions, light, fragile, or delicate.[21]

In the middle of a scheduled activity and working against the measured narrative
voice of Duret himself, the whims of *flânerie* unexpectedly emerged. One catches

the guest drinking tea, slyly observing details, and framing larger conclusions. No sooner had he appeared in the minute space between words and punctuation, however, than the *flâneur* retreated behind the conclusive description of the writer:

> All of which is to say that the Japanese has made more or less all things in his own image, for he is himself petite, and on average of a much smaller size than Europeans; the timbre of his voice is also more delicate, he has fewer needs, eats less, and above all he takes less space.[22]

The *flâneur* censored himself.

The next destination was China where, as in Yokohama, the Parisians were initially shocked by the degree of Europeanization, particularly in cities such as Shanghai. The disappointment of familiarity was quickly replaced, however, by an intense anxiety of otherness. Duret and Cernuschi were appalled by the poverty and odors of Chinese street life, by the lack of urban planning, and the total absence of infrastructure for foreign travelers. Cernuschi later remarked that China was like a vast cemetery. As retold by Edmond de Goncourt in his journal, "He [Cernuschi] spoke at length of the putrefaction of [Chinese] cities, the sepulchral cast of the countryside, the drab sadness and the terrible boredom that emanated from the whole country. China, he said, reeked of shit and death."[23] Duret's account was no better:

> The striking character, the dominant trait of the Chinese city is its grime, a dirtiness that has no name, a filth that offends all the senses at once. . . . At intersections and in front of pagodas people crawl in rags; there you are assailed by beggars covered in lesions and scabs, stricken with leprosy and ulcers, who have on their backs the vermin of several generations, and next to whom the beggars of Callot would appear to be gentlemen.[24]

What to do now in the face of such a repulsive alterity? Nothing, it seemed, could relieve the Europeans of their terrible discomfort. From a boat on the Yangxi River, Duret and Cernuschi saw the passing array of pagodas damaged by the Taiping rebellions, a spectacle that surely recalled the violence and destruction that had recently driven the European visitors out of Paris. A cursory view of the Chinese navy further reminded them of battle and strife: "What a navy of war! It is no surprise that with such armament, when in a clash with Europeans, the Chinese soldiers and marines react immediately by taking flight."[25]

There was, it appeared, no escape from their exasperation. Everything the travelers encountered only reinforced their impressions of a blighted nation. China both frustrated and exceeded their desire for radical difference, and the annoyance is palpable in Duret's text. He and Cernuschi then looked for consolation in the abundance of collectible objects and the satisfying order of acquisition. Rejecting the drift of the riverboat, the two visitors hoped to find in the presence of Beijing merchants and connoisseurs a structured framework of experience. The elite milieu of collectors and dealers in the capital indeed provided material compensation for the visitors' distress.

Duret recorded that in China they were compelled to abandon the collecting practices they previously enjoyed in Japan. Rather than being able to purchase cheaply hundreds of objects on a single occasion, in Beijing they could acquire only one article at a time, after hard bargaining, and always at an elevated price. Moreover, both the circumstances and the objects demanded a certain familiarity, and the European collectors had much to learn. Never losing his confident authorial voice, Duret wrote a disquisition on Chinese bronze production. Cernuschi, in the meantime, purchased from dealers in Beijing objects of considerable size and value. The bronze ceremonial vessel that he acquired remains, even today, the only *jian* of such large dimensions in a museum outside of China (Figure 11). In total Cernuschi shipped back to France over nine-hundred cases of religious statues, bronze ware, porcelains, prints, manuscripts, books, photographs, carvings, and architectural fragments.

On their return in 1873, Duret and Cernuschi began to interpret their experiences of travel and art collecting through writing and display. Newly reoriented in Paris, Duret resumed the vocation of the European connoisseur at ease in his judgements. His *Voyage en Asie* of 1874 divided the world into two unequal halves of west and non-west. The underlying assumption of Duret's account was that European travelers had the intellectual and cultural capacities to observe, to analyze, and hence to possess all that they encountered in the non-west. Like the Japanese prints that Duret acquired, his writing was also a way to collect Asia, to seize and to catalogue its otherness in his negotiation with the east. In his text Duret combined personal anecdotes with comments on the institutions, languages, family structures, customs, religious practices, and artistic achievements of the nations that he visited. Although presented as one man's observations, his

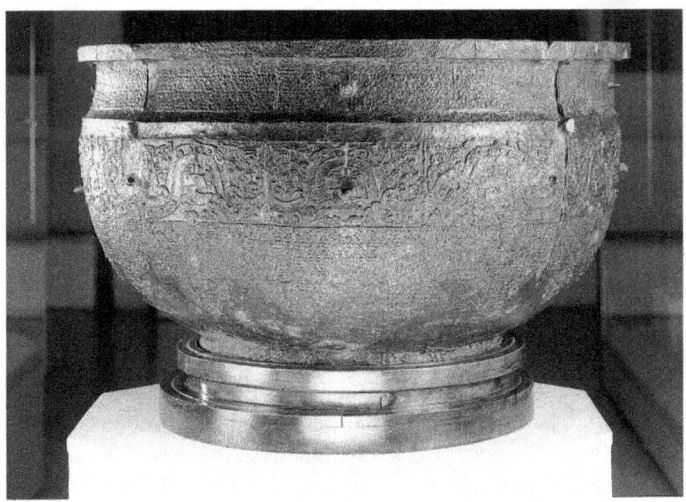

11 *Jian*, late fourth or early fifth centuries BCE

comments took the incisive tone of official reports. An example of Duret's assess-
ments:

> Whatever the distance in time that separates China from its beginnings, certain aspects
> belonging to the infancy of all peoples which have become unrecognisable, or that have
> entirely disappeared elsewhere through successive improvements, are scarcely modi-
> fied in China. In speaking thus, it is not only the modern states to which I compare
> China; one can go back in antiquity to Greece and Rome, and observe these nations
> evolve through the phases of civilisation that China has never attained, even today.[26]

Sweeping appraisals of this kind, as I have argued elsewhere, clearly distinguish the
ambition of Duret's text from his claim of a singular, autobiographical travel-
ogue.[27] Although he used the format of a personal memoir, with its emphasis on
eyewitnessed events and corporeal experiences to claim authenticity, Duret excised
from his account the very perils of *flânerie* that are so characteristic of travel and
excursion. Nowhere in the chronicle did he indulge in a random walk, or a chance
discovery that veered from the prescribed course. Suppressing the aimless incidents, Duret carefully schematized his peregrinations into a questionnaire of
Eurocentric evaluations.

Duret's itinerary was mapped in this manner through the lens of a larger order.
Travel, travel writing, and art collecting in the nineteenth century presupposed the
geopolitics of European empire building and were underwritten by colonial expansion into Asia. Indeed, Duret's voyage took place at a time of heightened French
interest in the region. After their recent defeat in the Franco-Prussian War, overseas conquest was regarded by some as a consolation for French humiliation at
home. Rivalry with Britain, whose presence in Asia was predominant, further
drove France to seek its own empire in Indochina.[28] Through his travel and publication of 1874 Duret actively participated in colonial debates of the time. Certainly,
he had no ideological objections to colonialism, and shedding patriotic bias – at
least for the moment – Duret even praised the British and Dutch colonization of
India and Java. The general impression of his text is a shrewd calculation of the
potential value of each country to France in economic, cultural, and political terms.

To reinforce the systematic and documentary nature of his voyage, Duret strik-
ingly refrained in his text from any hint of erotic response, or reactions to the sensual stimuli so abundant in the earlier travel writings of Théophile Gautier,
Gustave Flaubert, and Gérard de Nerval, to name only the best known. Ferguson
notes that in Daumier's drawing for the *Physiologie du flâneur*, published in 1841,
the *flâneur*'s gaze constitutes his central feature. It is, according to Ferguson, "a
gaze that begins in the activity of following women."[29] Duret and his epigone,
Guimet, apparently did not trail after women in the streets of Asia, but they were so
conscientious in their self-elected duty that they abstained even from scopophilic
pleasure. Duret's only detailed portraits were disapproving – the long passage on
Chinese paupers cited earlier, or the regret that old Japanese men wore European
clothes so ineptly as to "resemble monkeys."[30]

It is, of course, difficult to believe that nowhere in Asia did the European travelers find an opportunity for even a sliver of sensual, sentimental, or erotic interest. Duret's self-censorship, later emulated by Guimet, only pointed to that deliberate absence. Duret was determined to resist all temptation. At a ceremonial dinner of Japanese *haute cuisine*, a grand occasion of gustatory sensations, accompanied by the aural and visual animation of *geishas*, Duret was resolutely unmoved:

> Of the whole dinner I only managed to eat a couple of roast chestnuts, a crayfish extracted by chance from a flavourless bouillon, and a cup of rice. During this time one passed from guest to guest, and mutually invited each other to drink from small glasses into which the servants poured *saki*. It is an alcohol produced by the fermentation of rice; one drinks it hot, like tea, and its taste is not at all unpleasant.[31]

Having relented on the local beverage, Duret recomposed himself for a sober scrutiny of the twenty dancers, singers, and musicians who appeared:

> The ways things happen, one cannot imagine anything more decent. The Japanese dancer is wrapped from head to foot in a large robe of rich colours whose folds form a circle around her on the floor. While dancing, she does not change her spot and hardly taps her foot to mark the beat; her dance is all about gesture; it is above all a play of the head, from the top of the body to her arms. . . . Their songs have tempo and feeling; cadence and harmony are perfectly observed, and one fairly listens with pleasure; but there is almost no variety in the rhythm or the arias, and everything is delivered like a sort of continuous psalm.[32]

An effort of interpretation is required to argue that Duret gave in, despite himself, to the productive idleness and sensual luxuriance of *flânerie*. The tension between his tightly controlled narrative voice and the infrequent breaks, the rare bursts of spontaneity, allude once more to his radical disorientation in Asia.

Emile Guimet and Félix Régamey

Following the example of Théodore Duret, Emile Guimet, son of a rich industrialist in Lyons, requested a diplomatic passport and an official assignment from the French government to study the religions of Japan. Guimet invited an artist and fellow Frenchman, Félix Régamey, to illustrate his self-funded *mission scientifique*. The results were first published in 1877 as *Rapport du Ministre de l'Instruction publique et des beaux-arts sur la mission scientifique de M. Emile Guimet dans l'Extrême-Orient*. In 1880 Guimet produced a lavish volume entitled *Promenades japonaises: Tokio–Nikko*, containing his text and Félix Régamey's illustrations.

The journey of Guimet and Régamey in 1877 resembled the earlier trip by Duret and Cernuschi insofar as they too were accompanied by teams of porters, translators, guides, and government escorts. Perhaps on reading Duret's earlier account of Japanese cuisine, Guimet decided to hire a personal cook to protect himself from the surprises of local fare. Like Duret and Cernuschi before them,

Guimet, Régamey, and their extended entourage followed a prescribed itinerary through Japan. Guimet's journey in fact exactly adhered to the prior trajectory of Duret from Yokohama to Tokyo (Edo), to Kyoto via the *Tokkaido*, and finally to Kobe, where they boarded a ship for Shanghai. From China Guimet and Régamey traveled to India. As in the case of the earlier pair, Bombay represented for Guimet and Régamey the beginning of the return voyage to France. Each of these major stations – Yokohama, Shanghai, Bombay, and the Suez Canal – were strategic points in Western expansion in the late nineteenth century. The sequence of ports, cities, and sights toured by the Europeans was similarly influenced by the growth of Western presence in those parts of the world.

As Guimet pursued his investigation in Asia, Régamey recorded each encounter. Their peculiar relationship to *flânerie* was rendered in the artist's sketchbooks: a watercolor depicted Guimet in a litter, carried by porters through a park; a quick pencil sketch showed the Frenchman, notebook in hand, proceeding in a rickshaw that was pulled and pushed by two Japanese.[33] The physical act and sensation of walking, essential to *flânerie*, were mediated and even removed here by Guimet's porters (Figure 12).

Many of Régamey's illustrations published in Guimet's book described a still labor-intensive society, but there were also important signs of technological trans-formations in Japan. Only five years after Duret's passage, Guimet witnessed the remarkable emplacement of modern infrastructure during his visit. Already on

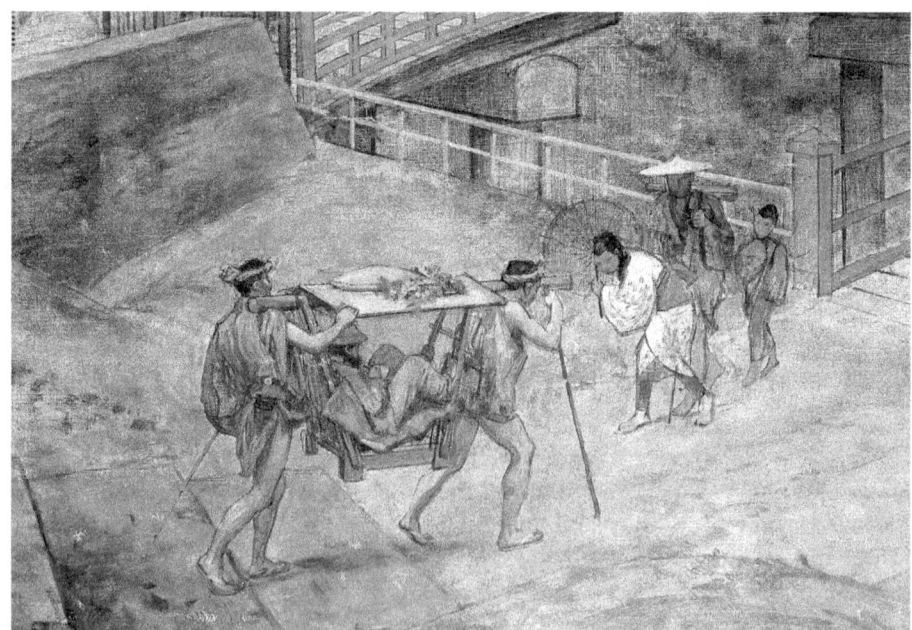

12 Félix Régamey, *The Sacred Bridge and the Ordinary Bridge at Nikko*, detail, 1876–78

page eight of *Promenades japonaises* Guimet related, in the manner of an eyewitness, the inauguration of the railroad in Japan. The emperor himself traveled by steamboat from Tokyo to Yokohama in order to board the train that conveyed him, "*without incident*," back to the imperial capital.[34] The French visitors, carried by local men from one site to another, witnessed the Japanese emperor being transported, at last, by Western machines. In the same way that the emperor could not indulge in aimless detours and promenades by train, the *flânerie* of the travelers was restricted by their porters.

Guimet's documentary ambition in Japan was appropriately enhanced by Régamey's quasi-ethnographic illustrations. In letters to his family, however, the painter wrote more candidly and incidentally about his experiences. "The old Japan is crumbling, the civilization moves forward in big strides, as they say; oil lamps, western hats, and umbrellas burst forth quite generally," Régamey complained in one letter home.[35] In another, written from Yokohama on 8 September 1876 to his brother Frédéric, Régamey exclaimed, "I write to you from the country of dreams." The reason for such a joyous tone? The artist elaborated in the second paragraph:

> And the inn with the little servants who greet the travelers with prostrations and words of welcome like birds chirping. Inside, one removes his shoes and socks, the girls wash your feet; the same girls drape over you a large garland of light fabric, and with their help you insert your arms into its capacious sleeves.[36]

However veiled the erotic appeal of this encounter, Régamey, in a private letter to his younger brother, gave a sense of the *flâneur*'s spontaneity; perhaps he even boasted a little of the pleasure that was strenuously avoided in the published accounts of both Duret and Guimet.

What Guimet emphasized in his report to the Minister were the concrete figures: "more than *three hundred* Japanese religious paintings, *six hundred* divine statues, and a collection of more than *one thousand* volumes."[37] One can fairly expect the italics in Guimet's enumeration. He was quick to add, however, that he was willing to share: "I have gathered considerable materials that I shall put at the disposal of anyone interested in the question."[38]

Upon their return home, Cernuschi and Guimet, brothers in travel and collecting, could not avoid a certain rivalry. Each traveler exhibited his collection of Asian art and objects at a prestigious institution in Paris within months of his return. Cernuschi displayed over a thousand objects at the Palais de l'Industrie in 1873, whereas Guimet presented his recently acquired treasures at the Trocadéro in 1878.

Although Cernuschi's voyage preceded that of Guimet by five years, the latter was actually first in donating his entire collection of Japanese religious artifacts to his native city of Lyons, in 1879. Guimet also announced the intention to establish a specialist library on the religions of China, Japan, and India, and a language school for both the French and "les jeunes Orientaux."[39]

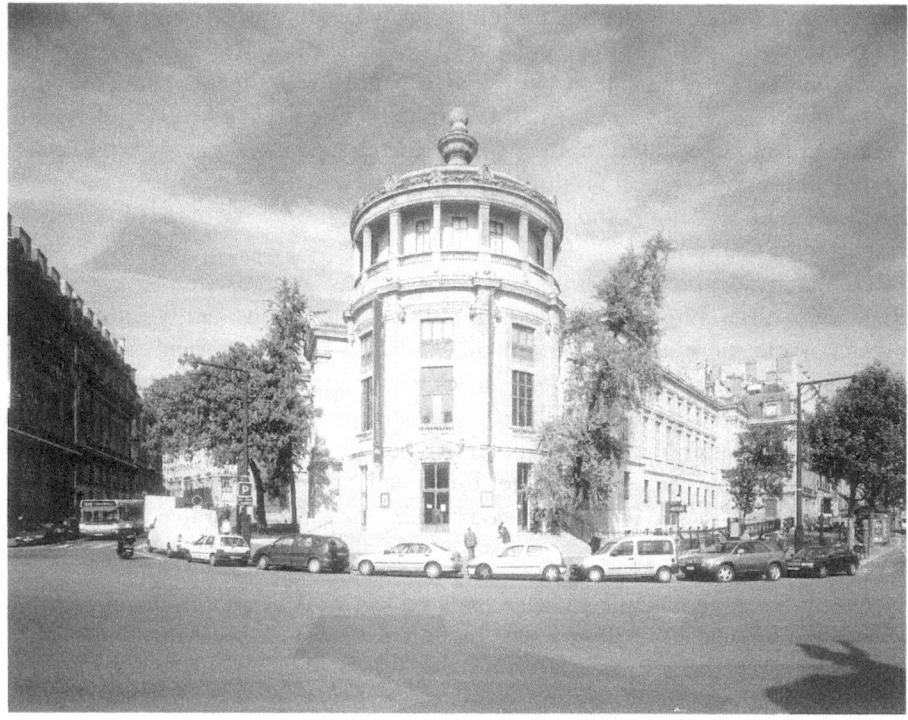

13 Exterior of Musée Guimet, Paris

Cernuschi, resident in Paris, in turn promised the city the gift of his mansion and his private collection of Asian art. The museum did not belong to Paris until the donor's death in 1898, but Cernuschi's bequest was immediately rewarded by the Legion of Honor. Not to be surpassed by Cernuschi's benefaction, Guimet uprooted his collection altogether from Lyons to the capital, where he had the museum exactly replicated (Figure 13).

Once the collections of Cernuschi and Guimet assumed their modern incarnation, the *flânerie* that accompanied their beginnings was frozen in the logic of museological display. The early traces of the *flâneurs* were both embedded and erased.

Notes

1 Salman Rushdie, *The Ground Beneath Her Feet* (Toronto: Vintage Canada Edition, 2000), p. 176. I am most grateful to the Social Sciences and Humanities Research Council of Canada for its support of this research project. I thank Aruna D'Souza and Thomas McDonough for their roles in the publication of the present anthology. I also thank Brian Grosskurth and Aron Vinegar for their very helpful comments. For my father.

2 S. Rushdie, *The Ground Beneath Her Feet*, pp. 176–177.

3 S. Rushdie, *The Ground Beneath Her Feet*, p. 177.

4 Notable examples in the massive corpus of scholarship are P. P. Ferguson, *Paris as Revolution: Writing the 19th-Century City* (Berkeley: University of California Press, 1994); R. Herbert, *Impressionism: Art, Leisure, and Parisian Society* (New Haven: Yale University Press, 1988); G. Pollock, *Vision and Difference: Femininity, Feminism and the Histories of Art* (London: Routledge, 1988); and J. Wolff, "The Invisible *Flâneuse*: Women and the Literature of Modernity," in *Feminine Sentences: Essays on Women and Culture* (Berkeley: University of California Press, 1990). E. Wilson argues, on the contrary, that it is the *flâneur*, not the *flâneuse*, who is invisible in her article, "The Invisible *Flâneur*," *New Left Review* no. 191 (January–February 1992), pp. 90–110.

5 W. Benjamin, "M [The Flâneur]," in *The Arcades Project*, trans. H. Eiland and K. McLaughlin (Cambridge, Mass. and London: Belknap Press of Harvard University Press, 2002), pp. 416–455, and also the essays "A Berlin Chronicle" and "Hashish in Marseilles" in W. Benjamin, *Reflections: Essays, Aphorisms, Autobiographical Writings*, trans. E. Jephcott (New York: Schocken Books, 1986).

6 P. P. Ferguson, *Paris as Revolution*, p. 81.

7 P. P. Ferguson, *Paris as Revolution*, p. 81.

8 Duret to C. Pissarro, autograph letter in Fondation Custodia, MS Paris 1978–A-8, cited in S. Inaga, "Théodore Duret (1838–1927): Du journaliste politique à l'historien d'art japonisant," unpublished thesis, Université de Paris VII, 1988, vol. 3, pp. 600–601 (all translations by the author unless an English source is cited).

9 J.-J. Rousseau, *The Collected Writings of Rousseau*, vol. 3, eds R. D. Masters and C. Kelly (Hanover: University Press of New England, 1992), p. 85.

10 J.-J. Rousseau, *The Collected Writings*, p. 85.

11 Discussed in D. Porter, *Haunted Journeys: Desire and Transgression in European Travel Writing* (Princeton, N.J.: Princeton University Press, 1991), p. 70.

12 T. Duret, *Voyage en Asie*, pp. 3–4.

13 T. Duret, *Voyage en Asie*, p. 4.

14 T. Duret, *Voyage en Asie*, p. 4.

15 T. Duret, *Voyage en Asie*, p. 14.

16 T. Duret, *Voyage en Asie*, p. 20.

17 T. Duret, *Voyage en Asie*, pp. 20–21.

18 I thank A. Vinegar for his close reading of an earlier draft of this essay.

19 W. Benjamin, *The Arcades Project*, p. 420.

20 W. Benjamin, *The Arcades Project*, p. 417.

21 T. Duret, *Voyage en Asie*, p. 8.

22 T. Duret, *Voyage en Asie*, p. 8.

23 E. de Goncourt, *Journal: mémoire de la vie littéraire*, vol. 11, ed. R. Ricatte (Paris: Fasquelle et Flammarion, 1956), p. 27.

24 T. Duret, *Voyage en Asie*, p. 75.

25 T. Duret, *Voyage en Asie*, p. 90.

26 T. Duret, *Voyage en Asie*, pp. 144–145.

27 See T. Chang, "Collecting Asia: Théodore Duret's *Voyage en Asie* and Henri Cernuschi's Museum," *Oxford Art Journal* 25, no. 1 (March 2002), pp. 17–34.

28 R. Aldrich, *Greater France: The History of French Overseas Expansion* (London: MacMillan Press, 1996), pp. 73–84.

29 P. P. Ferguson, *Paris as Revolution*, p. 89.

30 T. Duret, *Voyage en Asie*, p. 38.

31 T. Duret, *Voyage en Asie*, p. 47.

32 T. Duret, *Voyage en Asie*, pp. 48–49.

33 These and other drawings have been published in K. Omoto and F. Macouin, *Quand le Japon s'ouvrit au monde* (Paris: Découvertes Gallimard, 1990). See especially pp. 58, 64.

34 E. Guimet, *Promenade japonaises: Tokio–Nikko* (Paris: Charpentier, 1880), p. 8.

35 F. Régamey's letters are published in K. Omoto and F. Macouin, *Quand le Japon s'ouvrit au monde*, p. 148.

36 Régamey, letter of September 8, 1876 to F. Régamey, published in K. Omoto and F. Macouin, *Quand le Japon s'ouvrit au monde*, p. 146.

37 Guimet cited in B. Frank, *Le Panthéon bouddhique au Japon: collections d'Emile Guimet* (Paris: Réunion des Musées Nationaux, 1991), p. 26. Emphasis in the original.

38 B. Frank, *Le Panthéon bouddhique*, p. 26.

39 Guimet's announcement is quoted in B. Frank, *Le Panthéon bouddhique*, p. 33.

6

Transcrypts:
some notes between pricks

Simon Leung

The following is a script for a live/video work performed between 1991 and 1992 in New York and Los Angeles. In Los Angeles it was performed at Royce Hall, UCLA and at Los Angeles Contemporary Exhibitions (LACE). In New York it was performed at Graduate Center, City University of New York, at Anthology Film Archives, and at The Drawing Center.

"As I passed the *pistière* in the Rue de Bourgogne I saw M. le Baron de Charlus go in. When I came back from Neuilly, a good hour later, I saw his yellow trousers in the same *pistière*, in the same place, in the middle stall where he always stands so that people shan't see him."[1]

So Swann's butler describes the strange behavior of the Baron de Charlus and his predilection for the public conveniences that he comically misnames pistières, *adding for good measure that "M. le Baron de Charlus must have caught a disease to stand about as long as he does in a* pistière.*" Indeed the* pissotière *or* pissoir *(also known as* lieux vespasiennes, *or even by the English term "water-closets"[2]), first introduced on to Paris' streets in the early 1840s, proved suitable for much more than the relief of the* flâneur; *these public toilets were also notorious as spaces of male-male public sex.*

The pissoir *was originally introduced to the public spaces of the city as a means to discourage public urination, particularly on the distinguished landmarks of Paris's monuments. They proliferated during the years of the Second Empire, and became ubiquitous throughout Haussmann's boulevards, public squares, and parks – as witnessed in Charles Marville's well-known photographs of these structures, taken in the 1860s. Yet at the same moment that the* pissoir *was being championed as a boon to public hygiene, it was being condemned as a blight on public morality. Its sheltered space, public yet anonymous, was understood to enable and encourage sexual encounters among its male visitors, and indeed the Paris police regularly raided* pissoirs *from the 1850s onward as a means of discouraging such activity.*

Yet these repressive measures of the service des moeurs *were to a large degree fruitless. As a former chief of the vice police described it, the* pissoir *remained a favored site of* prostitution antiphysique *(male homosexual prostitution) and anonymous encounter:*

The water-closets, based on their design, are the cause of all this disorder. An entryway provides access to three stalls, separated by thin partitions in brick. When pédérastes choose a particular water-closet for their rendezvous, they pierce each of these partitions with small holes that permit two neighbors in adjoining stalls to commence unspeakable acts through it. Each day, city masons block the holes, and each evening they appear anew.[3]

Those very qualities that made the pissoir *an efficient and convenient piece of* mobilier urbain *also made it available for such a reinscription as a site of male homosexual activity. The boundaries between public use and private appropriation become inextricably blurred, and no amount of repair by the city's public works department could reinstate the clear demarcations so sought after by those charged with the surveillance and discipline of the streets and thoroughfares of the metropolis. Whatever the* flâneur's *pretensions to visual control of those spaces, in actual fact he was compelled to share them with such other, illicit uses of the modern city. Even more troubling, as the Baron de Charlus revealed, the* flâneur *may himself have partaken of such other use(s), sharing not only the same public space but also the same body.*

This is not, however, to claim the pissoir *as some sexual utopia. One often paid for one's encounters there, whether in coin or at the risk of disease (Swann's butler being closer to the truth than he knew) or arrest. As Simon Leung describes it in his 1991–92 performance work* Transcrypts, *the public toilet might better be thought of as a "heterotopia," a term coined by Michel Foucault to demarcate a type of space that is capable – in a single real place – of juxtaposing several incompatible sites (for example, urinal and sexual rendezvous), a site whose system of opening and closing both isolates it and makes it penetrable.[4] To paraphrase Leung, there may be many of us in the* pissoir, *but only some of us are, like the Baron de Charlus, in the tearoom, as it would become known in its American vernacular incarnation. Leung's work explores the complexities of this heterotopic space in its contemporary manifestations, but is not without its lessons for students of nineteenth-century urban space. And we might add that it has itself something of a historical character, performed as it was over a decade ago at a moment when (the then nascent) queer theory and art production were coming to grips with the impact of AIDS on sexual practices and their spaces. Transcrypts, that is, possesses something of a retrospective quality – a rethinking of a particular form of desire's inscription upon the public space of the city that was at once in defiance of its passing, during a time of political contestation over its meaning. –* Tom McDonough

I

It began in Paris. Two summers ago, two friends and I were walking along the Seine at dusk. Looking down at the edge of the river, I saw a pattern of movement which I immediately recognized. I suggested that we take a walk along the embankment under the bridges and closer to the water. My friends agreed. After seconds of walking on the embankment, it became unmistakable – this was a gay cruising spot.

Solitary men strode up and down the narrow strip with penetrating gazes made all the more penetrating by the darkening skies.

"This is a total cruise scene," I quietly whispered. My friends, neither of whom were gay, did not notice this. That is, they were oblivious to what was to me an obvious scenario until the scenario was named.

It began to rain heavily and we took cover under a bridge, where many men who were cruising also sought shelter. There arose a sense of uneasiness in me because although we were all enclosed in a relatively small space, some of us were there for sexual encounters and some of us were not. Our foreignness – we were obviously not French – augmented this awkward feeling. One of my friends innocently posed a question to me in English about the "scene" we were in and I quickly cut him off and asked him to not talk about this topic in such a compromising enclosure, where both "spectators" and "participants" are forced to seek common shelter from the rain. My extra-sensitivity produced a mildly indignant response from my friend. "Why not? After all, this is a public space." More than the old adage "the rich and the poor are not equal to sleep under the bridges of Paris," my friend's response in retrospect has made me think about my involvement with questions in this present context, in which all discourses are overdetermined to take on mythomorphic functions. My questions are: the question of space, and the question of ethics. That is, what does it mean to see or not to see, and how do we agree to behave so that we could speak with one another.

Let me take you back one more summer, when I was travelling alone, again in Paris. I had read in my guidebook that there existed, in the Conciergerie, a display of a replica of the last letter of Marie Antoinette, addressed to her cousin and written in pin-pricks. The image of the pin-pricked letter written by the captive queen denied pen and ink just before her execution moved me deeply. But when I tried to see this display I was confronted with the all too familiar sign encountered by disoriented tourists – "fermé." The sign read "closed." The part of the Conciergerie where the display was kept was under renovation. Disappointed, I walked around among the vast vaults and columns of the famous prison, feeling as though I were wandering through the sets for the last act of *Andrea Chenier*, just before the lovers walk off into the sunset . . . and the guillotine. It is within these two Parisian moments that I would like to frame this talk.

I would like to talk to you about "tearooms" – that is, public washrooms where men meet and engage in anonymous sex. My interest in this topic is both "theoretical" and "site-specific." I am interested in using tearoom sex both as a model for thinking about the subject in sexuality, especially in relationship to the writings of Lacan, and to recode some of the signals associated with this space which seem to have been crossed. In order to reach certain points we hope to arrive at, it is necessary to describe the tearoom as traversal, as moments, and, in this reading, the movement of a cinematic zoom, eventually focusing on a most ambiguous vanishing point.

First of all, one may describe the tearoom as a "heterotopic" space which is at once center and periphery.[5] Socially and topographically speaking, they generally exist on the borders of "the consciousness" of those not engaged in its activities, and are physically removed from the center of whatever architectural space they happen to occupy. This heterotopia is mapped upon the already peripheral and heterotopic space of public washrooms. That is why we think the truism "the best parties are in the bathrooms" both funny and ironic. Bathrooms are exactly the places not to throw parties. Especially tea parties. Still, I assure you there are many such tea parties being held as we speak. But before we enter, let me point out two features of heterotopic spaces: a) they always hold a function which is a part of the function of larger society, and b) they have their own logic and ethics predetermined by their relationship to larger society.

In a sense, the logic of how tearooms come into being is not unlike the story of the virus and its host, the story of an otherness within. This otherness may be despised, persecuted, or encouraged to grow. The virus, necessarily silent and invisible, is an agent searching for openings into the host body so that it itself can flourish. The host body thus must first be susceptible. Washrooms become tearooms only after a certain barrier has been broken. What I want to make clear, as you no doubt can imagine, is that this deployment of the viral metaphor is strategic, and itself parasitic upon another idea of another virus. For what ultimately makes a tearoom a tearoom is neither just the place nor its clients; nor just the activities, both physical and psychological; but the relationship between its inside and outside. After all, "the wholly-other," writes Levinas, "cannot be selved or samed." In other words, there may be many of us in the washroom, but only some of us are in the tearoom. The virus I speak of is thus never just person, place or thing, but an "economy." Just as its host and antibody agents are an "economy." Still, susceptibility to this economy cannot be articulated unless it shows symptoms. So the question is, "how to read?"

The space of this text is structured like a labyrinth. Complete with mirrors, opening and closing doors, and secret enclosures, the tearoom is a zone of many conflicting signs. At the simplest levels, there are the "writings on the wall" – the graffiti expressing desires, preferences and prejudices, arranging meetings, warning to others of the police; the cum stains; the glory holes . . ., etc. Often simultaneously layered with these signs are signs of dominant society's attempts to eradicate, discipline, and punish these desires – steel plates bolted into the walls to cover the holes, scrubbed and scratched out areas of the walls where faint and fragmented words remain, contesting homophobic graffiti, and official warnings of the presence of the police.

There are also other signs. Since words are rarely exchanged during tearoom encounters, there exists a complex choreography of rituals which produce and stabilize these other signs and their meanings during the course of an encounter. Knowing and repeated glances, extended lingering at the urinal, eyes peeking through cracks, tilts of the head, hand signals and a gently tapping foot under the partition between two stalls are all part of the silent tea dance. ("Tap foot for blowjob" is one of the most common graffiti one would encounter in an old-fashioned tearoom.)

The significance of this silence cannot be underestimated, for there is always too much at stake when a man is both compelled to signal, and forbidden to use voice, for his voice would render his desires naked and subject him to account. During these moments of signaling and decoding, all players are in effect playing "undercover," placing their bets against a field of silence. Is he trade or is he vice? Is that the look of interest or the look of disdain? Encouragement or rejection?

In some cases this duplicity is a doubly silent agreement. In other words, for some men it signals a betrayal, a double divergence, a split. I am not speaking merely about homophobia and the dramas of the "water closet," even though they do often converge on to the tearoom map. I speak here, of trauma. I would like to skip over the too-familiar terrain of the trauma individuals feel upon recognition of their sexual desire and the subsequent traumas they experience when these desires are measured against the social field. I would instead like to limit my discussion to the matrix of certain tearoom encounters, but recognizing that these different moments of trauma (and perhaps their repression or celebration) are intricately related in a field of signification. The trauma of this particular scene is fragmentation.

> We betray the fixed powers which try to hold us back, the established powers of the earth. The movement of betrayal has been defined as a double turning-away: man turns his face away from God, who also turns his face away from man. It is in the double turning-away, in the divergence of faces, that the line of flight – that is, the deterritorialization of man – is traced.[6]

This play of faces turning away is convenient for a discussion about tearooms for I think it is exactly this facelessness which makes tearoom sex such powerful and pleasurable experiences. I will return to this shortly. For the moment let me propose that for any good humanist subject engaging in tearoom sex, humanist subjects being what we all are in varying degrees, this turning away may first of all be one's own turning away from a seemingly consolidated sexual identity which is often left outside the tearoom, waiting like a specter. Such dissonance, as I've said, is not predicated exclusively on a simple homophobic conception of the self, for the stigma attached to tearoom sex with its associations of "clandestineness," "promiscuity," "anonymity," "emptiness," and faceless objectification is supposed to produce feelings of melancholic abjection in all subjects conditioned to invest in identities conceived to be whole and unfragmented, desiring love objects in equally whole and unfragmented packages. In one sense, this illustrates one reason why pornography produces guilt; in another sense, it marks the greater dilemma of one who must use language to speak, but cannot represent *one* self with the terms of that language. The further associations between tearoom sex and "filth" and the shame of this filth strengthen these feelings of fragmentation. The feelings of repulsion for shit, if we listen to Kristeva, are closely related to investments in the idea of whole and unfragmented identities, because "excrement and its equivalents (decay, infection, disease, corpse, etc.) stand for the danger to identity that comes from without: the ego threatened by the non-ego, society threatened by its outside, life by death."[7]

So this list brings us, finally, to a system of representation that secures a partic-ular cultural moment. That is, in an age when partners enquire about each other's sexual history and HIV status, tearoom sex is for some now also inevitably associ-ated with unsafe-sex, which *itself* has become an object of mourning. In his pow-erful essay "Mourning and Militancy," Douglas Crimp writes,

> Alongside the dismal toll of death, what many of us have lost is a culture of sexual possibility: back rooms, tearooms, bookstores, movie houses, and baths; the trucks, the pier, the ramble, the dunes. Sex was everywhere for us, and everything we wanted to venture: golden showers and water sports, cocksucking and rimming, fucking and fist-fucking. Now our untamed impulses are either proscribed once again or shielded from us by latex.[8]

I find this beautiful elegy for the "culture of sexual possibility" from the utopian 1970s and early 1980s rather uncanny, so perhaps now is a good time to enter one of the stalls. I want, nevertheless, also to seize this moment to resurrect the metaphor of the labyrinth, because when I said that the space of the text of the tearoom is structured like a labyrinth, I hope you did not take this to mean merely an architec-tural construction. "The labyrinth is where those without access to the thread of knowledge are condemned to lose their way."[9] My questions are, "what is the thread of this knowledge and how can it be used?"

The common implication one draws when one says that a sexual economy is structured like a labyrinth is that it is also a "trap" – that somehow one is isolated or imprisoned by one's desires. In the case of the tearoom this can be said to be literal-ized architecturally with the privatized stall, or the water "closet." But tearooms aren't necessarily traps – they are also gifts, seemingly gifts from the Father. Like all gifts, there are strings attached. To begin untying the strings, I would like to announce an object of fascination, namely the "glory hole," the transitional object which will take us to the second part of this paper. If I sound as though I am on the verge of celebration, then let me state again that my idea of the tearoom is exactly that it is heterotopic, and not utopic. To quote Leo Bersani in his description of another male-sex institution:

> Anyone who has ever spent one night in a gay bathhouse knows that it is (or was) one of the most ruthlessly ranked, hierarchized, and competitive environments imagin-able. Your looks, muscles, hair distribution, size of cock, and shape of ass determined exactly how happy you were going to be during those few hours, and rejection, gener-ally accompanied by two or three words at most, could be swift and brutal, with none of the civilizing hypocrisies with which we get rid of undesirables in the outside world.[10]

This generally describes power relations of desire in the tearoom. I would add, of course, race, class and most importantly age as important criteria for whether someone is "desirable." This can be poignantly felt in a tearoom, where most men are more "secretive" and have less time to read and register signs of desirability. If I were to again ask the question "how to read?," then we would see that the question has become more complicated, the stakes have risen. To read desire is to pose two simultaneous questions: "Do I desire you?" And "do you desire me?"

This necessarily frank assessment of value reminds one not only of the idealized insularity of romantic courtship, whether heterosexual or homosexual, but of another economy – that is, "economy" – "business." However, if this analogy can be drawn then one sees that this is decidedly not capitalism as we know it, for although one may have "value" and "assets," one rarely shows a profit. Profit would naturally signal another institution, like prostitution. Tearoom sex is more like the barter system, an economy of "the present" – one man contracts himself to be and feel like a commodity, to be protuberances and orifices which service other protuberances and orifices, with no planning for the future and no promise of justice. So from the verge of celebration we've reached a description which may sound a bit grim, but I do not mean it as such. For although like any economy we may resent the terms of such insider trading, this feeling as commodity, this "substitution" for a transcendental "self" for disembodied parts, is I think the very element which can teach us something about our conceptions of sexuality.

For this reason I will now focus on "the glory hole," a sexual model par excellence, because it is so formally elegant. The glory hole is not just another hole in the wall. No, it is bigger. Bigger than just any hole one can look through, because what makes a glory hole so "glorious" is that it can accommodate the circumference of an erect penis . . . which means it isn't *that* big. It is strategically placed: in a wall between two stalls, generally at hip level, so that a) a man can insert his penis into it easily, and b) it is around the eye and mouth level of someone sitting on the toilet on the other side. The glory hole, in other words, accommodates with maximum comfort and provides a pleasant view.

We speak thus, first of all, of scopic pleasure. I offer you a passage from the anthology *MEAT*, subtitled "how men look, act, walk, talk, dress, undress, taste, and smell. True homosexual experience from *STH*" (which stands for the journal *Straight to Hell*):

> I had been stationed in one of the booths about five minutes when he came in. He looked to see if there were any prospects in the other booths and took the booth next to mine. Luckily there was a big glory hole in our partition.
>
> As soon as he got settled I leaned back and looked through it. First I saw his huge hands with sun-bleached blond hair on them. His nails were wide and pink. I could see enough of his legs to tell he was muscular and tan. They too had shiny blond hairs.
>
> As he moved around his face came a little lower and he caught me looking at him through the hole. He was about 33 and the years had made a real man of him. He gave me a little nod and smile. I returned the smile. I looked right into his extremely light blue eyes with their white lashes and brows. He had longish blond hair which was straight and hung loosely.

I knew I had to move fast and his smile had encouraged me. I could feel my cock swelling and moving upward. I leaned back and spread my legs apart to display my hard cock. He moved closer to the hole to see it.[11]

Beside this gentleman from Ohio's evident arousal and excitement at having encountered what was for him an obviously sublime prospect, I want for our purposes to concentrate on his descriptions of vision, and how these various instances of vision are literally "centered" in respect to the glory hole. First, the other man comes in and looks around, probably through the cracks in the doors before settling on the booth next to our narrator's while our narrator sits in his own enclosed booth. Next, our narrator peeks through the hole and looks for signs which might adequately arouse him. What he sees are *parts* of this man's body – a hand, enough of his leg, his eyes, a smile. In short, fragmented scenes of the man's body which needs to be composed to render a "composite image" of *a* man in our narrator's fantasy. Naturally, this can never be totally achieved, since the clues are so scattered, and our narrator can see only one part at a time. The image of the other, in other words, is at best a multiplication of fragments, an obscure object of desire which hovers around the subject before settling down as an image, recognizable through a hole in the wall, a puncture in the screen.[12]

We now arrive at a stage where the glory hole takes on more than just a scopic function. It has in fact the possibility of many functions. But before we go on, let me register a mark of ambivalence located in the tension between "spectator" and "participant," "masquerade" and "display." More than the glory hole's status as a built-in invitation or built-in refusal to sexual pleasure, more than the tension between the possibility for something to remain an image or to integrate into the space and body of oneself, the problem at hand, it seems, is the nature of the other's constitution. A prick without a face. A floating signifier. When it "comes through," the effect, I assure you, is always uncanny. The image is that of an erect penis, engorged with blood, with hair, texture and smell, slowly pushing through a partition made of cold steel or marble, which enframes it like the head of a decapitated animal, decapitated, but alive. An organ without a body. It is very unhome-like.[13]

Freud tells us that the uncanny object arouses in us doubts as to whether what seems animate is indeed alive. He uses the example of the uncanny doll, an inanimate object to be played with, as something which can seem to come alive, feel alive, but whose life quality does not resemble that of the human; perhaps because it is too human, all too human. But we know that this player which has come through to our side is both alive and human. Or do we? Freud reminds us that the uncanny is not only something which ought to have remained a secret and hidden but has come to light; but also a structure, which in many cases couples with the anxiety of castration. At the risk of being too literal, "perhaps it shouldn't be forgotten that the organ that assumes this signifying function also takes on the value of a fetish."[14] I suggest that these models are not just literal, just visual, for the seduction scene alone is not sufficient. What is needed, still mute, is the contradiction springing from the incorporation itself. It ceaselessly opposes two stiff, incompatible forces, erect against each other: . . . "Two contradictory demands: that the Father's penis should neither come nor go." Without this contradiction within desire, nothing would be comprehensible. . . .[15]

Naturally, what threatens to wake us from our dreams of wholeness with its intrusion is itself an equivalent to a moment of condensation. Still, its entrance cannot be more vulnerable. Its daring in crossing the threshold can only have been riddled with hesitation and fear. So if you think our representation of masculinity has been a bit disorienting thus far, then step around to the other side.

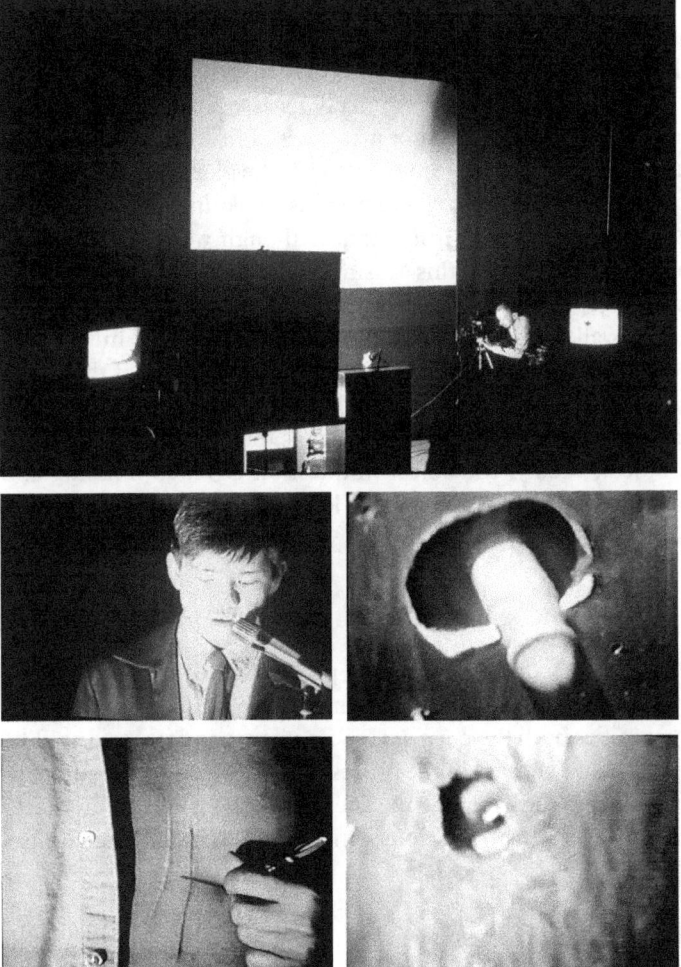

14–15 Simon Leung, *Transcrypts: some notes between pricks*, 1991–92

On this side we see a man who has placed his erect penis through the glory hole, literally plugging it. His hips pushed forward, pants around his ankles, like puddles, his hands grasping the ledge of the partition, barely hanging on . . . he's afraid to look down. He can't look down, because the space between his eyes and his sex had collapsed into no space at all, his stomach and chest, pressed against the cold partition. He saw that his sex had not disappeared into another man, but into the wall, for the other man can only be imagined. His other must now also exist only on the level of fantasy, for he cannot be seen, or felt, except by an organ which has disappeared to encounter a mouth. He wants to collapse into this mouth. But is it a mouth?! (He's being sucked through the hole!) Or is it something else? Like a hand, or an asshole? But if it is a mouth, is it the mouth of a man or a woman? Is it connected to a person? Or only something like a person? Oh, he's close! Is his sex being devoured? Has he engaged himself in a sacrifice he did not intend? What am I saying?!

Perhaps you've noticed that I have skimmed over something a bit too quickly in my haste to make that point. You will remember that before we entered I had expressed concerns about the tearoom and its infectious associations, particularly epitomized by the holes in its walls. I will stop just short of making my point, and put the problems of these troubled codes into the node of the glory hole and lead us out of the tearoom and to the post office, where we must pick up a letter from our dearly departed queen. Let me say that if it seems as though we now run risk of losing sight of our beloved object, then this "losing sight" may not be so much a supplanting, than a grafting.

The last letter. As we walk along I have the sinking feeling that it might have been sent COD, and with each day, the debt mounts. I wonder, in fact, if this is not yet another letter purloined from yet another French queen.[16] But unlike that other famous unseen letter, what I hold in my hand is perhaps too porous to sustain the ambition of such an object, even if the object in question is veiled, missing and unseen. It is here that I wish to put down that other letter, and inaugurate its disappearance with reading another form of inscription.

II

Let's begin at the beginning. That is, with the first prick. Already, we have a split. What we see is a tiny hole which has retained the mark of violence. What we say, prick, simultaneously signifies both the perpetrator of violence and its residue. The linguistic prick is a "split of subjectivity in the process of being held to *a* sexual representation."[17] It is a wonderment that language does not wish to contain more elements programmed to be this comical, this deferential, this bisexual. Language is a porous container.

The act of pricking *is* the sensation of being pierced *is* any painful stinging *is* a small mark or puncture made by a pointed object *is* the punctured object *is* the penis *is* to puncture lightly *is* to sting with a mental or emotional pang *is* to mark or delineate *is* to incite *is* a wound *is* a disagreeable person . . .

Verb and noun, agent and repository, the prick cannot decide. It is a punctured word, a phallic hole, a site of unborn, unrealized possibilities. The test is whether we can hold more than two concepts of this prick at once. Can we set the stage for so binary, so Oedipal a metaphor, can we let it flourish, like a virus, in our laboratory? Do we dare to let dissemination and repetition mutilate the unity of this signifier?[4] The answer is, of course, we don't have a choice.

The paper was given to you by your mother, so perhaps the tactile trace to her skin was already inevitable. But the hand of these traces reveals itself in images which betray its master – were they revelations or enactments of memory, enactments of the possibility of something else? Like the act of making pores, the pores on your mother's face, the surface of her cheek below her left eye, where "sight was saturated," where you had "no more eyes."[18] You don't notice it because you can think only one prick at a time, but what began to coalesce were fragments of masculinity, dispersed male body parts which you dare not put back together – maybe the face of a sailor dead for 150 years, frozen and preserved in the Arctic snows; maybe a hand beginning to grasp on to words, but before it can do so, the meaning of words are already falling through the holes; maybe a prick, a prick made of pricks, made to dissolve into a field somewhere, a ground to soak up the rain. And images of femininity that exceed themselves – like the Three Graces, like a smiling Louise Bourgeois with enough breasts for seven women. Perpetual Flowers. Undying Suns (sons). Maternal plenitude.

> A sweeter rose
> A softer sky
> An April day, that will not dance away . . .

One ponders the efficacy of such strategic methods for identification, for what arises is the spark you can only recognize as conflict. You look at these pricks and they keep moving, the needle at the end of the hand, like chess pieces on a board which only grows longer and wider. Where do you go? It would seem logical that if this pin entering the paper was destined to play out the violence of the primal scene from the view of the child, then the significance of the Father, the significance for which he has come to stand in this articulation as the third term of the Oedipal triangle, is at the same time the meaning of attachment to the Mother's body for the child. This is what I mean by enactment. The enactment of attachment in search of meaning guaranteeing castration, the moment of separation.

> There is an idea about the scar in the middle of our bodies.
> It is the idea that it is our center.
> But this center has no purpose, no sex.

> It is empty – an emptiness that refers to the attachment to a
> maternal space, an emptiness that refers to the separation
> from a maternal space.

> Following this logic, I asked myself a year later: "where is father?"

This is what I mean by enactment. The scaring convergence of the body of the father with the body of the mother in a binary play of castration on to the body of the child which is no longer the mark of deferment, no longer just the hand pricking an uncomprehending sheet of whispers, a sea of silence, but a line carved on the edge of sexual decipherability to demand once again the question, "where is father?" The hand that pricks and cuts and carves is also the tearing flesh, the sea of silence itself, all conspiring to reopen the groove between your legs in a return to a moment before your sex was named, and bound, and waiting silently in the crypt.

> What the crypt commemorates, as the incorporated object's "monument" . . . is not the object itself, but its exclusion, the exclusion of a specific desire from the introjection process: A door is silently sealed off like a condemned passageway inside the Self, becoming the outcast safe: "A commemorative moment, the incorporated object marks the place, the date, the circumstances in which . . . a desire was barred from introjection: like so many tombs in the life of the Self."[19]

This is what I mean by enactment: seeing the pores on your mother's face, the sound of a closing door. This confusion reminds you to think of something you read in a book or saw on TV about an inhuman beast, the nocturnal echidna, which to you looks like nothing but spiny pricks. But the echidna like you feeds its new-born with milk. She too is mammal. But Nature gave her no nipples, so her young must burrow into the skin of her swollen breasts, and break the skin, break the skin to drown in the sweetness of her milk. But does it know that it opens the skin of its mother just to drink? Or does it only want to retrace its steps? Back. The sound of a closing door.

"Never to receive pain(t)," a quiet plea, please don't. One of the drawings said plainly enough, "Never to receive pain(t)." There were fifty-five, how can you keep track? But it was not so plain, for in parentheses in the space below the word "pain" you had pricked a "t." Paint. Never to receive "pain(t)" . . .

> We have heard a good deal about Hegel's prediction of the death of art. Most of us here know that death, indeed sublation, is not just the dénouement of a story-line. It is also shorthand for a moment in a morphology. Let us remind ourselves of it: Hegel's *Lectures on the Aesthetics* offers us an epistemograph of the Mind, separated from its Knowledge, slowly closing the gap. Different varieties of art are the by-product of the Mind's separation from Knowledge. When the gap closes, art will no longer happen. In Absolute Knowledge there is no art.[20]

"T." T is for truth. Truth which can only stand next to the subject, next to the "I." Am I I or am I it. I or it. I confuse the two, the I and the It. Never to receive pain – T. No paint, no pigment, no liquid, no desire. We know fluidity to be the iconography of desire, we know it to find form in models and metaphors to oppose the solidity of models and metaphors like the phallus. But the hard prick is itself fleshy and porous, so porous, so open and so susceptible to invasion.

a disguising as of ships or guns to conceal them from the enemy – like a natural spring, holes sunk into the ground to get a source of abundant supply, a shaft resembling a container for a liquid as to gush or to flow –

Seeping, flowing, gushing through the pores; like water, like rain; the roof is leaking. And the queen, no longer a Queen, is she still pricking? Tracing the contour of each letter to make each letter Mean. Pricks to make up letters. Letters to make words. Words to mean . . . mean what? She had written "something" . . . she had addressed it . . . to her cousin. But did the letter ever arrive?! She fears now that it may never reach its destination! How could it have? It never left the prison . . . The roof is leaking! I must stop the leakage . . . I need something! Something! Something like a machine . . . To find a machine . . . to find a machine . . . find a machine that understands desire!! But surely no machine can account for every leak, every desire, changing, leaking, depending on which one is being addressed . . . to her cousin, Yes! But from the prison – but if it were only addressed and never sent. Could not have been sent . . . it could never have arrived . . . Surely no single machine could account for every leak! No! No! No! Give me anything! I need a tool, a washer. A plug.

And I'm a sucker for an orifice that shines
because you're mine, I walk the line.

His prick plugged. Perhaps he did not want to hear.

I sacrifice any thing come what may for the stakes of having you near, in spite of a voice, that cuts like a knife, it repeats, how it pricks up my ear . . .

Perhaps it's time to reconnect the two parties, although it must be a bad connection, with all the static, and the rain. Our friend, hanging by his fingertips, hanging on the other line, his prick plugged into the hole.

Did I hear correctly?
Did he suggest that I should mouth breath?
That my ear is an anus which needs to be vaginalized?

An asshole for an ear. How dare they cut me off! But this call must be put through! Hello?! This call has been paid for!

We find ourselves back in the tearoom. Yes, the moment before I was going to make my point. Yes. Allow me to collect myself. I was concerned about something.

Yes, the glory hole. I was concerned that in our undigested paranoia a node of possibility as complex as something like the glory hole should be collapsed into such a closed and unaccommodating sign. The view, as you remember, is really rather pleasant. That view, at the very least can be a model for safer sex, you might say, relocalizing pleasure through every glimpse. Look, our narrator and his friend, themselves mirrors . . . in a labyrinth. What is the thread of its knowledge? Is it veiled by the gaze? Covered by the refusal of a desire that is not returned? Blocked by the steel plate of the state? Glory has a price. There is no hole if there is no field.

> There was a little girl who had a blanket. The blanket got a hole in it. She wanted to
> get rid of the hole so she decided to cut it out. She cut it out and the hole got bigger.
> She cut that out, too, and the hole got bigger. Eventually the hole disappeared but so
> did the blanket.[21]

All in all, it's not just another prick in the wall. And the letter? Perhaps it must remain unseen, although I do say that we have a lot to learn from our dead queens. I offer you instead, the words of another captive, words of one blind man in the mouth of another, from *Samson Agonistes*, by Milton:

> O first created Beam, and thou great Word,
> Let there be light, and light was over all;
> Why am I thus bereav'd thy prime decree?
> The Sun to me is dark
> And silent as the Moon,
> When she deserts the night
> Hid in her vacant interlunar cave.
> Since light so necessary is to life,
> And almost life itself, if it be true
> That light is in the Soul,
> She all in every part; why was the sight
> To such a tender ball as th' eye confin'd?
> So obvious and so easy to be quench't
> and not as feeling through all parts diffus'd
> That she might look at will through every pore?[22]

©1992 Simon Leung

Notes

1 Marcel Proust, *In Search of Lost Time*, vol. 5, trans. C. K. Scott Moncrieff and Terence Kilmartin (London: Chatto and Windus, 1992), pp. 211–212.
2 A term that came into the English lexicon to denote a variation of the *pissoir* providing individual stalls.
3 François Carlier, *Deux Prostitutions, 1860–1870* (Paris, 1887).
4 See Michel Foucault, "Of Other Spaces," *Diacritics* 16, no. 1 (1986).
5 My use of the term "heterotopia" comes from Foucault's essay "Of Other Spaces."

6 Quoted from G. Deleuze and C. Parnet, "On the Superiority of Anglo-American Literature," in *Dialogues*, trans. H. Tomlinson and B. Habberjam (New York: Columbia University Press, 1987), p. 40.

7 Quoted from J. Kristeva, *Powers of Horror* (New York: Columbia University Press, 1982), p. 71.

8 D. Crimp, "Mourning and Militancy," *October* 51 (1989), p. 11.

9 D. Hollier on Bataille, in *Against Architecture*, trans. B. Wing (Cambridge, Mass.: MIT Press, 1989), p. 60.

10 This passage is taken from L. Bersani, "Is the Rectum a Grave?" *October* 43 (1987), p. 206. Although I am only quoting a descriptive segment from Bersani, the spirit of this text is very much indebted to his.

11 Quoted from *MEAT* (San Francisco: Gay Sunshine Press, 1981), p. 55.

12 Obviously, I have taken the tropes of the gaze from Lacan, and applied them to what I hope is an "expanding field." See J. Lacan, *The Four Fundamental Concepts of Psychoanalysis*, ed. J. A. Miller, trans. A. Sheridan (New York and London: W. W. Norton, 1978).

13 See S. Freud, "The Uncanny," in *Studies in Parapsychology*, ed. Philip Rieff (New York: Macmillan, 1963).

14 Quoted from J. Lacan, "The Signification of the Phallus," in *Ecrits*, trans. A. Sheridan (New York and London: W. W. Norton, 1977), p. 290.

15 Quoted from J. Derrida's forward to N. Abraham and M. Torok, *The Wolfman's Magic Word*, trans. N. Rand (Minneapolis: University of Minnesota Press, 1986), p. xv.

16 See *The Purloined Poe*, eds J. P. Muller and W. J. Richardson (Baltimore: Johns Hopkins University Press, 1988).

17 I have borrowed this phrase from J. Rose, "The Imaginary," in *Sexuality in the Field of Vision* (London: Verso, 1986), p. 210.

18 The images here are borrowed from the Emily Dickinson poem "I cannot live with You," (640), lines 33–34.

19 J. Derrida, forward to *The Wolfman's Magic Word*, p. xvii.

20 Quoted from Gayatri Chakravorty Spivak's lecture at the Whitney Independent Study Program, November 27, 1990.

21 This passage is from L. Tillman's novel *Haunted Houses* (New York: Poseidon Press, 1987), p. 10.

22 J. Milton, *Samson Agonistes*, lines 83–97.

7

Not the *flâneur* again: reading magazines and living the metropolis around 1880

Tom Gretton

It is not easy to understand metropolitan life; we need all the help we can get. In the second half of the nineteenth century one source of help was vital: general-interest weekly illustrated magazines.[1] Among the reasons for their success was the fact that they were able to deploy a mode of observation and appropriation which resembles that outlined in Baudelaire's "The Painter of Modern Life" (1863).[2]

The figure of the *flâneur* has had a long and successful life as a representation of the experience of being at ease in the metropolitan city, in a broadly three-phase history. The idea was developed in Paris by a set of "modern" writers who achieved success during the July Monarchy (1830–48). In the second half of the century the idea became a commonplace. In the period after 1900, and particularly after the First World War, ways of experiencing the metropolis which owe their force to the figure of the *flâneur* once again engaged the attention of the theorists. It caught the attention of Benjamin and of Kracauer, but also, though less directly, of Simmel. Then, a century after its first naturalization, the figure of the *flâneur* re-emerged, in profoundly modified and politicized ways, in the work of the situationists and of de Certeau, to such effect that the idea is once again an *idée reçue*. Here I want to draw attention to the fact that there was a period, from say 1860 to say 1910, perhaps the most intense period of the development of the modern imperialist metropolis and its spectacular culture, during which the figure of the *flâneur* seems to lie fallow, the object of no particular cultural interest; this essay will outline a possible explanation for this period of latency.

Looking at an illustrated magazine is not like looking at a work of art; reading an illustrated magazine is not like reading a novel or even a essay. But if it is not like those things, then what is it like? My answer is that during the two generations after 1860, reading an illustrated weekly was like being the *flâneur*'s better half, the painter of modern life. The general-interest weekly illustrated periodical emerged in London and Paris in the early 1840s, using pictures relief-cut on blocks of wood. Before the mid-1850s the illustrated weeklies had tended to treat their pictures as "illustrations": the text–image relation and page design suggests that pictures were presented as dependent signifiers. From the mid-1850s through to the triumph of the photomechanical half-tone after 1890, these magazines tended to display pictures as independent signifiers, neither their meaning nor their value being determined by the magazine's texts.[3]

The fallow period of literary interest in the *flâneur* corresponds quite neatly to the period in which the illustrated magazines relied for commercial success on the independent importance of their hand-originated prints of aspects of modern life, the period after the eclipse of the magazine as a set of texts-with-illustrations, before the impact of photo-journalism produced an initial recuperation of images by texts.

The developing metropolis of the 1830s gave rise to three distinct but convergent literary enterprises: the publishing fad for compilations of stories and pictures about metropolitan scenes and types, the promotion of the figure of the *flâneur*, and the development of the general-interest weekly illustrated periodical. This essay focuses on the idea of metropolitan experience as personified in the *flâneur* and mimicked in the illustrated weekly. Some of the major themes in this constitutive relationship of modernity were prefigured in the publishing fad (most intense in the 1840s). Among the better known of these compilations are *Le Diable à Paris* (two volumes, 1845–46, edited by Alphonse Karr), and *Les Français peints par eux-mêmes* (8 volumes, 1840–42, edited by Leon Curmer). The texts for such compilations were supplied by journalist-*littérateurs* such as Honoré Balzac, Jules Janin, or George Sand.[4] These ventures were open-ended: for as long as people bought volumes, the title might continue. These compilations were illustrated by artists such as Gavarni, one of Daumier's principle competitors, and in the 1840s a regular illustrator for the *Illustrated London News*. In such compilations, visuality is the major representational figure. The idea of the picture acts as the model for the sort of knowledge commodified: titles like *Les Physiologies parisiennes*, or *Tableaux de Paris* direct the reader/viewer to the visual representation of types, and offer a representation of modern urban experience as knowable because visible.

Baudelaire's 1863 essay entitled "The Painter of Modern Life" may be read as displaying a reluctance to endorse the concept of the *flâneur* as the best way to personify modern metropolitan aestheticizing hedonism. For Baudelaire other figures were as good as or better than even the "perfect *flâneur*": he suggests the incognito prince, the passionate observer, the *philosophe*, the human kaleidoscope, and above all the painter of modern life. One suspects that for Baudelaire the trope of the *flâneur* had outlived its interest. The *flâneur* had first appeared as a type of metropolitan spectator by 1806.[5] In the 1840s the figure was firmly established as a way in which to imagine metropolitan pleasure. Essays on the *flâneur* appeared in both *Les Français peints par eux-mêmes* and *Les Physiologies parisiennes*, demonstrating an originary link between the illustrated serial publication aiming to typify the diversity of metropolitan life, and the figure of the detached-but-engaged, private-but-public observer of the metropolitan scene.[6] Baudelaire's essay was written in praise of the work of Constantin Guys, who had been a sketch supplier for the *Illustrated*

London News since 1842. Baudelaire employs Guys in complex ways: he is a choric figure, he provides a way of developing a set of opinions on art and modernity which are clearly Baudelaire's own, and he embodies one of the types who are described and characterized. The essay has thirteen short sections with titles very like those deployed in the compilation genre. They are: Beauty, fashion and happiness; The sketch of manners; The artist: man of the world, man of the crowd, and child; Modernity; Mnemonic art; The annals of war; Pomps and circumstances; The military man; The dandy; Woman; In praise of cosmetics; Women and prostitutes; Carriages. The dandy is one of the types that the painter of modern life, himself the subject of Baudelaire's observation, can characterize as he searches for modern beauty; that is, the convergence of the contingent and the transcendental in the ground-level life of the metropolis.[7] Baudelaire was writing about a magazine illustrator, presenting him not as a journalist, but quite clearly as an artist. Thus the essay transfers the power to represent, which in the *Illustrated London News* so evidently belongs to the collectivity which produces the periodical, on to one of its many artist-illustrators.

Like other illustrators of modernity, Guys had a certain fame at the time. He was known as a man about town as well as a sketch artist: the Goncourt brothers, novelists, diarists, and mover-shakers in the art world, record his persona, in their diary for April 23, 1858, in the guise of a recollected conversation:

> a strange, varied and changing man, copying himself and renewing himself . . . , his verbose conversation overflowing with asides, zigzagging from idea to idea, going off the rails, losing the thread and finding it again, not letting your attention wander for a minute, holding it through the impact of his speech: explosive, figured, so highly colored you can almost see it, like contrast in a painting. An eloquence at once voluminous, inimitable, and unexpected, where all of a sudden, your attention threatening to slip away, he grabs it back with a low-life image, or a slang phrase, or maybe by the emergence, from all this disorder and flashiness, of a long word from the discourse of the German philosophers, or by the way he will define the object under discussion by a technical term from art.

> He evoked a thousand things on that walk through his memories, throwing into the conversation from time to time handfuls of ironical observations, sketches, recollections, landscapes, paintings, profiles, streetscapes and street-corners, sidewalks where chorus girls in thin pumps splash by, shell-torn cities, blood-soaked and disemboweled, with the rats already scurrying towards the field hospitals. Then on the other side, – rather like in an album in which you find a quotation from Balzac on the back of a drawing by Decamps – there issued from the mouth of this man social silhouettes, insights on the English and the French races, a comparative philosophy of the national character of these Peoples, all new, not one that had grown mouldy in a book, two-minute satires, one-word pamphlets.[8]

Whatever its oddities as a portrait, this passage is (low-life and gruesome dimensions set aside) an effective representation of the intellectual experience of consuming an illustrated weekly.

For Baudelaire and the Goncourts the literary text which evokes a compendium of visualized differences was the dominant way of understanding metropolitan experience, and for them the individual visual artist was the figure on the basis of whose perceptions such texts could function, and in whose subjectivity the texts found their key metaphor. But it seems to me that this metaphorical figure was itself a personification, not of the metropolis, but of the illustrated weekly. The painter of modern life wanders along the boulevard, isolating from the flow of experience a succession of still images, and in communicating them offers to his fellow observers a sense of discrimination and a sense of acceptance, a sense of detachment and a sense of participation, a sense that they are in the modern world, but not carried along by it as trash by a river. The Goncourts, Baudelaire, and all those who celebrated in text the power of visual art to see to the heart of modern things, made a double displacement, from the visual to the textual, but also, logically prior to that, from a particular anonymous and collaborative genre to its representative artists.

My argument here is that "the medium is the message." Karr, Balzac, Baudelaire, and the Goncourts, all at work in the infancy of the illustrated weekly, were responding to the same cultural need as it was, but their professional interest in the universal adequacy of textual modes of representation made them unable to recognize that the new genre had the tools required to deal with one key representational task posed by the modern metropolis, that of permitting its dominant denizens to imagine their dominance as delightful. This essay will offer a demonstration that this adequacy was achieved by the construction of a genre which in significant respects mimicked the metropolis. To be precise, it mimicked the version of metropolis which was also being articulated (though less adequately) in text through the figure of the *flâneur*. The illustrated weekly and the metropolis, on different scales and within different parameters, share the same characteristics; their relationship, to coin a phrase, is fractal.[9]

The Illustrated London News (*ILN*) began publication in 1842. Only one of its various competitors, *The Graphic* (1869–1932) achieved anything like the same status. *L'Illustration*, closely modeled on the *ILN*, started in 1843; in 1857 *Le Monde illustré* appeared. The total sale of general-interest illustrated weeklies in 1870s France was something over 100,000.[10] Given that such periodicals were sold in large part into cafés, *cercles* and other foci of bourgeois sociability, as well as into bourgeois households, and that many week-old issues were sold on to humbler destinations, we can posit a high number of readers per copy. Surviving representations of the readership in easel painting typify the readers of the illustrated weekly as female members of high-bourgeois households. Representations in such places as journal title heads and index illustrations tend to show both men and women reading the magazine, enacting a domestic bourgeois sociability (as distinct from the solitary recreation typified by reading a novel). The sociability associated with such journals was not in fact exclusively domestic, nor exclusively the province of either men or women, as the next paragraphs will demonstrate. Indeed, textual representations in the illustrated weekly of their readers suggest that those who produced the journals believed that their version of the metropolitan experience was one which was available to, and consumed by, women as well as men. Texts in *Le Monde illustré* repeatedly represented the Salon as having a cultural role linked to its own, and as being a specifically metropolitan (rather than national or *mondain*) form: art and the mass of the *grand public* meet in the illustrated periodical each week, as they do on Sundays during the Paris Salon. On April 21, 1880, apropos of Carolus Duran's portrait of the Comtesse V…, the centrefold image for that week (p. 251), the editors have this to say:

> It was the *Monde illustré* that first gave a full development to its artistic part, displaying, week after week, reproductions of artworks from the current year; these have been an inexhaustible source of subjects either elevated or gracious or heart stirring. Alongside our news pictures, which always have to be a little brutal in their execution, these works provide, in the collected *Monde illustré*, a review of the fine arts which is of high value, and, we believe, highly appreciated by our subscribers. And, of course, the annual exhibition of the fine arts is one of the most notable attractions in Parisian life: painters and sculptors size each other up there, art's dilettantes go there to check on art's progress and to applaud its successes: and furthermore the public, the mass public, which floods in through the doors of art's stronghold on Sundays, finds there both its favourite entertainment and an artistic education.

Readers are encouraged to distinguish between the week-by-week procession of news-pictures and the "artistic part," even though the discrimination in terms of "finish" which is indicated by "always . . . a little brutal" is quite difficult for a twenty-first-century observer to sustain.

This passage takes it for granted (*d'ailleurs*) that the journal functions for its readers as the Salon does for Parisians: it is a constitutive space of metropolitan modernity. It sees the journal's role as mixing pleasure and instruction in a way that feminizes the "grand public" through the use of the age-old trope of pleasure and instruction, and classes its own cultural position as bourgeois/dominant. This is a two-edged discourse, since in a range of ways it invites the readership to identify with the journal, thus projecting on to them an equivocal gender position, both dominant and receptive, both pleasured and pleasuring.[11]

Despite plenty of such self-promoting textual and iconographic representations of the regular readership of the magazine, we will never know who did read *Le Monde illustré*, nor what they made of the experience. But we can work on interesting clues. Each week the magazine printed a rebus. Readers could send in their solutions to the puzzle; the names of successful solvers were listed alongside the solution. To solve a rebus various sorts of looking must be deployed; here the pleasures of sight are closely connected to the pleasure of mastery. The most common pseudonyms for rebus-solvers are "Oedipus" and "The Sphinx," both of them in this context allusions to the relation between the bourgeois man and the mother-city; the rebus thus itself becomes an emblem of the *flâneur*-position. The complex riddle posed by the rebus might best be solved collaboratively. Collectivities such as subscriber groups based in cafés produced many winners; here, as in the figure of the *flâneur*, the myth of the observer meets the practices of the participant.

In the first six months of 1880, there were 25 rebuses. The weekly number of winners varied from 1 to 59. There were 351 correct responses in all; 159 names appear at least once. There are regular solvers: the "café central" in Tarare (Burgundy) sent 19 correct solutions, "le Bichon du cercle de Mézières" 15, the Officine-club in Toulon 12. Bouta de Chissay solved the problem 9 times, "Bouta et Bichette" 5: this is the leading solver who is not named as a member of a collectivity, and seems to represent a woman, then two women. A hundred and fifty-one solutions (90 names in all) come from private citizens, or at any rate cannot be identified as by groups or individuals from cafés or clubs. A hundred and six come from cafés or from individuals located in cafés (42 café-names in all). "Le Sphinx du grand café de la Paix, Saumur," guesses correctly 9 times; Wallior in the café de la Paix in Versailles once. Ninety-four correct entries are submitted by members of *cercles* or clubs (27 *cercle* names in all). Many of these groups convened in cafés. Sometimes distinctions are hard to make: I have counted "un groupe d'abonnés de la brasserie de Ruoms," in Marseille as a club, like "les abonnés du salon de coiffure Jany" (x 3), and "les abonnés du salon elegant" (x 4), both also in Marseille. Thirty-seven of the names I have classed as private are likely to be café *noms de plume*: "l'homme-singe de Nevers" (x 2), or "une admiratrice de l'Oedipe du Café de l'Univers au Mans" (himself x 9), or her own "admirateur" (x 1).

The gendering of the solvers is predominantly, but not exclusively, masculine; we can name 16 winners as female, with another 4 family-related names ("toute la famille," "Maman et bébé"). Mme la Comtesse de Sèze succeeds from Champgueffier, as (separately) do Mlle Lydie Rouzé, Marguerite Sauvage, and Marie Sauvage of the Café Poillon in Lille, Veuve Herrier or Vera d'Achut (x 4), both from Paris. Mmes A. C. from Oulmes (x 6) hide their identity, but cryptonyms are no more common for women than for men (unless women are hiding behind men's names). Among other cryptonyms we note a number of personas named after street activities: "deux employés sur le pave" (x 2), "les types du cours Devilliers, à Marseille" (x 6). Both an anonymous and an individuated solidarity with the journal is permissible, though in many cases we are shown a persona rather than a subject: but that is also the way of the Boulevard.[12]

Four names are identified as writing from Paris, 52 names have no location attached to them, 100 come from the provinces, 3 from outside France. There is no particular geographical bias, except for the under-representation of Paris, which had roughly 10 percent of the population of France at the time. I suppose that many of the unlocated names come from Paris, and that a large part of the sociability and the imagined community constructed via the rebus and projected via its list of winners was actually metropolitan, as well as being symbolically so. With between thirty- and forty-thousand weekly sales, these 159 names represent under half a percent of the copies purchased. This active, responsive, commodified-public-sphere consumer-group was predominantly male, and predominantly responded to the journal as a collectivity, or as an individuated member of a collectivity; typically as a member of a recreational group meeting in a café or a café-like club. Bourgeois actors, even *mondain* actors, felt at home in this public space, and countesses, widows and students all felt entitled to make themselves known.

This inscribed readership was located both in a commodified national-metropolitan public arena, and in numberless private worlds, offering traces of private lives which, though unknowable, still share pleasures with us, offering glimpses of existences that mimic and intersect with, but do not impinge on, our own. That is to say, this inscribed readership has no features which run counter to my interpretation of the illustrated periodical as sharing a cultural logic with the boulevard-as-consumed-by-the-*flâneur*, and many features which converge with or reinforce it.

Illustrated weeklies broadly resembled each other. They were 16 pages long (in smaller and poorer capitals maybe 8, sometimes, particularly in London, 24 or even 32 pages). They were mostly about 360 mm high by about 270 mm wide. They would normally have three columns of text per typeset page, with something approaching half of their editorial space given over to illustrations. In the earliest years this proportion had been lower, though the number of pictures per issue had been higher. In 1842 the *ILN* published thirty illustrations per issue, and *L'Illustration* provided approximately that number through the 1850s. By the mid-1860s a sharply reduced number of considerably larger pictures (whole- or half-page images, rather than pictures taking up less than a quarter of a page) was becoming the norm. This annual flow of discrete texts and pictures represents the unknowability of the metropolis as effectively as the accumulated novels of Balzac's *Comedie humaine,* or Zola's Rougon-Maquart cycle, represent its knowability. This representation of the unknowability of that which is represented is reinforced by the fact that the illustrated weekly is on the edge of the ephemeral: while the *ILN* was collected in many patrician and institutional libraries, neither *The Graphic* nor any equivalent French paper was nearly so fortunate. A great torrent of things known, things curious or significant, flows through the illustrated weekly: through it, not into it. Like the metropolis, the illustrated weekly is a river, not a lake; in this it is quite unlike a literary text, or an artist's oeuvre.

The illustrated weekly offers the observer a huge archive. But it is not only enormous, it is also interestingly unchartable. There were plenty of highly productive cultural institutions in the metropolis: the annual Paris Salon showed thousands of paintings, several hundred new novels were published in London and Paris each year, scores of new plays were staged. But such cultural production always had mechanisms of selection and valorization attached: Salon-goers knew which score of paintings had to be seen, novel readers which novels had to be read. No such mechanisms were ever developed to winnow the "worthy" texts and images in the illustrated weekly from the dross: that work was left, it seems, almost entirely to the reader, and almost entirely to his or her own criteria. Mimicry of the *flâneur* emerges here also. That which is a problem for the historian was an opportunity for the observer seeking the pleasures of random contact and capricious appropriation; the medium, in its refusal to deliver one sort of message, effectively delivered another.

If the medium is the message, how did the medium function, and how can we describe its functioning in a way that permits us to consider this as its message? My answer will come mostly from a consideration of the nature of the particular facts, pleasures and values that the magazine offers its consumers in any one issue, but there are also some general points to be made about the sorts of space and time that the illustrated weekly offers to our understanding. The space constructed is complicated and unstable. The illustrated weekly is like the metropolis in that it is not possible to see it all at once; like the city it has a great deal of interiority, and attention paid to one element of its contents is attention denied to another aspect. In this it is unlike a narrative text, in which attention to one part of its contents entails attention to the others. The notion that interiority could be extirpated, that the whole might be made visible, is a fantasy which was nurtured in the nineteenth-century discourse on the city, not least in the illustrated magazines. But of course the observer cannot see the whole of the city, and of course the reader cannot see the whole of an illustrated weekly all at once: just as every facade conceals an interior, every recto page has its verso; furthermore, exhaustive sequential readings are very difficult and distinctly absurd. The journal's space mimics the city's in another rather more simple way too. The city can be mapped, and has specialist places and structures, though some are contested and most are in fact used for a range of practices. The journal also has its (relatively) specialist spaces: in the case which I will discuss, the front cover, with its ambition to emblematize the week, the season or the mood; the centerfold, with the most delightful, most spectacular or most collectible pictures, and so on. However, here also nothing is precisely predictable, though texts are always more predictable than pictures.

As well as two versions of space, one in which surveillance is possible and one in which occlusion is the necessary condition of revelation, the illustrated weekly incorporates two versions of time: it represents cyclical time through its predictable periodicity, and it represents the "modern" time of progress, in which things are never the same twice, in which the new always supersedes the old. Any "news" periodical must, of course, have this contradictory effect, but several aspects of the illustrated weekly combined to make it particularly evident. Lead times for producing wood-engravings were inevitably longer than lead times for texts. Thus illustrated weeklies did not compete in the market for news scoops, though they took pains to be up-to-the-minute. They relied on the newness of their pictures, rather than on news stories; on the dosages of the stylish, the exotic, the unforeseen, the picturesque, and the sublime which they could fit into their pages. Novelty rather than news, and variety rather than sobriety characterize their production.

The next section of this essay consists of a guided tour, as it were, page by page, of one number of one illustrated magazine, *Le Monde illustré* for February 14, 1880. This is in several ways a distorting way of dealing with any such magazine, because the images and columns of text presented are transformed by being reproduced in a different medium and genre, and because the magazine's images, and the messages they convey, are fundamentally transformed by being forced into a structuring narrative, given that the a crucial aspect of the illustrated weekly was that its structure disarmed coercion and refused narrative. Not only that, it refused the sort of purposeful I've started-so-I'll-finish attention which reading a newspaper article (or a chapter in a book) rewards; no start-up investment *appears* to be required to look at a picture.

The front cover for the week of February 14, 1880 is very modern-metropolitan with its fashionable location and cast, but at the same time it integrates the modern with the cycles of the year and the lifetime, and with the *longue durée* of the Christian faith (Figure 16). The couple are dressed as Pierrot and Pierrette, and as such evoke both sentimentality and sophistication; they refer to theatricality, and represent the spectacle of the modern city. The picture shows the fleeting moment

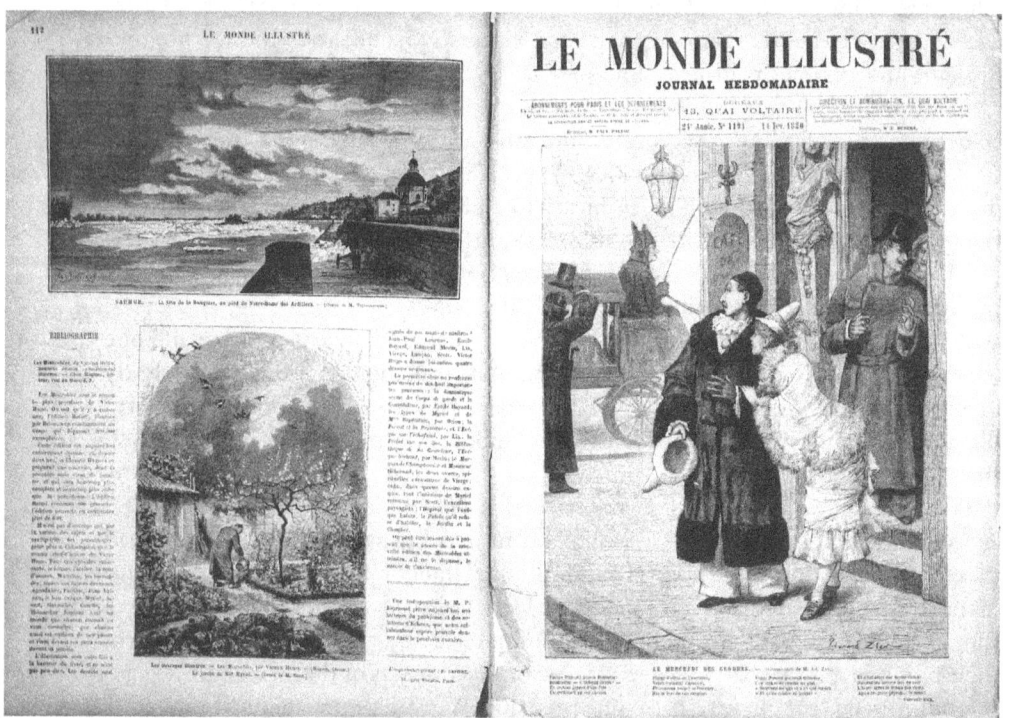

16 *Le Monde illustré*, 14 February 1880, p. 97 ("Le mercredi des Cendres"), and p. 112 (ice on the Loire, and a picture from a new illustrated edition of V. Hugo, *Les Misérables*)

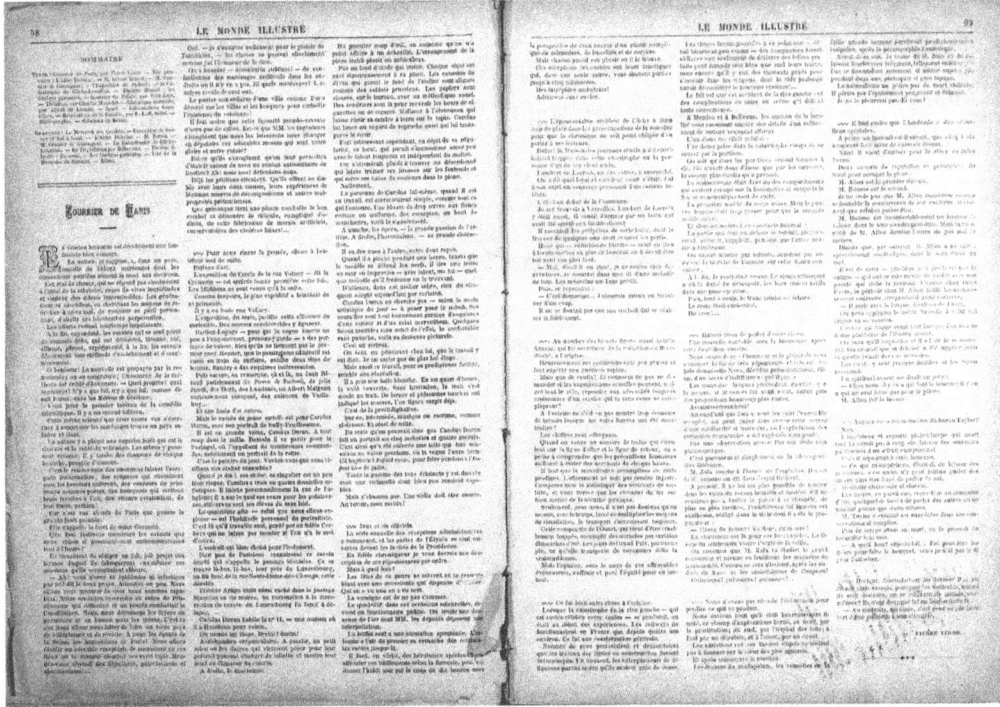

17 *Le Monde illustré*, 14 February 1880, pp. 98 and 99

on the street, and the way that the metropolis can reveal, for those with eyes to see, the convergence of the contingent and the transcendental; it also shows how urban spaces both interior and exterior may offer themselves only as alluring glimpses or vague suggestions of architectural form. This may be a banal image, but it does its work well; it gives the reader/viewer a position which is at once immersed in the metropolis and above it, because able to apprehend it both as action and as allegory. The back page, shown in the same figure, will be discussed at the end of this account.

Pages 98 and 99 (2 and 3 of this number) are covered in text (Figure 17). It is printed in three columns, without much page design or typographical excitement; printed rather light, too: on the high-speed presses of the time, it was not easy to get a good impression on to both sides of a sheet of newsprint. Pictures are printed on one side of each sheet, texts on the other, and the whole is collated so that any particular opening shows either text sides or image sides. The modern metropolis too is diverse, being made of different sorts of neighborhoods folded into one another, demanding and rewarding different forms of attention at different moments. The metropolis, like the illustrated weekly, is emblematic of the division of labour, of the increasingly effective zoning of the spaces of work and of recreation.

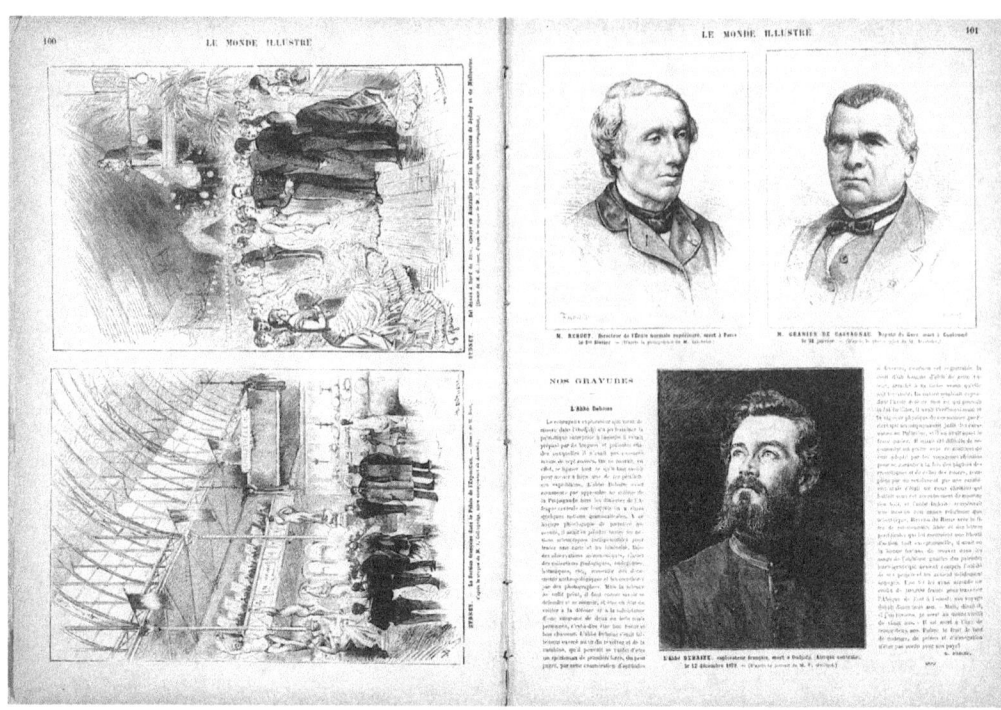

18 *Le Monde illustré*, 14 February 1880, p. 100 (drawings from Sydney) and p. 101 (funerary portraits)

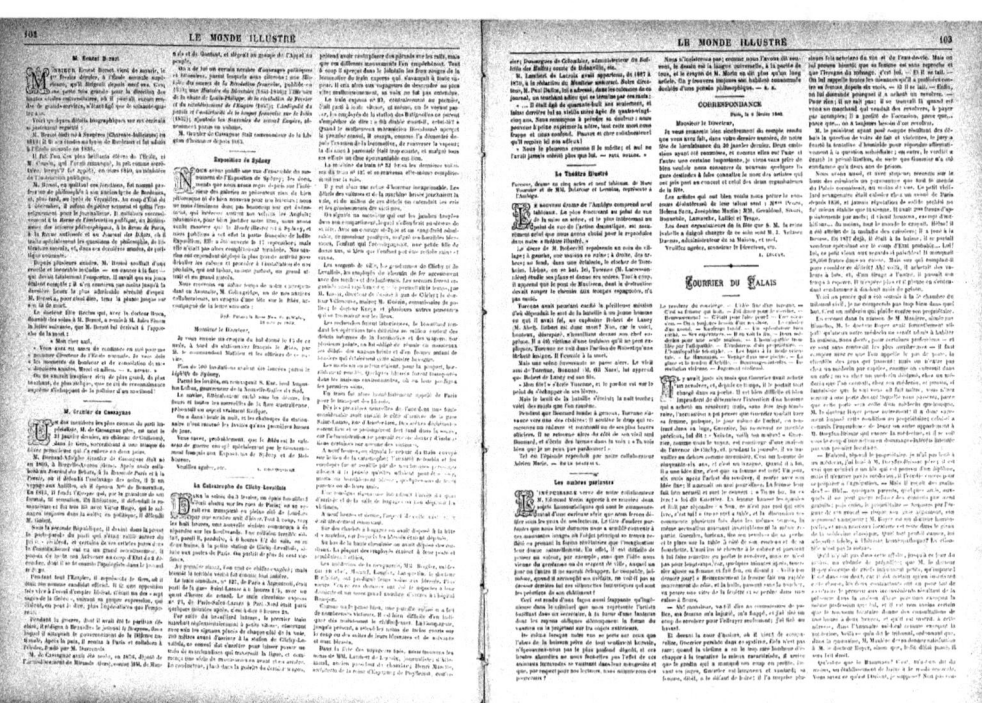

19 *Le Monde illustré*, 14 February 1880, pp. 102 and 103

In the next opening, pages 4 and 5 (100 and 101) the space of the emblematic, the typical, the summative (as on the front cover), is replaced by the space of news (Figure 18). Here we are shown two sketches of the French pavilion at the International Exhibition in Sydney, Australia. These pictures represent the necessary symbiosis of metropolis and empire. The metropolis is only the "mother-city" because it is the focus of global patterns of trade, influence, and culture: unless the metropolis can represent the presence of its *colonia* as a dimension of the mother-city's selfhood, it will represent itself merely as a city.

The next page shows us three portraits, of eminent men recently deceased. The metropolis is a focus of culture, of the representation of the nation in the political arena, as well as being the centre of a global influence. It is convenient that these three portraits should be of men who have contributed to the reproduction of these metropolitan functions: one died bringing Western health-care and the word of Christ to French central Africa, one at his post as director of the Ecole normale supérieure in Paris, and one, a *député*, in his chateau in his constituency. Symbolically, they all died in the metropolis, and so they are symbolically laid to rest here.

The text section entitled "Nos gravures" (Our engravings), starts on this page, and continues on the next two (Figure 19). This section gives a commentary or parallel information on most of the pictures in this issue: the front cover, the back page and a full-page reproduction of a Salon painting in the centerfold are passed over in silence. "Nos gravures" very seldom provides a text which is featured as being the occasion for the illustration, or as providing an authoritative version of its meaning or value. Rather, "Nos gravures" tends to provide additional anecdotes or tangential essays; these expand, rather than control, the pleasures of the image. A section on current court cases follows: it is a regular feature, but almost never produces illustrations.

Next we come to the centerfold (Figure 20). Over these two pages, the journal often reproduces a single image. It was not unusual to print a double-page centerfold picture (often of a reproduced painting) with no text on the back, though centerfold images were more normally printed with text on the verso. This week there are two pictures. On the left is a reproduction of a painting from the 1879 salon, of a bourgeois suburban heaven in which nature is perfectly annexed and controlled, the relationship between interiority and exteriority perfectly managed, and in which the play of social difference between ages and genders is a matter of relaxed observation, pleasure a matter of the appreciation of surface. The right-hand picture reminds us that getting from the metropolis to its dependent countryside is not always easy, that this modern *douceur de vivre* has its risks. On February 3 there had been a fatal train-wreck on the line from Paris to its downriver recreational suburbs, including Argenteuil and Asnières: Impressionist country. There was a comment on the calamity in the February 7 issue, but no picture; now we are given an extraordinary elegiac image of the aftermath of the catastrophe, and thus admitted to another encounter between the contingent and the

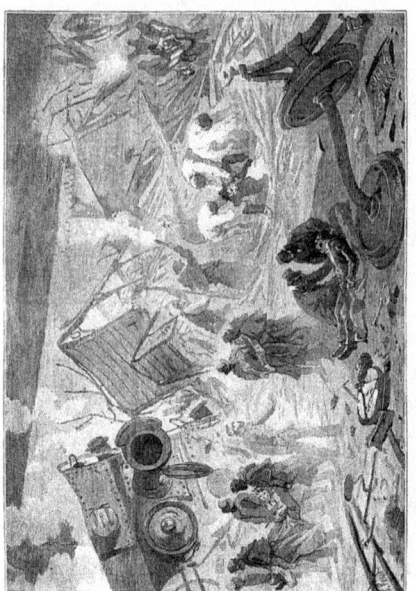

20   *Le Monde illustré*, 14 February 1880, p. 104 (*Le Tir*: Ballavoine), and p. 105 ("La catastrophe de Clichy Levallois")

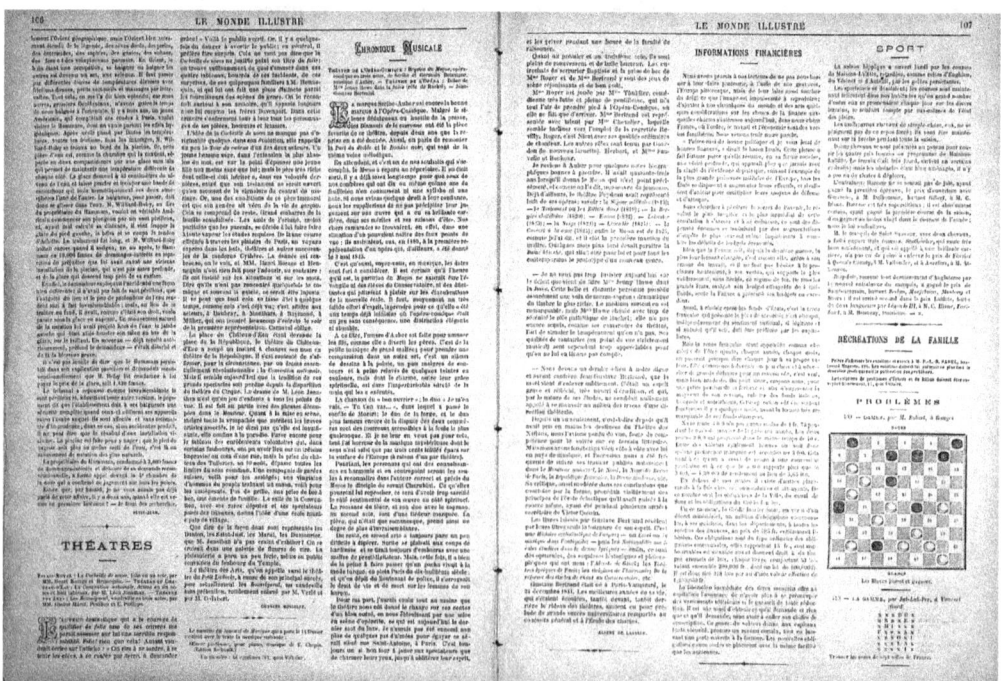

21   *Le Monde illustré*, 14 February 1880, pp. 106 and 107

transcendental; one which operates this fusion not only on the level of subject matter but also on that of the pictorial resources deployed, both highly journalistic and eruditely painterly.[13]

Next, another pair of text pages (Figure 21). The week's theatrical and musical performances dominate the left-hand page; on the right the stock exchange and horse racing each have a column, and the "Family recreations" section begins with a draughts problem and a word-square puzzle; readers are invited to send in their solutions, and given the necessary information to do so. As we have seen, while these games are announced as family recreations, they also serve and represent the sociability of the café.

The next page has a "tableau" from a play which has opened in the past week (Figure 22): like the text pages which preceded it, this is a regular feature, and emphasizes the fact that commercialized leisure is at the core of the metropolis's compulsion: Baudelaire, Benjamin, and the illustrated weekly all agree on this. The next page has a couple of moralizing sketches, of miscreants made into emblems by their shadows; in features such as this the satirical tradition of Daumier and his companions finds a late and faint echo – sometimes a comic Salon review, once a month a strip-cartoon series on some aspect of metropolitan life, at other times whimsy such as this.

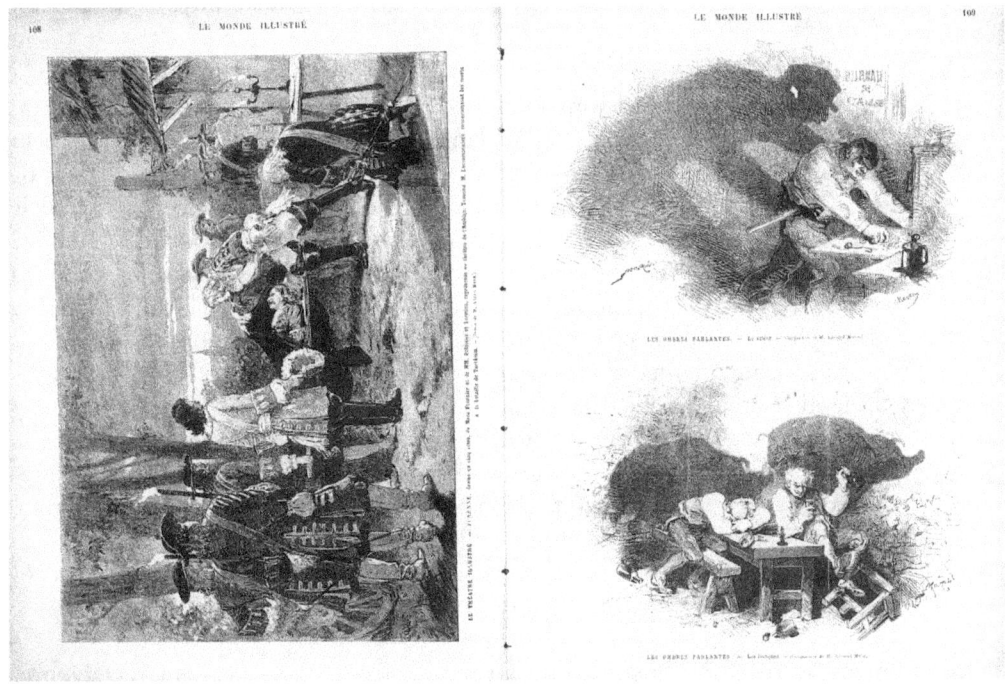

22 *Le Monde illustré*, 14 February 1880, p. 108 ("Le théâtre illustré"), and p. 109 ("Les ombres parlantes")

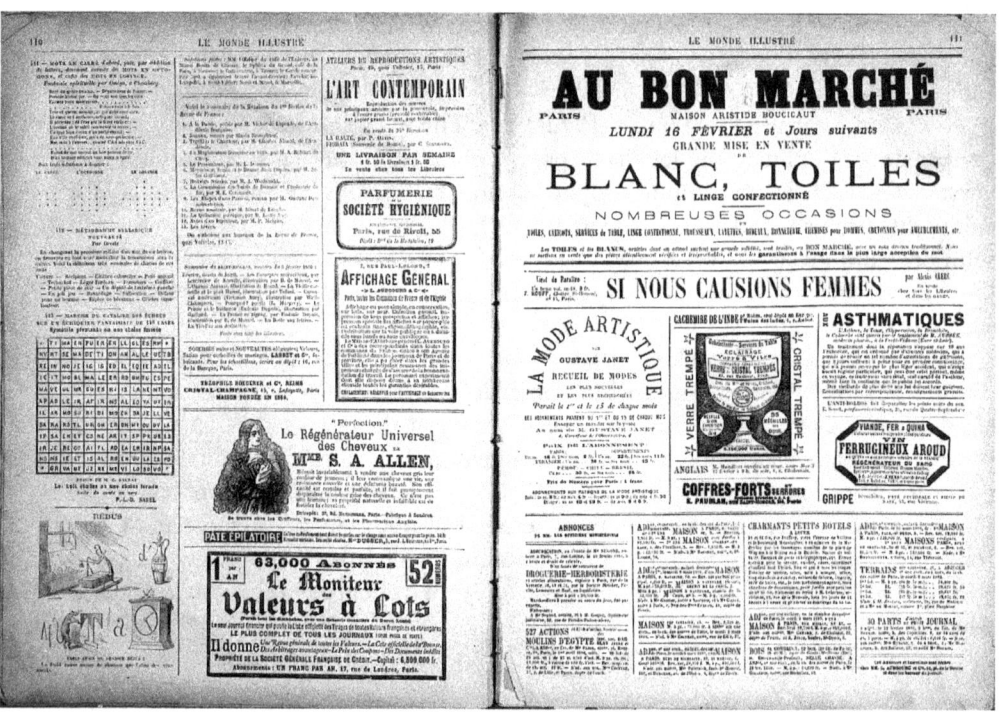

23 *Le Monde illustré*, 14 February 1880, pp. 110 and 111

Next is another text opening (Figure 23); there are plenty more puzzles, and though we have been told that they are family recreation, the list of the most recent competition winners reads: MM. Oedipe du café de l'Univers, au Mans; Bouta de Chissay; le Sphinx du grand café de la Paix, à Saumur; le café central, à Tarare; le cercle sancerrois; Eureka; Ko-Long-Bo, à Saint Vallier; Nono et Millet, à Marseille. This page has the first of the advertisements; these dominate the next page also. In 1880 the transition from text-based advertising to display advertising with graphics was taking place. The display of a commodified culture of consumption is here contributing to the spectacle of the illustrated weekly, almost on the same footing as editorial matter.

The last page (see Figure 16), which sometimes also holds advertisements, in this case carries an image for a story which had been heavily featured in the previous week's number: the accumulation of ice floes on the Loire at Saumur. It also carries a promotional article for an illustrated version of Victor Hugo's *Les Misérables*; at least three of the book's illustrators were regular contributors to *Le Monde illustré*.

Three features of the illustrated weekly were crucial to its success as a fractal representation of the metropolis. The first was the sharp division of labor between text openings and image openings, and the relatively loose interpellation of images by texts (setting aside the quick categorization which is entailed by the caption), so that the texts in "Nos gravures" offer additional or tangential information for the print, rather than an interpretative straightjacket. In the illustrated weekly, pictures do not have to be escorted by a text. In this issue, three of the major images are left "to speak for themselves"; the consumer of the illustrated weekly is not in any sense obliged to be its "reader." The fact that he or she often needs to turn the journal through 90 degrees to look at pages in comfort makes the same point in a different way: this is not an orderly publication; it does not concentrate on "text-like" satisfactions; the *dérive*, random delectation, the glance, the gaze, interventionist bodily activity are all rewarded, at least as much as is an orderly perusal. The air of the illustrated journal, like the air of the city, makes the reader/citizen free: that the freedom is conditional, and arguably chimerical, is as true in the one case as in the other.

The second point is that this sort of pleasure-seeking appropriation of the pictures in the periodical is also promoted through a tendency to invest in the "spectacular" value of the illustrations, in distinction, though not necessarily in opposition, to their "informational" value. The train-wreck is reported in this way. The use of *sfumato* effects makes it hard to work out that the smash actually took place in a station. It is also hard to disentangle the different trains involved, but the composition is very striking, the art historical references canny, the play of forms and textures considered and ingratiating. This tendency to make sure that every story makes a picture, that, in Bryson's terms, the figurative should both exceed and in a sense marginalize the discursive, can be seen at every turn.[14] Through the illustrated weekly, the metropolis can indeed offer us a quasi-painterly visual pleasure. We are invited to see the modern world, with its suburban pleasures, its fog, its violent train-wrecks, through the eyes of the painter of modern life.

The third point comes as a counterpoint to the last. Isolating pictures from "their" texts, piling on to the individual picture the pleasures of a decontextualized attention, might be thought to represent (and to produce) a form of focused and particularizing experience quite inappropriate to the idea of the metropolis as a mighty river, full of experience as of water, in which the observer can only drift or fish. It seems to me rather that what the illustrated weekly encouraged was freedom to fix upon this or that object of appropriation in constant consciousness of the other. As with the painter of modern life figure, this cultural formation passes the power to produce meanings from the thing observed to the observer; from the city to the stroller, from the journal to the reader.

One convention which I have not been able to discuss with reference to this number of *Le Monde illustré*, but which was used constantly in the period, is the collaged page: the report in which images, sheaves of sketches or handfuls of finished pictures, are gathered and assembled in a composite construction or overlapping with each other, and turned into an object of delectation by the journal, ready for us to ignore, scan, or synthesize into an impression. This is another resource for the illustrated weekly in its attempt to represent an experience which is overflowing with things which provoke delight and the urge to classify and arrange; overflowing both with differences and with instances of difference. It accomplishes this effect partly by representing variety as such, but it also does it by being, like the collaged page, itself various, excessive, too much to take in: eight pages of illustration, with up to a score of pictures a week, twenty-one column feet of differentiated short texts, representational labor accumulating in unmanageable heaps on a side table. The illustrated weekly represents a plethoric form of experience, and is at the same time itself a plethora of experiences, too much, too rich, to hold in consciousness *as a whole*. I am content to think that in this double representational effect the illustrated weekly once more mimics "the metropolis," something which is at once too much, and a representation of too much. We can only deal with this excess, or with that, by developing our confident discrimination, our sense of distinction.

Through the figure of the painter of modern life, Baudelaire criticizes the urban dandy-idler because of his lack of discrimination, his inability to see beyond his narcissistic reflection. It may indeed be that the effect of the illustrated weekly is to reinforce just such narcissistic self-regard, but if so this effect is achieved through a contradictory process. The page-to-page and issue-to-issue arrangement of the illustrated weekly succeeds in, as much as it nourishes and rewards, the attitudes which Baudelaire attributes to the painter of modern life: the constant search for encounters between the contingent and the transcendental; the search for that beauty of which relish for the everyday is the necessary doppelgänger; the quest for modernity, and in that quest, the chance discovery of the modern; the pleasurable perception not of the self but of the other.

I have given a reading of the illustrated weekly as though it were a fractal representation of the metropolis, addressing its "readers" as metropolitans, providing them with a resource through which they might imagine themselves as such. If it was in any measure through the forms and contents of the illustrated weekly that the landed elites and bourgeois groups of Europe's imperial heyday came to terms with the relationships between globalization, nation-building, and class formation (that is, with the metropolis) then the illustrated weekly is worth a second glance. It emerges from my way of looking at the illustrated weekly that the distinctive nature of metropolitan experience is that it constantly incorporates its external other: that is, the metropolis as a space of representation includes all those who turn or who are turned to face it.

In terms of gender politics the effects of such an interpellation are complicated, but some things are clear. Following Elizabeth Wilson's argument that the *flâneur* represents as much the attenuation of masculine power as its triumph, we may argue that the mimicking of the (anxious or triumphalist) cultural style of the painter of modern life in the illustrated weekly makes the dialectics of pleasure and instruction, "masculine" visual activity and "feminine" visual receptivity, too complicated, too nuanced, to be mapped on to any simple schema of triumph and subjection. We may also argue that through the mediation of the illustrated weekly, at any rate, the possibility of "joining in" to the metropolis was not anything like as gender-specific as the figure of the *flâneur* has seduced us into supposing it to have been. Where has the invisible *flâneuse* been? Under our nose, in the illustrated weekly. But she has been there with the *flâneur*, who also became functionally invisible from around 1860 to around 1910. Invisible, because neither of them were needed in order to represent a constitutive "metropolitan" cultural style; the illustrated weekly did the job more adequately than either of them could have done it, alone or together.

Notes

1 D. Reed, *The Popular Magazine in Britain and the United States 1880–1960* (London: British Library, 1997) offers a useful starting place. D. Kunzle, "*L'Illustration*, journal universel, premier magazine illustré en France, affirmation du pouvoir de la bourgeoisie," *Nouvelles de l'éstampe* 43 (January–February 1979), pp. 8–19, provides a context. Earlier versions of the present essay were given to the Bartlett School of Architecture at UCL in 1999, to the UCL History of Art Research seminar in 2000, and at the 2001 CAA conference in Chicago.

2 First published in *Le Figaro* in 1863; a good text in C. Baudelaire, *Curiosités esthetiques, l'art romantique*, ed. H. Lemaitre (Paris: Garnier, 1962).

3 T. Gretton "Text and Image, Figure and Ground: Page Design in Nineteenth-Century General-Interest Weekly News Magazines in England and France."(Paper given at Edinburgh University department of Fine Art, November 2004.)

4 Among the first was A. Bazin de Raucou, *L'Epoque sans nom* (2 vols, Paris: Mesnier, 1833), in which the *flâneur* is presented as the *littérateur*'s alter ego. Relevant recent literature includes: J. Weschler, *A Human Comedy: Physiognomy and Caricature in 19th-century Paris* (London: Thames and Hudson, 1982); A. Sheon, "Parisian Social Statistics: Gavarni, *Le Diable à Paris*, and Early Realism," *Art Journal* 44, no. 2 (Summer 1984), pp. 139–148; R. Sieburth, "Une ideologie du lisible: le phénomène des 'Physiologies'," *Romantisme: revue du dix-neuvième siècle* 15, no. 47 (1985), pp. 39–60; S. Le Men, L. Abélès, and N. Preiss-Basset, *Les Français peints par eux-mêmes* (Paris: Réunion des musées nationaux, 1993).

5 E. Wilson, "The Invisible *Flâneur*," *New Left Review* no. 191 (January–February 1992), pp. 90–110.

6 The essay in the former (*Les Français peints par eux-mêmes: encyclopédie morale du dix-neuvième siècle*, vol. 3 (Paris: L. Curmer, 1840), pp. 65–72) is by A. de Lacroix; that in the latter (*Les Physiologies parisiennes, illustrées par MM. Gavarni, Cham, Daumier [etc.]* (Paris: Aubert, n.d. [1840])) is by L. Huart.

7 C. Baudelaire, *Curiosités esthetiques*, pp. 455–456 and 468.

8 This text, taken from E. and J. de Goncourt, *Journal. Mémoires de la vie littéraire, vol. 1 1851–65*, ed. R. Ricatte (Paris, Robert Laffot, 1989), p. 346, is repetitious and excessive; some of it very hard to pin down. Compare L. Huart: "The *flâneur* can compose a whole novel – out of nothing more than a simple meeting on an omnibus with a woman with a lowered veil – then in the next instant give himself over to the most elevated of philosophical speculations concerning society and humanity" ("Le *flâneur*," in *Les Physiologies parisiennes*, p. 8). Translations by the author.

9 *OED*, 2nd edn: *Fractal*: A mathematically conceived curve such that any small part of it, enlarged, has the same statistical character as the original.

10 *Histoire générale de la presse française*, vol. 2, eds C. Bellanger, J. Godechot, P. Guiral, and F. Terrou (Paris: P.U.F., 1969), p. 302; and vol. 3 (1972), pp. 191 and 387.

11 The "grand public" is, of course, here gendered both as masculine and as feminine, as recipient and as donor: it "penetrates in floods" before finding pleasure as well as instruction.

12 "Bichon" is a kind of spaniel; "abonné" means subscriber. "L'homme-singe" is the ape-man. "Admirateur" is a male admirer, "admiratrice" a female one. "Salon de coiffure" is a hairdresser (gender of clients unspecified). "Deux employés sur le pave" is (freely) two bureaucrats out on the street.

13 For more extensive discussion of these images, see T. Gretton, "Difference and competition," *Oxford Art Journal* 23, no. 2, pp. 152–153.

14 N. Bryson, *Word and Image: French Painting of the Ancien Regime* (Cambridge: Cambridge University Press, 1981), pp. 12–14.

8

The *flâneuse* in French fin-de-siècle posters: advertising images of modern women in Paris

Ruth E. Iskin

Fin-de-siècle posters, an innovative mode of large-scale full-color advertising, played an important role in portraying middle- and upper-class women as fashionable *flâneuses* in Paris.[1] This essay analyzes a selection of French advertising posters, proposing that the *flâneuse* was quite visible in the visual culture of the 1890s. Situating poster images of women in the city within wider discourses of their time, the essay draws on visual, literary, and historical sources to interpret meanings and roles of these images in their historical context. The debate on the *flâneuse* initially emerged as an offshoot of scholarship about the *flâneur*, the nineteenth-century Parisian man, whose chief occupation was mastering the city with idle walking and detached looking.[2] While earlier studies neglected the emergence of women in the city, since the 1990s an increasing number of scholars have studied the presence of women in the nineteenth-century metropolis, shifting the focus on women's exclusion to studies about women in the city.[3] These latter studies have demonstrated that women increasingly became part of the modern metropolis and that a feminine stroller or *flâneuse* emerged both in historical practices and in literary representations by the late nineteenth century.

Most recently Lynda Nead in her study of London argues that the mythology of the *flâneur* wrote women out of the city and obscured diverse historical practices of women and cultural debates about women's increasing participation in metropolitan life.[4] While Nead focuses attention on British visual culture, most studies have examined primarily textual sources, paying little, if any attention to images, and none have focused on posters. Before analyzing a selection of French posters that visualize the *flâneuse* in the city, I will briefly discuss nineteenth-century references to the *flâneuse*, the relationship between women's *flânerie* and late nineteenth-century consumer culture, and the role and material culture of posters in the era of *flânerie*.

As Janet Wolff demonstrated, the *flâneuse* was absent from many of the discussions on the nineteenth-century *flâneur*. The *flâneuse*, however, was not entirely invisible in nineteenth-century discourses. She appeared in the title for the entry of the 1866–79 edition of the Larousse *Grand Dictionnaire*, "*Flâneur, euse*." The defi-nition, which follows, "a person who strolls, or has the habit of strolling," ("*per-sonne qui flâne, qui a l'habitude de flâner*") is gender neutral, while the rest of the text explicitly refers only to the *flâneur*.[5] Balzac notes in 1845 that "respectable women" ("*Les femmes comme il faut*") "promenade on the boulevards" but "amuse them-selves by shopping," ("*s'amusent à marchander*") and "pass by quickly and without meeting anyone."[6] Although he did not explicitly name it, Balzac acknowledged respectable women's *flânerie* while noting its limitations. He also astutely identified the common strategies of shopping and walking quickly, which women used to retain their respectability in the city.

Walter Benjamin, who recognized the link between *flânerie* and consumer cul-ture in the late nineteenth century, stated, "the department store is the last prome-nade for the *flâneur*. There his fantasies were materialized."[7] Since nineteenth-century department stores catered primarily to women whom they considered as the typical consumer, one may well paraphrase Benjamin thus: the department store became the promenade for the *flâneuse*. There her fantasies were materialized. Indeed, in Zola's 1883 novel *Au bonheur des dames*, which was based on extensive research on the development of the department store in nineteenth-century Paris, the author wrote: "it was for woman that all the establishments were struggling in wild competition."[8] As historian Lisa Tiersten notes, the department store enabled women to take up the position of *flânerie*, continuing their "urban promenade unmolested . . . circulating freely. . . . The very scale of the place, the sense of open space seemed to make the store a city in itself."[9] Moreover, writing in 1880, Jules Clarétie recognized that the department store was the *flâneuse*'s milieu. However, he refers to "*flâneuses*" as "hysterics," defining them as "worldly women," who are kleptomaniacs, women who sometimes steal for the joy of stealing.[10] Clarétie's interpretation of the *flâneuse* as hysterical reflects nineteenth-century ideas about women's deplorable lack of self-control in the face of aggres-sive retailing strategies. It may also be part of a "modernist denigration of consumption."[11]

Mark Poster proposes that an important task for historians is to "circumvent the modernist denigration of consumption," which "goes back to Enlightenment assumptions about progress, reason, and masculinity as the active transformation of the world," if we are to write "histories of 'mass' society that allow for critical positions other than that of the autonomous, rational individual of the liberal and Marxist traditions."[12] For middle- and upper-class women during the fin-de-siècle, shopping offered an acceptable context for a cultural and social relationship to the metropolis that transcended buying goods. As historian Erika Rappaport points out: "a shopper might have lunch out, take a break for tea, and visit a club, museum, or theater. Shopping also involved discussing, looking at, touching, buying, and rejecting commodities."[13] This is not to say that shopping, on its own, was equiva-lent to *flânerie*, but rather that it provided the socially sanctioned context for respectable women's *flânerie*. Furthermore, walking in the city, according to Michel de Certeau, is an active enunciation that affects social space.[14] Though de Certeau's analysis is oblivious to the role of the cultural constructs of gender in such enunciations, applying his insights to women's walking in the city during the nineteenth century is productive. In the period in which the ideology of separate spheres associated women with the domestic sphere women's walking in the city signifies an affirmation, a trying out, transgression, and an "appropriation of an 'I'." Using de Certeau's concepts further – women's *flânerie* as speech act implies rewriting not only the physical boundaries of territorial access, but also the socially engendered internal limits of feminine identities.[15] Walking and *flânerie* in the pre-automobile culture of the late nineteenth-century metropolis were a necessary condition for advertising posters.

The advertising role and material culture of posters in the era of *flânerie*

The large, bold-colored images of posters enabled passers-by to apprehend them while walking. This was crucial in an era in which walking, in general, and *flânerie* in particular, were still central to urban life. In Paris of the 1890s "People had the time to stroll, . . . and . . . gaze upon that picture gallery of the boulevard which the poster-hoarding had become."[16] Georges d'Avenal notes in 1901 that the impact of posters was tied to their iconicity which enabled spectators to apprehend them quickly: "The ideal poster," he wrote, necessitates no reading, one takes it in at a single glance "despite oneself," "merely by letting one's gaze fall on it."[17] Iconicity differentiated late nineteenth-century posters from earlier ones, and also set them apart from late nineteenth-century advertising in newspapers and periodicals. The latter were dominated by words, while posters embedded words within their images. When advertising in journals included images at all, it was mostly limited to small, minimally articulated black-and-white pictures. In contrast, posters attracted the eye with large-scale easily readable images and brilliant colors. Posters used numerous visual strategies to attract attention in the midst of distraction of the street or boulevard, on which they were displayed. Furthermore, they attempted to influence the behavior of their viewers. Deputy François-Emile Villiers stated in 1880 that a drawing "startles not only the mind but the eyes . . . stirring up passions, without reasoning, without discourse."[18] This was particularly worrisome since "a drawing strikes the sight of passers-by" addressing "all ages and both sexes, . . . speaking even to the illiterate."[19]

The fact that women were increasingly participating in urban space and were among the key targets for poster advertising must be considered when analyzing late nineteenth-century poster icons of women in the city. Many of the posters discussed in this essay, which depicted women in the city, both featured and courted the gazes of modern women for the pragmatic reason that women were considered the primary consumers. Posters were generally commissioned by those who could invest in the promotion of their products and establishments, such as department stores. At this early stage of the advertising industry, advertising agencies were still in their infancy. Thus records that reveal a specific agency's or artist's aims in reaching a particular audience through a specific ad (which are readily available for the twentieth century), are generally not yet available for this period. A rare glimpse at the intention of advertisers to appeal to the type of woman depicted in advertising images can be gleaned from a caption under an advertising image in a 1900 supplement to the British journal *The Poster* directed at the advertising trade. The caption, which reads, "This Show Card will Catch the Eyes of Mothers," makes an explicit connection between the young mother depicted in the ad advertising a Borax Starch Glaze and the targeted consumers. Note that the British advertisement chooses to represent the Victorian mother strolling on the street with her offspring rather than occupied with motherly duties in the domestic space. To understand late nineteenth-century posters it is crucial to consider their overall advertising role and specific goal of addressing targeted consumers. This perspective has been largely absent from art historical studies that tend to focus on posters as art.

With few exceptions, art historians specializing in late nineteenth-century art have tended to treat fin-de-siècle posters primarily as part of the oeuvre of a canonical artist such as Toulouse-Lautrec, as sources for artists such as Seurat, or as related to styles such as Art Nouveau, while specialized studies of poster artists tend to focus on their stylistic evolution. To broaden the investigation, this essay examines a selection of fin-de-siècle posters as a new form of mass-media communication in the context of *publicité*, the late nineteenth-century French term for the emerging fields of advertising, publicity and marketing.[20] Many of the innovations introduced in poster design reflected the artists' creative responses to the complex demands of advertising and the conditions of poster display in the city. This, of course, does not detract from the creative achievements of individuals. Rather, it highlights the functions of posters as a late nineteenth-century communication medium as well as aesthetic objects of art, graphic arts, design, or decorative arts. By visualizing modern women at the very site where they, along with men, were increasingly looking at the city spectacle, fin-de-siècle posters resonated with certain historical changes.

The *flâneuse* in fin-de-siècle French posters

The rise of the so-called New Woman and popularity of icons of modern women in advertising posters were interrelated. Posters, which depicted urban women with agency, participated in reshaping women's identities in the 1890s and early 1900s because they converged with a period in which the reception of such images was taking place in the midst of dynamic changes. Feminist demands, congresses, and numerous articles in journals during the 1890s, brought debates on the New Woman to public attention during the decade of the flowering of fin-de-siècle posters. Fin-de-siècle debates about the New Woman's desires to enter the public sphere addressed her participation in leisure activities in the city, work outside of the home, and legal and political rights. Economic interests and new modes of advertising played an important role in forming new icons of modern women as part of complex cultural changes which were not limited to politics and suffrage. Though these changes were much contested, portraying active women in the city was less threatening in a commercial poster advertising a department store or a bicycle, than in a political context. Posters could thus visualize attractive icons of modern women in the city prompting the assimilation of such images into mainstream culture.[21]

The anonymous 1894 poster advertising Vendroux biscuits features an idealized leisurely viewing of posters, rather than a mere casual look while walking by (Figure 24). The scene highlights a *flâneuse* and includes a *flâneur*. Out on a stroll with her dog, this fashionable *flâneuse* is stopping to look at a poster that catches her eye. Her bright red dress accessorized with matching hat, umbrella, and red dog leash, draws attention to her. The corseted figure and chic outfit were sure to attract gazes of *flâneurs* on the street. The poster, however, presents her as a spectator as well as spectacle. It stages her in an idealized city space in which the *flâneur* next to her is as oblivious to her nearby presence as she is unconcerned with his. The scene thus establishes the city as a safe space for a woman stroller. It presents a public space in which multiple possibilities of looking and desire coexist as if in

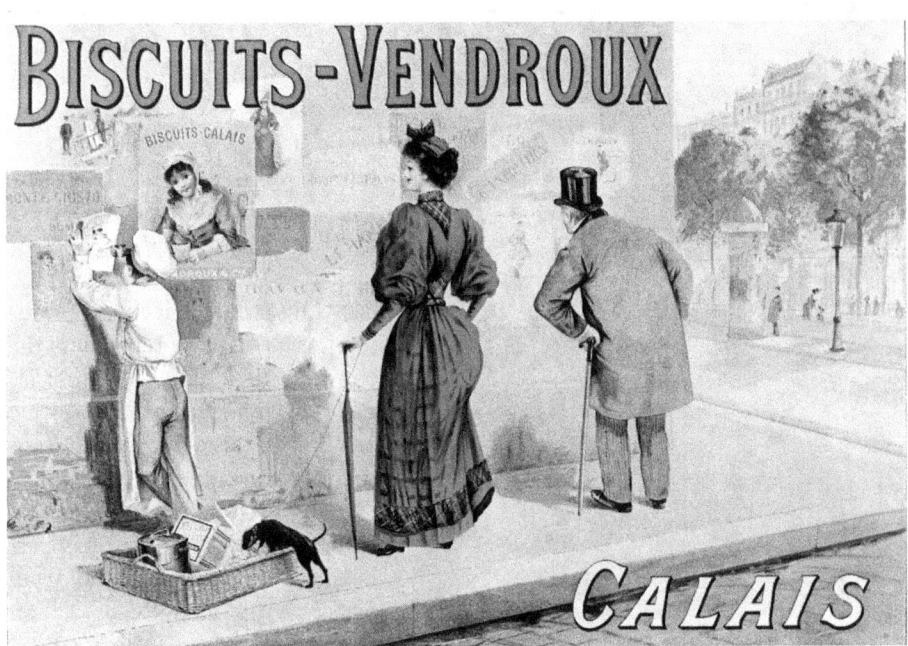

24 Anon., *Biscuits Vendroux*, 1894, poster

their own imaginary separate spheres even though the spectators share the same pavement. The masculine *flâneur* is leaning forward peering at a poster advertising the café-concert Alcazar, while the more detached *flâneuse* stands upright looking in the direction of a poster advertising biscuits from a greater distance. Though her dog indulges in sampling the goods, the worldly woman, bemused spectator, and potential consumer, is a composed, rather than hysterical, *flâneuse*.

Hugo d'Alési's 1895 poster features the Parisian *flâneuse* looking at a *bouquiniste*'s display (Figure 25). The striking icon of a hatted and gloved metropolitan woman is dramatically silhouetted against the glowing sunset sky. Out on a stroll on board of the Seine she has stopped to look at a lithographic print taken from the portfolio labeled "*Centenaire de la Lithographie, Galerie Rapp*," an exhibition celebrating the one-hundredth anniversary of lithography at the Rapp gallery (which this poster advertises). The *flâneuse* is the protagonist of this urban scene. She is the feminine version of the "*flâneurs des quais*," who, as the Larousse states "do not allow a single day to go by without casting their habitual glance *(donner son coup d'oeil habituel)* at the displays of the *bouquinistes*."[22] Defined by her cultivated gaze and fashionability, she performs both with the expert touch of an actress who knows she is observed by an audience. She occupies central stage while the faintly sketched miniaturized top-hatted *flâneur* looking at another *bouquiniste*'s display in the distance is barely visible on the margin of the picture (near the Eiffel Tower). The poster portrays her urban presence as unchallenged by the *flâneur*'s gaze.

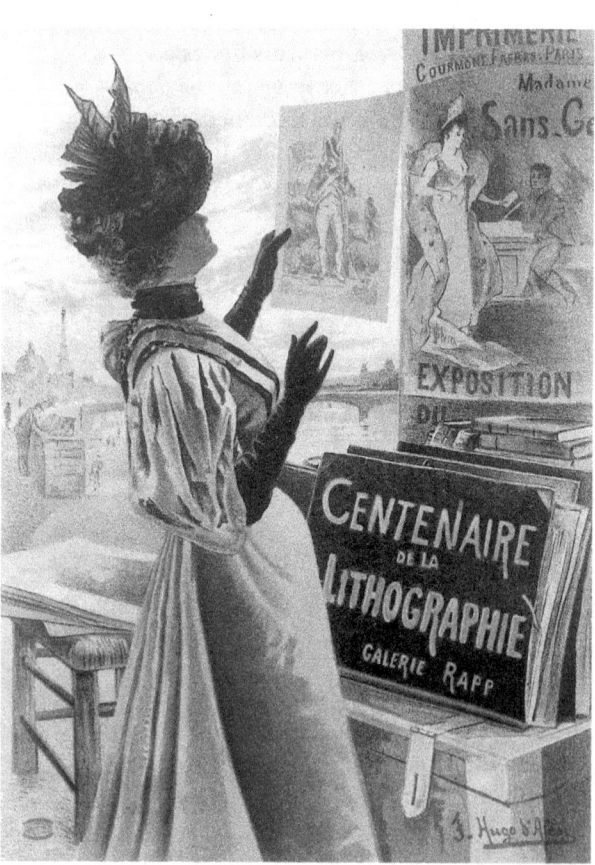

25 Hugo d'Alési, *Exhibition of the hundredth anniversary of lithography, Rapp Art Gallery*, 1895

This kind of icon of a contemporary *flâneuse* represents the converse of a fantasy femininity so often depicted in fin-de-siècle posters. It is the diametric opposite of the sexually provocative "Chérettes" who dance down from the sky into the café-concert in Chéret's posters, or the alluring figure in *Affiches-Pichot* by an anonymous artist, which advertises a print shop by that name.

The provocatively posed, bare-breasted, winged victory figure is a sexualized woman catering to a desiring masculine gaze. Defying gravity, her feet barely touch clouds in a celestial sphere that is nonetheless marked as a Parisian sky by the miniaturized Eiffel Tower on the horizon. Often given a set of wings, these kinds of seductive feminine figures are suspended above ground – floating, flying, levitating, hovering, ascending or descending. Their bare feet dangling above ground are unsuitable for walking. The *flâneuse*, on the other hand, is grounded in the city, "botanizing on the asphalt" fully clad in a stylish outfit.

Clearly, posters attempted to appeal to women's gazes when they advertised feminine fashions and accessories, beauty products, cosmetics, and household goods. But some posters also appealed to women when promoting a range of other products such as bicycles. Many of the posters that advertised bicycles to women tapped into late nineteenth-century discourses on women's new freedoms, and promoted bicycles as a new form of transportation, sport, and recreation in Europe as well as across the Atlantic. Writing in 1897 about "La Bicycliste," the French author, Georges Montorgueil notes that the far-reaching influence of the bicycle was "more violent than any revolution, it has entered customs, turned traditional opinions on their head, erased fearful resistances and put pressure on old police ordinances on costume."[23] Numerous posters of the late nineteenth century, which represent women on bicycles as an icon of freedom and mobility, make sense when read in this context. For example, Phillipe Chapellier's *Petit, Cycles et Automobiles* (n.d.) promotes the company's bicycles by featuring a modern woman cycling down the Champs-Elysées sporting what at that time was considered a comfortable "rational dress." It shows women populating the boulevard on foot, on a bicycle, in a carriage, and in a new automobile. The cyclist draws interested looks from the couple riding in a chauffeured automobile, particularly from the elegantly attired woman passenger. Though women (and men) tend to be on display on the boulevard, this bicycle rider is also portrayed as herself gazing at the spectacle. The fact that she is looking sideways rather than straight ahead suggests that her look is for pleasure, not navigation. She is a consumer of bicycles and a modern *flâneuse* on wheels. Posters of this type must have had an impact on the contested zone of the street by injecting an icon of modern women into the public imagination. They invited the identification of women who wished to be independently mobile.

If Chapellier's poster presents women's free mobility on the boulevard as a fait accompli, Georges de Feure's 1894 advertisement for the *Paris Almanach* hints at tensions on the Parisian street (Figure 26). The *Paris Almanach* was an illustrated publication, published by the prominent Parisian publisher and book and print dealer Edmond Sagot.[24] Sagot must have commissioned this poster to advertise his establishment as well as the *Paris Almanach*; thus his address appeared in the front, while the window display of his establishment was depicted in the background. The poster portrays a self-assured upper-class elegantly dressed woman walking in the densely populated city carving out a physical and psychic space. Unchaperoned, she deftly navigates her way with the help of the *Paris Almanach*. Showing her looking at

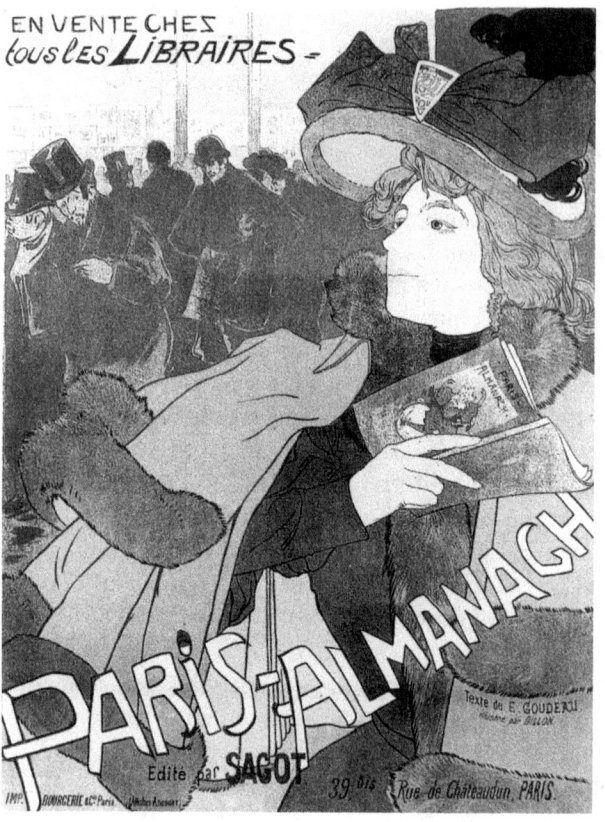

26 Georges de Feure (Georges van Sluiter), *Paris Almanach*, 1894

the portable volume, the poster suggests the utility of the Almanach while furnishing an alibi for her status as a respectable *flâneuse*. Whether a Parisienne or a tourist, the poster features her interested gaze, showing her lifting her head from the volume, looking intently at a particular site. Note, however, that it also makes explicit the conditions of her *flânerie* – always a spectacle for masculine gazes, such as the gaze of the top-hatted man in the back (on the upper left). While registering these tensions by including the male *flâneur*'s gaze in the background, the poster features her *flânerie* and shows her as continuing unfazed. Directing her gaze outwards, she is claiming the street as a space for her sightseeing at a time when a woman's respectability could still be open to question when she walked in the city on her own. The poster promotes the *Paris Almanach* to women by featuring a woman who claims her dignity and independent mobility, practicing a new kind of presence on the metropolitan street. This *flâneuse* is fully aware of the need to negotiate her walking and looking in the city. This poster not only portrays a respectable *flâneuse*, but also inserts her gaze into the conflicted mix of gazes that make up metropolitan street spaces of the 1890s.

Leonetto Cappiello's 1905 poster, *Paquet Pernot* advertises a brand of packaged biscuits by featuring a stylish *grand dame* as a consumer who is the reigning persona inside the shop (Figure 27). Her authority is established by her stature, comportment, and extraordinary elite designer outfit. Though Thorstein Veblen's oft-quoted theory has popularized the notion that women consume primarily to display their husbands' wealth, this type of poster emphasizes a different message.[25] In contrast to Veblen's theory, these posters often portray the woman consumer as herself deriving a new status through acts of consumption. They imply her agency and play up the woman's persona rather than merely her husband's wealth. Though her haute couture fashion most likely reflects the husband's wealth, it also establishes her consumer role as an urban experience that mixes shopping with fashionable city outings. This kind of poster appeals to women by portraying their activities as pleasurable in their own right. For example, *Paquet Pernot* invests the upper-class woman wearing a flamboyant outfit with the authority of taste and class. Her extravagant toilette, whose plumed hat adds to her height, magnifies her social standing by depicting her as towering over the shop clerk, contrasting her stature with his deferring stance. Though it portrays a scene inside a shop, the poster subtly imports into the interior the passing silhouette of a woman walking-by seen through the window. We are reminded that shopping is part of a broader urban experience, which includes walking in the city.

Théophile-Alexandre Steinlen's 1896 six-foot poster *La Rue (Affiches Charles Verneau)*, which advertises the print shop Verneau, represents a mix of classes, genders, and ages on the dense Montmartre street (Figure 28). Though most of the women are walking by unmolested, a tense encounter is taking place on the right. A pot-bellied middle-aged businessman in black suit and gold watch-chain almost blocks the path of the hatted and gloved *bourgeoise* in white attire. She is determined to exclude his intrusive maneuver by pointedly averting her eyes and tilting her head as she walks by. He directs an aggressive gaze at close range towards the working-class girl who is carrying the *bourgeoise*'s large package. In self-defense, the girl looks straight ahead and keeps walking. Steinlen highlights one shoe of each woman pointed forward, making the point that the *bourgeoise* and the girl are marching by despite this obstacle. The artist intensifies the urban drama by placing the *bourgeoise*'s advancing foot perilously close to the gleaming black shoe of the man who has squarely planted himself in her way. It is a tight choreography of body language, ogling, and fending off unwanted gazes — gendered strategies played out in the charged social spaces of the city.

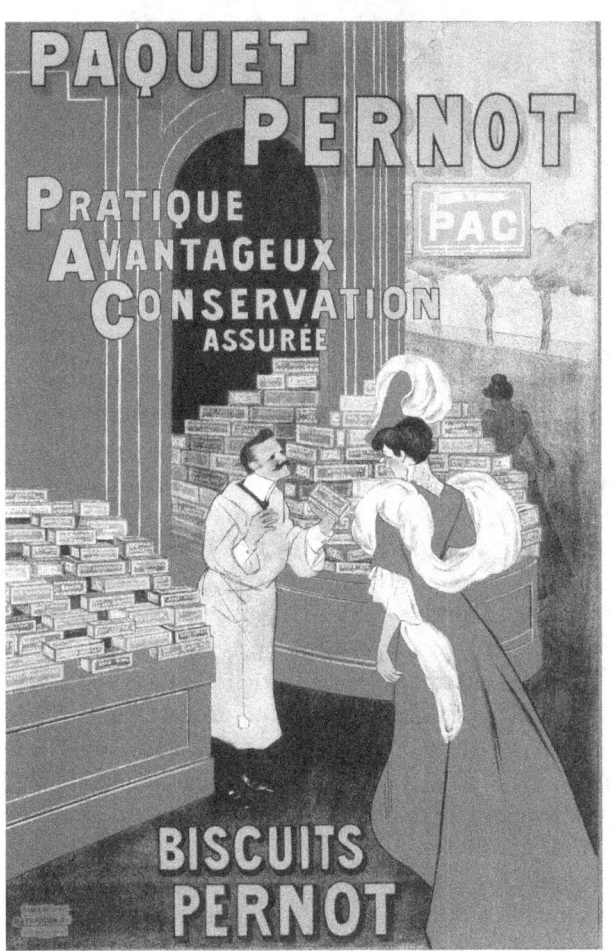

27 Leonetto Cappiello, *Paquet Pernot*, 1905

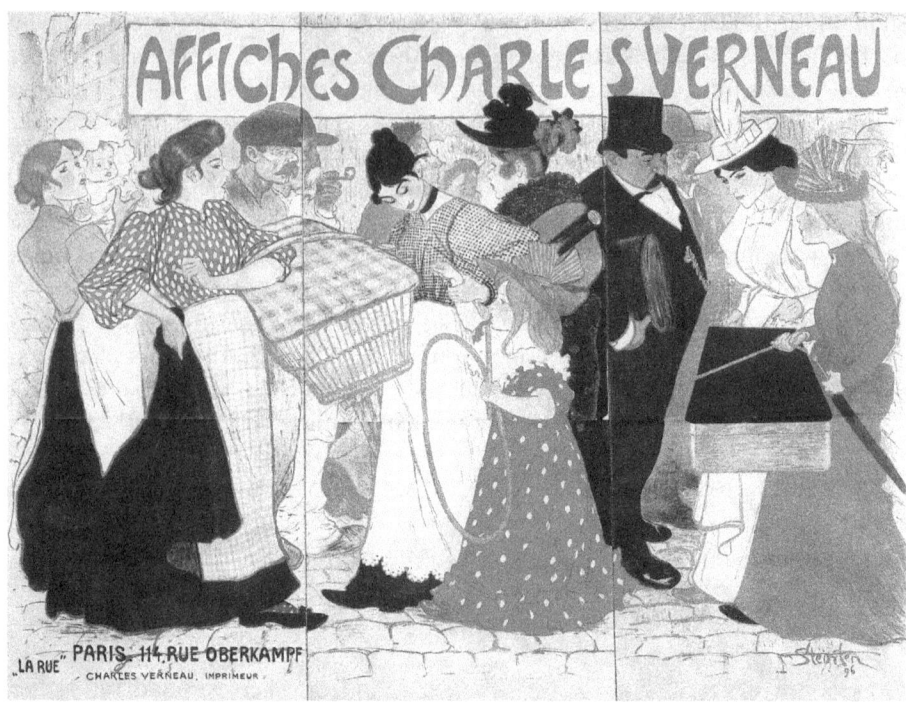

28 Théophile-Alexandre Steinlen, *La Rue Affiches Charles Verneau*, 1896

Flâneuses, flâneurs, and literary discourses

The metropolitan street was a contested zone for fin-de-siècle women, yet women were increasingly venturing into it with more independence than would have been possible earlier on. As we learn from late nineteenth-century novels, journalism, and diaries, women adopted new practices. While the young artist Marie Bashkirtseff longs for unchaperoned mobility in the Paris of the late 1870s, the novelist Colette, writing *Claudine à Paris* some twenty years later, describes Claudine asserting her independence.[26] When Claudine decides to go shopping in a department store and her father orders her to take her maid along as chaperon, she responds by feigning surprise: "I opened my eyes as wide as saucers. 'Gracious, of course I'm going out by myself – what's wrong?'" and proceeds to do as she wishes.[27] While walking alone in the city did not in and of itself constitute *flânerie*, revising social constraints, which enabled women to walk alone or in each others' company without compromising their respectability, made feminine *flânerie* possible.

Ménie Muriel Dowie (considered one of the most important British New-Woman novelists and herself an adventurer) describes a fin-de-siècle woman's passion for the kind of *flânerie* Victor Hugo was famous for – observing the metropolis from the upper level of omnibuses. In her 1895 novel *Gallia*, Dowie portrays

Margaret Essex – a young middle-class British woman who had studied painting in Paris – as passionate about observing London from the upper level of the omnibus. Though "the train is nearer and quicker," she strongly prefers the omnibus: "for real exhilaration, give me the top of an omnibus on a fine afternoon in London," and "without its omnibuses London would lose half its charms for me."[28] This may be surprising, given that the upper level of buses, a favorite vantage point for Victor Hugo's observations of Paris, was closed to women in Paris around 1857.[29] It would be misleading, however, to assume that this prohibition applies across the board to other cities or dates, and such restrictions in Paris were evidently lifted later in the nineteenth century. Indeed, women were depicted on the upper level of the Parisian bus in journalistic illustrations by the 1890s.

In contrast to poster images such as those discussed in this essay, various literary representations, including Zola's *Au bonheur des dames*, stereotype women as weak-willed or hysterical. To brand women as "hysterical" *flâneuses* may have functioned to displace masculine anxieties. Elizabeth Wilson, who recognizes the *flâneur* as a cultural construct and an influential fiction, associates it with a crisis in masculinity, a "projection of angst," brought about by "the violent dislocations that characterized urbanization."[30] By constructing the detached *flâneur*, masculine identity could claim a position of rational self-control, while femininity was identified with susceptibility to the manipulations of consumer culture. Some scholars have argued that woman was "unfit for *flânerie* because she desires the objects spread before her and acts upon that desire."[31] Certainly, late nineteenth-century discourses attributed supreme detachment to masculine *flâneurs* and its diametric opposite – an inability to resist consumer temptations – to women.[32] However, it is problematic to maintain that only women were subject to the provocation of desire by commodity spectacle.

Biographies of some of the nineteenth century's most celebrated *flâneurs* yield information that demonstrates that the stereotypically gendered discourses did not necessarily match lived practices. Balzac, for one, was a compulsive buyer of luxury goods, decorative objects, furniture, and antiques, leading an exasperated colleague to state that, "selling oneself to the upholsterer for the next two years is the act of a lunatic!"[33] Nonetheless, Balzac's identity as *flâneur* has been constructed selectively from the historical record to focus on his "descent into the street" as "a great moment in literature," as his biographer Graham Robb, for example, describes it.[34] Balzac's walks through Paris were not limited to incognito observations and detached *flânerie*. They also included succumbing to temptations and uncontrollable buying, spending extravagant sums of money (some 100,000 francs in a three-year period). One could argue that Balzac was a collector rather than a mere consumer, because his excessive spending was primarily on decorative objects, but this ignores the overriding common traits of buying compulsively and lacking control. Balzac himself likened his lack of control to "the demon of gambling."[35] Furthermore, Balzac's acquisitions often did not live up to the quality and attributions he believed they had when buying them for large sums of money.[36] Perhaps the insistence on the supreme detachment of the *flâneur* was a case of protesting too much. The social construct of the detached *flâneur* may well have functioned as a reassuring denial at the historical moment when seductive commodity spectacle threatened Enlightenment ideals of reason.

Conclusion

What was at stake in women's *flânerie* in the late nineteenth century? Since *flânerie* necessarily involved venturing beyond the physical and psychic boundaries of private space, at stake was access to the city, redrawing the boundaries of feminine "respectability," and reformulating feminine subjectivity. Feminine *flânerie* represented a contested quest for freedom, while the *flâneur's* free access to the city was taken for granted. Rita Felski notes that women were entering the city in greater numbers both as workers and as consumers, exerting pressure on the ideology that associated women with the private sphere.[37] As we have seen, this development was accompanied by new representations of women in the city. Some late nineteenth-century posters visually enunciate respectable forms of feminine *flânerie* by depicting women looking while walking in the city, or enjoying other forms of mobility.

It could be argued that during the late nineteenth century advertising images that feature women in the city replace an ideology of confinement with an ideology of consumption for women. On one level this may well be the case. However, late nineteenth-century women were enticed to consume certain products and services with messages that opposed confinement, and stressed freedom and mobility. These poster images encouraged women not only to patronize shops, but also to walk and socialize in the city, travel, and visit resorts. They portrayed new women pursuing diverse pleasures of *flânerie* from browsing on the bank of the Seine, to bicycling on the boulevard, walking on the street, shopping, or sightseeing. They also depicted the cosmopolitan woman who traveled to explore unfamiliar regions.[38] Though theories about advertising were in their infancy, in his 1899 article "Symbolism in Advertising," Karl Kloufe notes that poster advertising works through "subtle insinuation," by suggesting "a train of thought that will bring the loiterer by a series of brain exercises to the article advertised." As Judith Williamson states (discussing twentieth-century advertising) "we, and those goods, are interchangeable, they are selling us ourselves."[39] In selling late nineteenth-century women a variety of goods, these kinds of posters sold women their new "selves." Though posters used diverse strategies to sell a host of different products, many of them associated middle-class women with a lifestyle that entailed access to public spaces of the metropolis. Thus poster images of a respectable *flâneuse* who enjoys a new mobility in the metropolis, altered not only modernity's cityscapes but also its psychic spaces of identities.

This essay has historicized the theorization of the *flâneuse*, taking into account visual and literary representations as well as modern women's experiences and aspirations. While diaries provide records of the lived experiences of their authors, other descriptions of the *flâneuse* in journalism and novels are valuable in two respects. First, they indicate that women's *flânerie* was considered possible in the late nineteenth century. Second, they suggest that late nineteenth-century discourses on *flânerie* were not exclusively on the male *flâneur* (which was itself established in nineteenth-century journalistic and literary accounts). If we expect all the same traits attributed to the masculine *flâneur* – his degree of unfettered freedom and supreme detachment – in practices and representations of feminine *flânerie*, we might well conclude that feminine *flânerie* was not possible. But if we consider representations of women in the city along with modern women's increasing active participation in the city, burgeoning mobility, and practices of walking, looking, and enjoying a variety of urban pleasures, than we may well conclude that a feminine *flânerie* became integral to urban modernity by the late nineteenth century.

For women to assume the freedom to practice *flânerie* in the metropolis meant stepping out of the conceptual and physical segregation of the gendered territories of "private" and "public." Ultimately the demands for, and gradual advances towards, women's education, entry into professions, employment opportunities, wages, and the vote, exceed the definition of a respectable feminine "*flâneuse*" if we understand it narrowly as focusing only on the pleasures of the city. Women's *flânerie* was entangled with commodity spectacle. Its symbolic resonance, however, was deeper and its urban geography broader, because *flânerie* brought the modern woman into a wide range of engagements with the city. Thus if the construct "*flâneuse*" continues to resonate, it is because it represents women's increased access not only to the physical territory of the modern metropolis, but also to a symbolic geography of a modern public sphere.

Notes

1   This essay discusses issues that are further investigated in my book on *Impressionism, Parisian Consumer Culture and Modern Women* (Cambridge University Press, forthcoming). It draws on a portion of my essay "The Pan-European Flâneuse in Fin-de-Siècle Posters: Advertising Modern Women in the City," *Nineteenth-Century Contexts* (Vol. 25, no. 4 [2003]), pp. 333–356 and is printed with permission. Thanks to all those who made valuable suggestions to this work in its various phases, especially J. Bristow, N. Caputo, S. Guilbaut, M. Iskin, Z. Kezer, J. Rudolph, M. Ryan, R. M. San-Juan, D. L. Silverman, C. Whiting, and C. Cuevas-Wolf. Special thanks to G. P. Kucich, and the anonymous readers for very helpful comments. Thanks to P. H. Reill, director of UCLA's Center for Seventeenth and Eighteenth Century Studies, S. Levine and S. Canning, for opportunities to deliver early versions of this work and for their comments, and to audiences at the CAA and at lectures at UCLA, the University of British Columbia, and Michigan University, Ann Arbor. For supporting the research and writing of the essay and the larger project of which it is part, I am grateful to the Ahmanson-Getty fellowship at UCLA's Center for Seventeenth and Eighteenth Century Studies; the Killam post-doctoral fellowship and the Green College Research

Scholar Award at the University of British Columbia; the Mellon at the Penn Humanities Forum, University of Pennsylvania; and the Ben Gurion University for a faculty research grant supporting reproductions.

2 J. Wolff's essay, "The Invisible *Flâneuse*: Women and the Literature of Modernity," [1985] repr. in *Feminine Sentences: Essays on Women and Culture* (Berkeley: University of California Press, 1990) pp. 34–50, first articulated the exclusion of women from the literature of modernity on *flânerie*. Though her essay denied the existence of the *flâneuse*, it opened up a productive space for further studies. G. Pollock's essay, "Modernity and the Spaces of Femininity," in *Vision and Difference: Femininity, Feminism and the Histories of Art* (New York: Routledge, 1988) pp. 50–90, analyzed women's exclusion from the Paris of the Baudelerian *flâneur*. It claimed a place for Mary Cassatt and Berthe Morisot in a revised modernist narrative, relating their painting of domestic scenes to the artists' lack of access to the metropolis. Pollock's essay, however, did not re-examine the stereotypical association of women with the private sphere in light of the changing conditions in the late nineteenth century.

3 See E. D. Rappaport, *Shopping for Pleasure: Women in the Making of London's West End* (Princeton, N.J.: Princeton University Press, 2000), E. Wilson, *The Sphinx in the City: Urban Life, the Control of Disorder, and Women* (London: Virago Press, 1991), D. E. Nord, *Walking the Victorian Streets: Women, Representation, and the City* (Ithaca, N.Y.: Cornell University Press, 1995), A. Friedberg, *Window Shopping: Cinema and the Postmodern* (Berkeley: University of California Press, 1993).

4 L. Nead *Victorian Babylon: People, Streets and Images in Nineteenth-Century London* (New Haven and London: Yale University Press, 2000).

5 p. 436 (translations are mine unless an English source is cited).

6 H. de Balzac, "Histoire et physiologie des boulevards de Paris," in *Traité de la vie élégante*, preface and notes by L. Lumet (Paris: Bibliopolis, 1911), p. 224. [*Le Diable à Paris*, vol. 1 (March–April 1845)].

7 W. Benjamin, *The Arcades Project*, trans. H. Eiland and K. McLaughlin (Cambridge, Mass.: Belknap Press of Harvard University Press, 1999), p. 895.

8 E. Zola, *The Ladies Paradise* (Berkeley: University of California Press, 1992), p. 69. See R. Bowlby, *Just Looking: Consumer Culture in Dreiser, Gissing, and Zola* (New York: Methuen, 1985). On Zola and the representation of women's gazes in late nineteenth-century visual culture see R. E. Iskin, "Selling, Seduction and Soliciting the Eye: Manet's Bar at the Folies-Bergère," *Art Bulletin* 77, no. 1 (March 1995) pp. 25–44.

9 L. Tiersten, "Marianne in the Department Store: Gender and the Politics of Consumption in Turn-of-the-Century Paris," in *Cathedrals of Consumption: The European Department Store, 1850–1939*, eds G. Crossick and S. Jaumain (Aldershot and Brookfield, Mass.: Ashgate, 1999), pp. 119–120.

10 J. Clarétie, *La Vie à Paris* (Paris: Victor Harvard, 1882 [1880]), p. 492.

11 M. Poster, "Culture and History: The Cases of Leisure, Art, and Technology," *French Historical Studies* 18, no. 1 (Spring 1993), pp. 131–135.

12 M. Poster, "Culture and History," p. 135.

13 E. D. Rappaport, *Shopping for Pleasure*, p. 5.

14 M. de Certeau, *The Practice of Everyday Life*, trans. Steven Rendall (Berkeley: University of California Press, 1988 [1984]). A. Friedberg notes that for de Certeau, "the *flâneur*'s movements" were "'pedestrian speech acts'." A. Friedberg, *Window Shopping*, p. 38.

15 M. de Certeau, *The Practice of Everyday Life*, pp. 97–99.

16 J. Laver, *19th-Century French Posters* (London: Nicholson and Watson, 1944), p. 10.

17 G. d'Avenal, "Le méchanisme de la vie moderne: la publicité," *Revue des deux mondes* 2 (January–February 1901), p. 649.

18 *Journal officiel de la République française*, June 8, 1880, pp. 6, 212–6, 213, cited in M. R. Levin, "Democratic Vistas – Democratic Media: Defining a Role for Printed Images in Industrializing France," *French Historical Studies* 18, no. 1 (Spring 1993), p. 95.

19 M. R. Levin, "Democratic Vistas – Democratic Media," p. 95.

20 A recent exhibition catalogue includes a section on commerce and communication, *The Power of the Poster*, ed. M. Timmers (London: Victoria & Albert Publications, 1998). For an introduction to 1890s French posters, see P. D. Cate, "The French Poster, 1868–1900," in *American Art Posters of the 1890's in the Metropolitan Museum of Art*, exhibition cat., ed. David W. Kiehl (New York: Metropolitan Museum of Art, 1987).

21 For the role of posters in depicting modern women see R. E. Iskin "Popularising New Women in Belle Époque Advertising Posters," in *A Belle Époque? Women and Feminism in French Society and Culture 1890–1910*, eds D. Holmes and C. Tarr (Oxford and New York: Berghahn Books, 2005).

22 P. Larousse, *Grand Dictionnaire universel du 19e siècle* (Geneva and Paris, 1982 [1866–79]), p. 436.

23 G. Montorgueil, *La Parisienne* (Paris: Librairie L. Conquet, 1897), p. 186. Police ordinances forbade women to wear pants.

24 The small, thin paperback volume included monthly calendars along with illustrations and journalistic writing describing seasonal activities in Paris.

25 T. Veblen, *The Theory of the Leisure Class: An Economic Study in the Evolution of Institutions* (New York and London: The Macmillan Company, 1899). Though displaying the husband's wealth was one of the roles of fashion, as E. Wilson notes, Veblen disregarded the fuller role of fashion in urban life "as communicative text as well as source of pleasure." E. Wilson, "The Invisible *Flâneur*," *New Left Review* 191 (January–February 1992), p. 99. For a critique of Veblen see J. Lears, "Beyond Veblen: Rethinking Consumer Culture in America," in *Consuming Visions: Accumulation and Display of Goods in America, 1880–1920*, ed. S. J. Bronner (New York and London: Norton, 1989).

26 M. Bashkirtseff, *The Journal of Marie Bashkirtseff*, trans. Mathilde Blind (London, Paris, and Melbourne: Cassell & Company, 1890), p. 347. Colette, *Claudine in Paris*, trans. Antonia White (New York: Farrar, Straus, 1958), p. 35.

27 Colette, *Claudine in Paris*, p. 35. In Britain too, opinions on the need for chaperons were changing. See E. D. Rappaport, *Shopping for Pleasure*, and Nord, *Walking the Victorian Streets*.

28 M. M. Dowie, *Gallia* (London: Everyman, 1995) pp. 69–70.

29 W. Benjamin, *The Arcades Project*, p. 432.

30 E. Wilson, "The Invisible Flâneur," p. 109.

31 P. Parkhurst Ferguson, "The *Flâneur* On and Off the Streets of Paris," in *The Flâneur*, ed. K. Tester (London: Routledge, 1994), p. 27. J. Wolff concurs that women cannot be considered *flâneuses* since shopping precludes the "detached and aimless strolling of the *flâneur*." J. Wolff, "The Artist and the *Flâneur*: Rodin, Rilke, and Gwen John in Paris," *Feminine Sentences*, pp. 111–137.

32 Zola, for example expresses the nineteenth-century dichotomy in *The Ladies'*
    Paradise, contrasting the supreme masculine control of Mouret, the owner of the
    Paradis des Femmes, who invents its innovative marketing, with the loss of control of
    women shoppers.

33 This was the comment of Latouche, Balzac's agent and editor, who was his "closest
    friend and bitterest enemy." Cited in G. Robb, *Balzac: A Biography* (New York: W. W.
    Norton, 1995), p. 150.

34 G. Robb, *Balzac*, p. 70.

35 G. Robb, *Balzac*, p. 367.

36 G. Robb, *Balzac*, pp. 366–367.

37 R. Felski, *Beyond Feminist Aesthetics: Feminist Literature and Social Change*
    (Cambridge, Mass.: Harvard University Press, 1989), p. 19.

38 This is further discussed in my essay in *Nineteenth-Century Contexts*.

39 K. Kloufe, "Symbolism of Advertising," *The Poster* 2 (January 1899), p. 9. J.
    Williamson, *Decoding Advertisements: Ideology and Meaning in Advertising* (London:
    Marion Boyards, 1978), p. 13.

9

Why the Impressionists never painted the department store

Aruna D'Souza

For Emile Zola, whose larger literary project was concerned mainly with investigating the social and economic underpinnings of Second Empire France, with interrogating this modern way of living that seemed both radically new and inevitable, writing a novel on the theme of the department store seemed crucial.[1] When *Au bonheur des dames* appeared in 1883, it was clear that the real protagonist in this "phantasmagoric hymn to the marvels of modern commerce,"[2] despite the putative love story between heroine and hero, is the department store itself. The text comprises a meticulous accounting of the ways in which such cathedrals of consumption "[shook] up and reinvigorated commerce in France," in Zola's words, by introducing fixed prices, by encouraging browsing, by revolutionizing store design and product display, and most importantly by transforming shopping into a leisure activity for the urban bourgeoisie.[3]

It is clear that Zola chose the subject of the department store precisely because it was one of the most visible features in the changes that took place in Paris from the mid-nineteenth century onward – a product of Haussmannian renovations as well as of economic and social transformations that would profoundly transform the way life was organized for working- and middle-class inhabitants of the city. In contemporary tourists' guidebooks, breathless with their accounting of the sights of this capital of the nineteenth century, the Bon Marché, the Louvre department store, Le Printemps and La Samaritaine were regularly included on the "must-see" lists.[4] So apparent was their centrality to Paris's reputation as a modern metropolis that even critics of Impressionism recognized it as a potential subject for the painters of modern life: in Duranty's 1876 text, "La Nouvelle peinture," the "magasin de nouveautés" is cited as one of many scenes appropriate for the painter's brush, while Huysmans, on the occasion of the 1880 Impressionist exhibition, wrote that there was still much left to paint: "All of modern life is still there to be studied; hardly any of its multiple facets have been perceived and recorded. There is still more to do: official galas, salons, balls, glimpses of family life, the life of the artist and the bourgeoisie, the stores . . ."[5]

And yet, despite the fact that the *grand magasin*, both as an architectural entity and as a commercial institution, was a central feature of the modernity that Impressionism purported to represent, there exists no depiction of the department store by an Impressionist painter. It remains for us, then, to ask why. The search for an answer to this question will require us to look at the ways in which commerce was depicted by the painters of modern life, in order to discern the horizons of that system of representation; Degas's images of millinery shops will stand as a limit case in this regard. It will also require us to examine the institution of the department store itself: through an investigation of the popular culture of this temple to modern shopping, it will become clear that the department store was constructed as a sort of blind spot in the literature and visual culture of the bourgeois man – the *flâneur* – and as such, was more or less unrepresentable via a mode of painting – Impressionism – which arguably organized itself around the ocular range of that city stroller.

To discover the logic behind this occlusion of the *flâneur*-artist's gaze: such is the task that presents itself. Given the fact that the department store was a site of commerce (though, as will be discussed later, it was the site of many other things, too), one might ask how commerce as such *could* be represented within the terms of modern life painting. It is a curious fact that for all the ways in which Impressionism gives evidence (and itself formed a part) of consumer culture in later nineteenth-century Paris, it rarely pictures the transaction of buying and selling overtly.[6] Commerce is depicted implicitly throughout Impressionist and modern life imagery – in the fashions, décor, and leisurely activities of the people depicted, for example – but almost nowhere is it depicted explicitly, despite the fact that life in Paris was increasingly organized, for most of its middle-class inhabitants, around such business transactions.

Those few Impressionist images which do deal directly with commerce are rarely discussed in terms of the specificity of their subject matter in relation to the economics of buying and selling.[7] When they have been discussed at length, Degas's pictures of millinery shops, to take one of the most important examples, have generally been placed within the context of a nineteenth-century popular mythology which saw *modistes* as sexually available young women, available to the *flâneur*'s gaze as well as to other of his desires – as paintings about shopping for sex *rather than* shopping for goods, in other words. Hollis Clayson's analysis situates Degas among the wide range of artists who engaged with such a mythology, relying upon imagery such as cartoons and Epinal prints to make her case that "for some late nineteenth-century Parisians, the millinery shop seems to have always denoted elusive, commercialized sex."[8] She does not find the Degas images particularly erotic themselves, nor does she find in them explicit references to such myth, but rather argues that "the tensions in the pictures are Degas's way of acknowledging the legend of the millinery shop as a *magasin-prétexte*."[9] Eunice Lipton, while drawing upon much of the same contextual material, comes to a somewhat different conclusion: noting the matter-of-fact, decidedly unerotic depiction of hat-makers and sellers in Degas's pictures, she finds that the artist actually *resisted* the prurient sexuality of many popular depictions of young, pretty hat-makers in favor of a focus on the seriousness of the milliner's craft.[10]

Both interpretations offer a set of conditions for looking at these images that foregrounds sexuality and sexual commerce, while acknowledging that Degas does not seem actively to exploit such themes in these instances. Neither seem particularly interested in the actual depiction of commodity production or commercial transaction contained in the series.[11] However, it is precisely because Degas's pictures engage the theme of commerce and the commodity in a (relatively) unencumbered way, in order to reflect on the notion of buying and selling as such, that they form an important and interesting exception in the field of Impressionist image-making. Treated from this point of view, outside of the issue of clandestine prostitution, they are no less complicated nor any less immersed in the issue of gender.

The series, probably begun in the early 1880s (perhaps 1882), consists of at least sixteen pastels and paintings. Degas seems to have been interested both in the interaction between customer and salesgirl, and in the more contemplative activity of the artisans who made the hats. The most famous examples of the former announce fairly explicitly their interest not only in the issue of the vanity of the *bourgeoise*, but in the issue of class differences between buyer and seller of goods as well. Take, for example, *At the Milliner's* (1882, Metropolitan Museum of Art, New York), in which the salesgirl is bisected by a free-standing mirror becoming nothing more than a modestly attired hatstand, while her customer is lost in contemplation of her own image. Such visual treatment of the shop girl is common in Degas's pictures;[12] and while such a radical restriction, occlusion, or even erasure of the working woman in these pictures may be interpreted as a clear statement of the class dynamics inherent in the commercial transaction, there is in fact a great deal of ambiguity as regards the relative social rank of the characters in these images. In one of the oddest pictures of the series, a version in the Annenberg Collection (1882–84), a bare-headed woman sits on a diamond-patterned couch in luxurious *salon*, adjusting the fit of a hat on a young woman seated next to her; the intimacy of their pose, the intertwining and overlapping of their limbs, suggests that they are friends of equal station out on a shopping trip, but the fact that one of the women is hatless and coatless implies that she is, in fact, the saleswoman helping her client, in which case her close and informal relation to her client – and the fact that she is seated, not standing – is not just unexpected, but improper.[13] The remarkable painting in the Art Institute of Chicago (1884/90), depicts a milliner in drab dress and gloves sitting behind a table full of hats, one of which, elevated on a stand, overlaps the figure almost as if it sits on her head (Figure 29). The ambiguity of the milliner figure is in line with the relatively imprecise class signifiers found in other pictures from this group: her aristocratic air may derive from the fact that in at least two pastel preparatory sketches, she is shown to be a hatted client examining a potential purchase; and while wrist-length gloves were

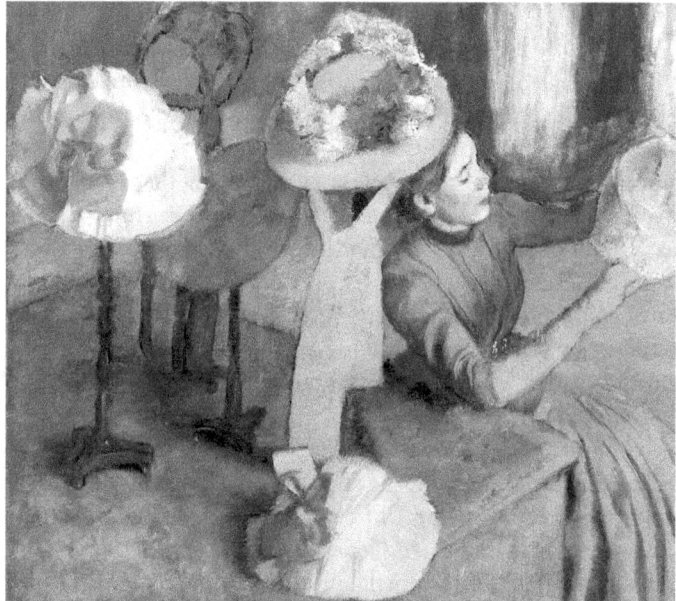

29 Edgar Degas,
The Millinery Shop,
1884/90

commonly worn by milliners, the elbow-length gloves on this figure were more
likely to be found on their customers.

   One might wonder at such kinds of imprecision in the work of an artist who was
so concerned with the classification of individuals within the terms of class and
social station.[14] There seem to be two possible explanations for these strangely
ambiguous images that are both particular to Degas and revealing with respect to
the conceptual and visual limits of Impressionism more generally. The first of these
has to do with Degas's discomfort with the intersection of money and art-making.
Degas's reasons for preferring to depict small boutiques rather than the bustling
grands magasins and the contradictory class markers within the images themselves
are likely rooted in his well-known anxieties about the commercialization of art
through the expansion of the "dealer-critic" system of art speculation, a phenomenon in which the Impressionist group played a formative role.[15] While ironically
referring to his paintings as "mes articles" – a term which gave them the commodity status of those goods sold in the arcades and boutiques of Paris – he simultaneously built up an oeuvre in which commerce and art's relation to it was worked
out in visual terms. In works such as *A Cotton Office in New Orleans*, entrepreneur-
ship is recast as leisurely, even aristocratic, capitalist activity, utterly dissociated
from notions of business-like hustle and the market. Moreover, while taking charge
of the "marketing" of the Impressionist exhibitions, Degas was careful not to
appear too immersed in their commercialism, attempting to define himself as a
genteel *amateur* and fine craftsman, as opposed to a professional artist, and therefore a tradesman.[16]

In this context, Degas's choice to paint the type of shops he did was significant, as Marilyn Brown points out:

Depicting *modistes* in small, self-operated boutiques rather than in large department stores, Degas seemed to admire in these working class women a quality which he could identify as an artist, in spite of his higher-class status: the shared capacity of being artisans producing and marketing handmade luxury commodities in an increasingly industrialized, consumer society.[17]

To read the milliner figures as stand-ins for the artisan-painter, especially if that painter had his own ambiguous and even ambivalent relation to the aristocracy, would indeed account for some of the unclear signifiers of class and station in these images. Degas's insistence on depicting his subjects, producers and sellers of wares, in the particular role of artisan, highlighting their devotion to and propensity for their creative task, is a way of distancing his own role as producer and seller of paintings from the venal realities of business.[18]

While Degas's discomfort with the Impressionists' role in the increasingly commercial art economy may have been an extreme case among his peers, it suggests one reason why other Impressionist painters shied away from the depiction of scenes of overt commerce in their work, especially those that took place in the department store. Already uneasy about negotiating their reputation as "independents" – and, paradoxically, increasingly reliant on that label to generate sales – it is not unlikely that many modern life painters were eager to avoid a too-close association with the world of shopping. This was especially the case since department stores like the Bon Marché had begun to exhibit and sell paintings and sculpture by the mid-1870s in halls "conceived in the grand style of a Louvre museum gallery."[19] In popular culture, too, viewing artwork was increasingly associated with the department store phenomenon of browsing, and it became a trope of caricature to show female Salon-goers looking at paintings in a mode akin to window-shopping, studying them for the latest fashion trends.[20] If, as Michael Miller argues in his excellent study of the Bon Marché, the spectacle of the department store was one whose goal was to transform bourgeois culture into consumer culture by commodifying its artistic pursuits – by holding music concerts, providing reading rooms, and mounting art exhibitions – then artists like the Impressionists had to find means to carve out a role that balanced their economic needs with their desire for autonomy and their commitment to "the painting of modern life," a life that was more and more associated with shopping.[21]

The second possible answer to the question of the imprecision of class and social station in Degas's images of millinery shops is more interesting, and has more far-reaching implications regarding the limits of the Impressionist's gaze in relation to the world of commerce. It starts, in fact, with a fairly banal observation: the fact that these pictures were studio fictions, many posed by Degas's friend Mary Cassatt, who was not necessarily even depicted wearing her own clothes.[22] As such, they may lack the veneer of realism that seems apparent in other of his directly observed and acute scenes of social life. That the pictures failed to achieve an "accurate" transcription of their subject was noted by Degas's critics: "Degas does not go beyond the short anecdote," complained Gustave Coquiot.

> His paintings and drawings of milliners are not by any means ravishing successes. . . . If Degas cannot give you the complete character of all these women, so be it! . . . [B]ut, in truth, he could have gone beyond photographic documentation, this so-called painter of "modern truths." . . . He never considered what could really be at the center of feminine thinking![23]

Coquiot's comment is curious. While it is more likely that he was lamenting the loss of feminine sentimentality and prettiness in the face of Degas's documentary "objectivity," it also seems to suggest that what was lacking in the artist's work was a specifically feminine viewpoint: that what Degas's images of millinery shops picture is not a woman's world, but a woman's world imagined by men. This should not surprise us – after all, Degas may have been less schooled in the etiquette of the millinery shop than he was in that of the wings of the ballet or the dance studios of Paris, given that while the bourgeois *flâneur* had access to the latter of those spaces (and the young women who worked there), the *luxe* boutiques that Degas depicts were hardly accessible to him in the same way.[24] These salons were rarely the site of mixed-sex shopping in the mid-nineteenth century; the Annenberg picture seems to represent, in fact, a very private haute-couture-type dressing room, to which men would probably not have had access under any circumstances. He could only depict them in his mind's eye, in other words, as a space off-limits to his presence.

Such an approach, in the depiction of scenes of shops and shopping, was not at all unusual in modern life painting of the period. Take, for example, James Tissot's painting of *The Shop Girl* (c. 1883–85), part of his series of paintings on the theme of *La Femme à Paris*, in which a saleswoman holds open the door for the departing customer (whose place the viewer occupies in front of the canvas), while in the background, another young woman is ogled by a top-hatted gentleman walking by the shop window (Figure 30). Because the shop in question seems to specialize in lace and trimmings – hardly catering, then, to the male customer – we are left with two interpretive possibilities: first, that the viewer/departing customer is conceived within the painting to be a woman, in which case the signs of sexual invitation embodied in the saleswoman would seem inexplicable;[25] or second, that the claims to realism in the painting – the accuracy of detail, the effort at documentation present here – merely disguise the fact that, as a space more available to women than men, the *flâneur*-artist could only experience that space via a fantasy of power and control. That the salesgirl seems to flirt with the customer is not merely part of the larger mythology of the working woman in this period – it is intimately bound up with one of the few ways, in the representational terms of the historical moment, that the *flâneur* could access the place in which she worked.

While Tissot can only imagine male access to the space of the lace shop in terms of such a fiction hinging on a titillating transvestitism of the viewing subject, Degas

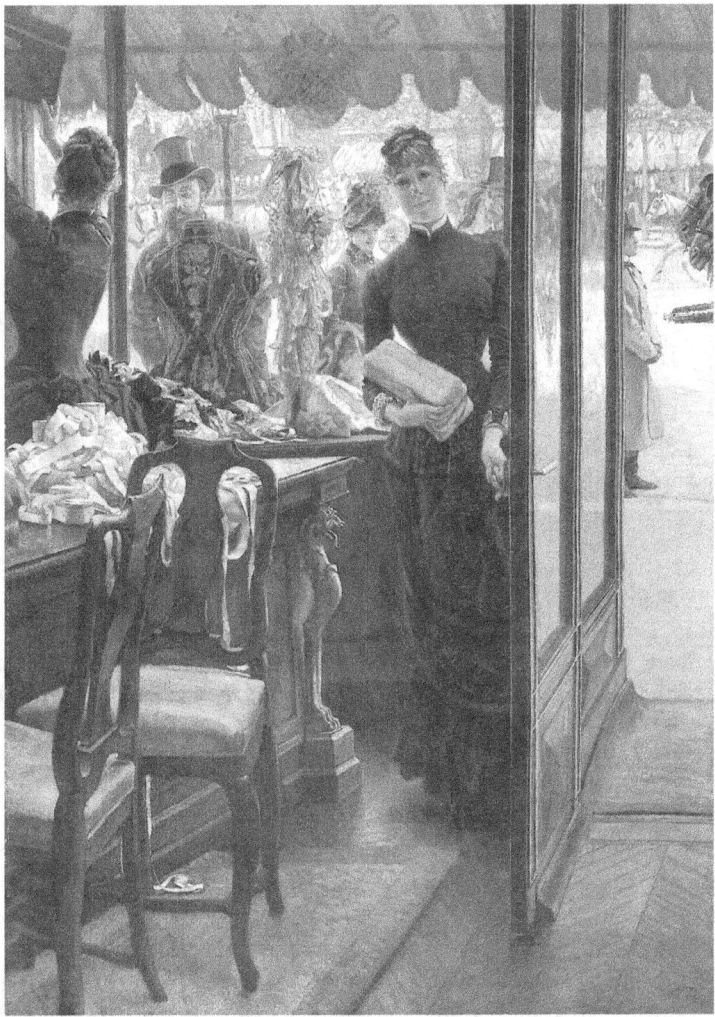

30 James Tissot, *The Shop Girl*, c. 1883–85

insists upon a quite different construction of the position of the male viewing subject. In their claim of allowing visual access to a site which might otherwise be off-
limits to the artist's gaze, Degas's milliner pictures have much more in common
with his pictures of women at their toilettes, with which they were shown at the
1886 Impressionist exhibition, than might at first be obvious.[26] Displayed under
the title *Suite de nus*, those images have provoked countless questions about the
class of the woman depicted, given the artist's seemingly unusual access into a very
private feminine space.[27] Perhaps in order to explain the painter's access to women
in their most intimate moments, the bather images have been seen most often in
terms of voyeurism, with an imaginary "view through a keyhole" justifying both

the subject and the structure of the images in question: Gustave Geffroy, in his review of the 1886 exhibition, wrote that "the artist wanted to paint a woman *who did not know she was being watched*, as one would see her hidden by a curtain or through a keyhole."[28]

For many of the pictures of women in hat shops – a similarly inaccessible space for the *flâneur* – the device that frames and structures our view is not the keyhole but the *vitrine* or shop window. In fact, a number of Degas's milliner scenes – especially the Museum of Modern Art's *At the Milliner's* (c. 1882) and the Art Institute's *The Millinery Shop* (1884/90) – are composed to suggest that they are scenes glimpsed by a passer-by on the street: the cut-off, glancing view on to the scene, the elevated viewpoint, and the unself-consciousness of the observed women all contribute to the effect, as does the fact that Degas, very unusually, began glazing his oil paintings as well as his pastels in the 1880s, the glass in the frame suggesting the *vitrine* of the represented shop. At the time that these two milliner paintings were exhibited at the last Impressionist exhibition in 1886, the British writer George Moore commented on this innovative perspective:

> Perhaps the most astonishing revolution of all was the introduction of the shop window into art. Think of a large plate-glass window, full of bonnets, a girl leaning forward to gather one! Think of the monstrous and wholly unbearable thing any other painter would have contrived from such a subject; and then imagine a dim, strange picture, the subject of which is hardly at first clear; a strangely contrived composition, full of the dim, sweet, sad poetry of female work.[29]

While some commentators have found in this "shop-window composition" evidence for the idea that Degas imagined his viewer as a bourgeois *woman* out window-shopping, I find this highly unlikely.[30] Rather, I see these images as very specifically providing the only visual access to this subject that was possible within the terms of Impressionism: that of the botanizer on the asphalt, the *flâneur*, as he makes his way through the city streets, glancing through windows all the while. What I would like to argue is that the ambiguities present in these works are the result of an enforced distance – here imagined as a view through the shop window – between the *flâneur*-artist and his subject, a distance that was strangely out of sync with the assumption of total visual possession of the city offered by the fiction of *flânerie*.

If the increasingly close relationship between art exhibition and consumer culture was one reason that the Impressionists never painted the department store, another, more crucial one is found in the intersection of visuality and bourgeois masculinity in the figure of the *flâneur*. In "Modernity and the Spaces of Femininity," Griselda Pollock proposes to chart the spaces of modern Paris according to the late nineteenth-century ideology of a "separation of spheres," to create a symbolic map rooted in the ideology of gender rather than in any physical or architectural organization of space.[31] As such, Pollock's argument needs to be read not as a literal accounting of what men and women could *see* in modern Paris – what spaces they actually had access to, what sights/sites were authorized or forbidden to men or to women. Rather, hers is a map of what bourgeois men and women could be *seen to see*. Organized around the psychoanalytic concept of the gaze, Pollock's work signals to the reader that what she is interested in is the way in which the bourgeois subject, especially the female bourgeois subject, was constituted through vision: it was not simply that painters like Morisot or Cassatt could not go to the *cafés-concerts* or wander on the streets, it is rather that they could not *picture* those activities and retain their designation as respectable women of a certain class.

If Pollock is correct to say that the range of Impressionist subjects maps the *flâneur*'s gaze (she follows Baudelaire on this point), the question arises as to why he could not be seen to see the department store – why this space could not be pictured according to the terms of modern life painting. The answer has to do not with the reality (architectural, commercial, social) of that space – how it was built or how it was used – but rather with how its use was coded, what could be admitted as to its use. The department store and the mix of commerce and sexuality which it came to represent was not simply something that Impressionism *happened not* to see, but rather something that that mode of painting, organized as it was around the *flâneur*'s gaze, *could not* be seen to see: could not picture, in other words.[32]

How was male access to the department store represented? Certainly, there seems to have been a shift from images of the massive *magasins de nouveautés* of the 1840s and 1850s when men as often as women were depicted as clients, to those of the *grands magasins*, or department stores, after the mid-1860s.[33] These later images of the department store proper, especially those published as part of the stores' publicity campaigns by magazines such as *L'Illustration* and *Le Monde illustré*, tended to show male customers not as consumers, but as patrons of the more intellectual and cultural pursuits ostensibly offered by the businesses, especially the reading rooms or paintings galleries in establishments such as the Bon Marché and the Grands Magasins du Louvre, which proposed ways to pass the time for those not interested in shopping.[34]

This is not to say that men did not shop in the department stores; in fact, for all the recent work on the architecture of the *grands magasins* as evidencing a tailoring of built space to the needs of women,[35] it was equally the case that the layout and design of the stores was directed towards the particular desires of men. The department stores pictured male use of their spaces as primarily that of relaxation and edification – and we do well to remember that most of the images (and the copy) from articles appearing in the popular press on the subject were marketing tools produced by the department store itself, and do not form any sort of journalistic record of the actual use of the space – at the same time as the male customer was courted with as much vigor as the female. The decision of most nineteenth-century department stores to place the menswear on the street level of the store, for example, often with access via a separate entrance, or to place women's lace and lingerie departments on a higher floor, was geared towards minimizing men's potential embarrassment at having to mix with the female clientele.[36]

Deflecting the male customer's squeamishness about shopping – an activity that was increasingly coded as "feminine" in the last third of the nineteenth century[37] – had an added benefit for the stores themselves: it allowed the establishments to sell themselves (to husbands and fathers, one presumes, as much as to female shoppers) as "safe" spaces for a proper woman to go out in public. One advertisement for Le Printemps department store capitalized on both the privacy this arrangement afforded women shoppers, and the petty bourgeois fantasy of social advancement (Figure 31). In an image composed of fourteen vignettes, we witness a series of encounters in the store, overlooked by quasi-mythological personifications of Le Printemps and other heavenly attendants.[38] Amid scenes that express the characters' wonder at this new machine for selling – at the functioning of the elevator, the

31 "Les Grands Magasins du Printemps," *Le Monde illustré*, 11 April 1874

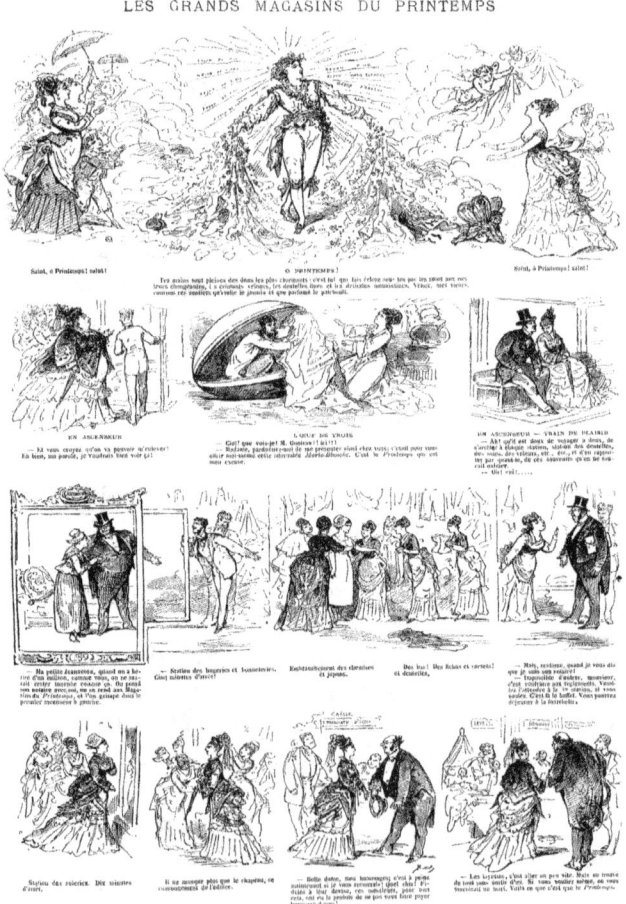

selection and range of merchandise, etc. – we see a narrative involving a young woman named Jeanneton and her solicitor. "My dear Jeanneton," says the lawyer, "when one inherits a million francs, like you have, you cannot remain turned out in such a manner. You must take your solicitor with you, make a visit to the Magasins du Printemps, and climb the first staircase on the left." Later on, after witnessing the solicitor and his young charge in various departments, we find him in a state, facing a store employee who refuses him entrance to one of the floors: "But, Madam, I tell you that I am her solicitor!" The employee calmly replies, "It is not possible for you to enter, Monsieur – it is against the rules. If you would like, you can wait on the 7th floor, at the buffet. You can have some lunch." When Jeanneton descends from her transformation at the hands of the fashionable sales assistants, her lawyer is ecstatic: "Beautiful lady, my compliments: I could hardly recognize you! How chic! True to their motto, these gentlemen have the wisdom to not make you pay too much for all this!" They leave the store, Jeanneton's male companion eager to go out and find her a husband suitable to her new station in life. This advertisement plays on many fantasies and anxieties, not least of which is the anxiety over women's entry into public space, something that the department stores not only invited, but depended upon for their very existence. While the bumbling solicitor in this comic advertisement expresses outrage at his being barred from a floor of the shop that specializes in stockings, corsets, and other lacy underthings, the reader is meant to read that exclusion as one of the attractive features of the shopping experience, as attractive as the low prices and quality goods.

This exclusion of men from some floors of the *grands magasins*, and the extent to which the shopping experience was coded as a female one – almost all department stores referred to their customers in their advertisements and other publicity materials as *les dames* – had a flip side. For all that this type of segregation was desirable both from a male and female perspective as a way of portraying the shopping experience as eminently safe and respectable, there emerged a comic trope in the popular literary and visual culture of the period that expressed a deep masculine anxiety over what, exactly, was taking place in those off-limit spaces. A fictional account entitled "Les Magasins du Mauvais Marché" that appeared in *La Vie Parisienne* in 1876 – a magazine whose target audience seemed to be the savvy man-about-town – tells the story of a young, *haut bourgeois* named Lionnel, who enters into a wager with a friend to prove that, as he believes, there is no such thing as an honest woman (Figure 32).[39] They chose a victim from the crowds at the Opéra, a young, pretty *bourgeoise* from the provinces. Over the next twenty-four hours, Lionnel is rebuffed in his attempts to make an acquaintance with the woman by M. du Martoy, her suspicious and jealous husband. Finally, the night before the couple is to leave Paris, Lionnel sees his chance: Mme du Martoy is scheduled to spend the day at the Mauvais Marché department store.

That morning, Mme du Martoy's overprotective spouse drops her off at Le Mauvais Marché. The young woman is nervous at being left alone in such a bustling and chaotic place. Her husband reassures her – "It is a completely

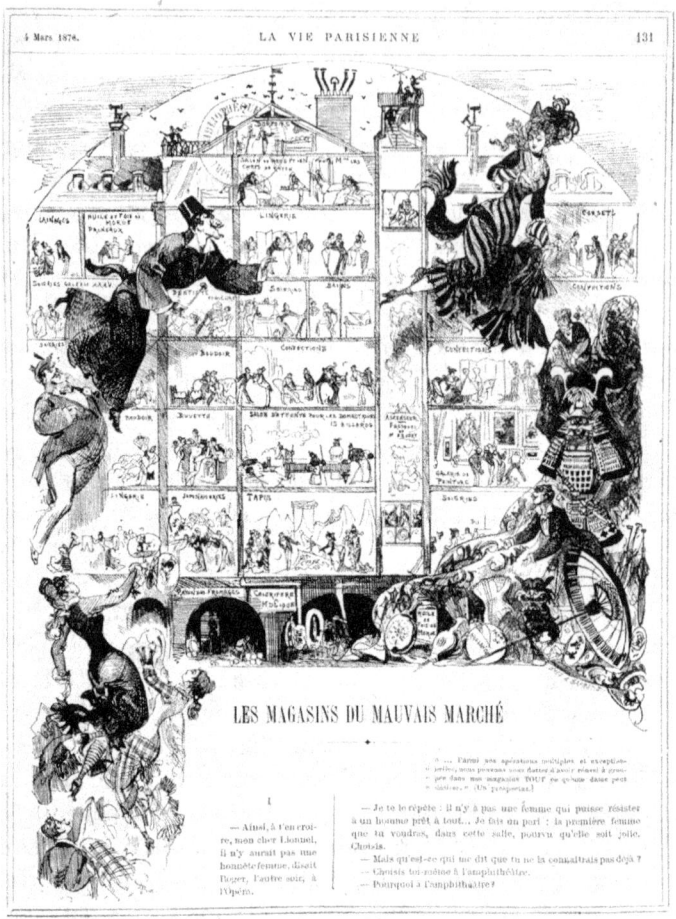

trustworthy establishment . . . I would never leave you this way at the Louvre or at
Printemps, but here it's different" – and arranges to meet later. Lionnel, seizing
the opportunity of finding Mme du Martoy alone, springs into action, discarding
his coat and hat and picking up a box of merchandise, pretending to be a salesman;
he approaches his victim and, all the while making his sales pitch, interjects a
whispered entreaty to the woman to meet him privately. Mme du Martoy is sur-
prised to see her acquaintance selling garters at a department store, but is hardly
displeased. Availing themselves of the convenient department store service of
hiring a sales assistant to gather one's list of merchandise without having to actually spend the time shopping, Lionnel takes her to a private meeting room which
he has filled with goods culled from the store's massive selection, transforming it
into a boudoir of seduction. As Lionnel proceeds to win his bet, M. du Martoy is
left standing on a street corner, increasingly anxious as to his wife's whereabouts,
lamenting his decision to leave her alone in such a corrupting place:

He was truly a provincial fellow; a woman, according to him, could never venture alone in Paris without exposing herself to the most serious dangers. If he had left her alone in the Mauvais Marché, it was only because the store's reputation for morality would shelter her from all unwanted approaches. Why hadn't he done like everyone else? Why hadn't he planned to meet his wife in front of the statue of the Virgin of Bouzingot [a popular meeting place in the store]? That's what it was there for.

Hardly quality literature, to say the least, but the features of this tawdry tale – the corrupting gadabout, the innocent provincial husband, the naïve but not entirely unwilling wife, and the department store not only providing the opportunity for a secret and anonymous assignation but also the merchandise one needs to seal the deal – are commonplace in popular culture from the period.[40] And it is interesting to note that, while the department store in these accounts is portrayed as a place in which wives engage in secret and nefarious activities precisely because of their husbands' lack of interest or inclination for shopping, the story in question in fact takes particular care in describing exactly the sort of commodities that assisted Lionnel in his game of seduction, the language often sounding like advertising copy:

A double-thick carpet, into which one literally sank, with a white background and bunches of cherries with bright green leaves. The octagonal room was lined from floor to ceiling with pink satin silk and gold buttons, like a railway car, quilted like a priest's overcoat and perfumed like a sachet of handkerchiefs. The mirror-covered ceiling reflected the carpet below. In a corner, a slightly inclined sofa . . . covered, as if attached with four pins, by a shawl in pink crêpe de Chine with blue flowers and green leaves, and bordered by a fringe. Add two cushions, and you have a sort of ceremonial bed on which a princess would sleep, fully clothed, in ancient times.

In this and countless other stories and images from the period, male access to the department store was pictured as extremely particular: the bourgeois, provincial husband only bothered to visit the hardware and furniture departments during his visit to the Mauvais Marché – and even that limited interest in shopping is presented as a sign of his faltering masculine authority in the story – while the *haut bourgeois* Casanova was successful precisely because he managed to transform a corner of the most public of places, the department store, into an extremely private one. In this latter case, especially, the story makes it clear that Lionnel was only able to do so because of the vast array of products available in this temple of commerce, so that even though Lionnel was not at the Mauvais Marché to shop, he certainly took advantage of the goods on offer. More importantly, the reader of this story, who was presumably meant to identify with the cad Lionnel, became, without having to leave his armchair, a vicarious consumer whose narrative pleasure was inextricably tied to the accounting of fabrics, upholstery, and *objets d'art* that were central to this torrid tale. One could argue, on the basis of this story and many more like it that are peppered through the popular journals of the day, that the images that were key in constructing the bourgeois male subject as someone not only disinclined towards but excluded from the sphere of consumption were those very images that inspired his own desiring gaze upon the commodity, that turned him into a species of consumer despite the fact that shopping was an activity – in the symbolic economy of the separation of spheres – allocated to women.

It was not until the 1890s, with Felix Vallotton's series of woodcuts and panel paintings of department stores that the iconography would enter, if only briefly, the avant-garde repertoire (Figure 33). There are a number of reasons one could offer for the willingness of this artist to embrace a subject matter that had been anxiously rejected by earlier modern life painters: first among these has to do with the Nabis group's very different understanding of the relation between art and commercial culture than that held by Impressionism, such that artists moved seamlessly between the creation of paintings and café advertisements, or fine art and decorative objects; second, the Nabis artists, especially those involved in a more *intimiste* approach to painting, embraced the "feminine" worlds of domesticity, women's work, and privacy in a way almost unprecedented in the history of modern painting.[41]

And even so, while Vallotton may have found it appropriate to depict the Bon Marché, his vision still retained traces of the *flâneur*'s anxiety in the face of that site. Both his triptych painting and his woodcuts on the theme are unusual in that they show male sales clerks seeing to the needs of their female clientele: while this adequately mirrored the reality of who was being employed by the department store before the turn of the twentieth century, it was rare to find a depiction of the commercial realm, whether in the popular press or in the exhibition hall, that did not elide the desiring (male) consumer's gaze with the desiring (male) sexual gaze, and

33 Félix Vallotton,
The Bon Marché, 1893

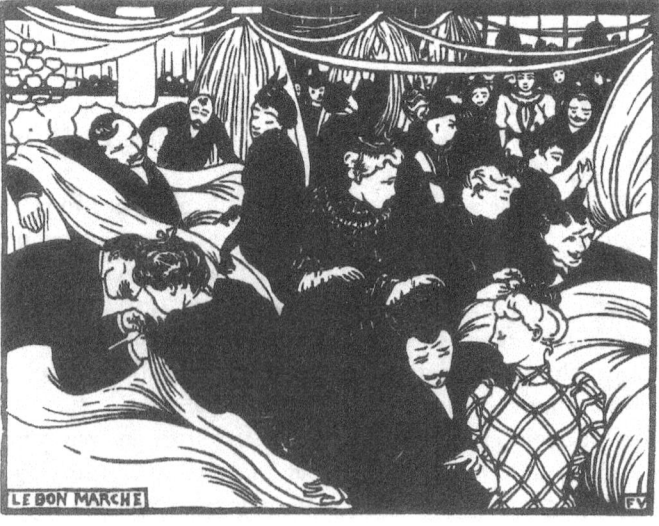

therefore image the salesperson as a woman.[42] This is not to say, of course, that desire – even the sexual kind – is not the primary theme of Vallotton's work. Indeed, the woodcut of 1893, with its undulating rhythms of swaths of linens, obsequious salesmen, and swooning female shoppers, presents the department store as the site of an almost endless series of intimate encounters between anonymous men and women, and thus this world of private, feminine sovereignty becomes, for Vallotton, as pathetic and suspect as the bourgeois interior with its occupants' hypocritical claims to fidelity, as pictured in works such as *Le Mensonge* from the *Intimités* series of 1897–98. What has changed here is not the coding of the department store as a feminine space, or a space of subversive female desire, but rather the lens through which such a mythology could be pictured. No longer interested in maintaining the fiction of the *flâneur*'s masculine authority, more invested in the world of anxious battles between the sexes, Vallotton could depict the department store, finally, for what it represented in the bourgeois, masculine imagination: a site where the separation of spheres was revealed to be a sham, where the careful, exclusive boundaries that had been drawn around public life were consistently and insistently transgressed.

Notes

1 Faculty support grants from Purchase College, State University of New York underwrote the research and illustration of this text. I would like to thank E. McBreen, T. McDonough, and T. Garb, all of whom provided invaluable comments. This piece is dedicated to my sister, Suneeta D'Souza, who naturally comes to mind when I think about shopping.

2 K. Ross, "Introduction: Shopping," in E. Zola, *The Ladies' Paradise [Au bonheur des dames]* (Berkeley: University of California Press, 1992), p. v.

3 E. Zola, *Correspondances (1880–1883)*, ed. B. H. Bakker (Montreal: Presses de l'Université de Montréal, 1983), p. 329; cited and translated in K. Ross, "Introduction," p. xi.

4 For example, Baedeker's 1898 guide to Paris lists not only the names and locations of the stores, but gives a sense of their uniqueness and history, as well. K. Baedeker, *Paris et ses environs: manuel du voyageur* (Leipzig: Karl Baedeker, and Paris: Paul Ollendorf, 1898), p. 41. Later on in the guide, in an exposition of the sights in the Faubourg Saint-Germain, the Bon Marché is singled out as an architectural curiosity in the neighborhood (p. 255).

5 Quoted in M. Simon, *Mode et peinture: le Second Empire et l'Impressionisme* (Paris: Hazan, 1995), p. 248, n. 202. All translations are mine, unless otherwise noted.

6 On the topic of Impressionism's imbrication in late nineteenth-century consumer culture, see R. L. Herbert, *Impressionism: Art, Leisure, and Parisian Society* (New Haven and London: Yale University Press, 1988); as well as more recently R. E. Iskin, "Impressionism, Women, and the Public Sphere of Modernity" (Ph.D. dissertation, University of California at Los Angeles, 1997), and her article, "Selling, Seduction, and Soliciting the Eye: Manet's *Bar at the Folies-Bergère*," *Art Bulletin* 77, no. 1 (March 1995), pp. 25–44.

7   See, for example, the literature on Manet's *Bar at the Folies-Bergère*: the fact that this
    painting represents an instance of buying and selling commodities has been explored
    only relatively recently by art historians, though writers such as T. J. Clark have made
    much of the class and sexual implications of the relationship between buyer and seller.
    See R. E. Iskin, "Selling, Seduction, and Soliciting the Eye," as well as a number of the
    essays in *Twelve Views of Manet's Bar*, ed. B. R. Collins (Princeton, N.J.: Princeton
    University Press, 1996).

8   H. Clayson, *Painted Love: Prostitution in French Art of the Impressionist Era* (New
    Haven and London: Yale University Press, 1991), p. 131.

9   H. Clayson, *Painted Love*, p. 130.

10 E. Lipton, *Looking into Degas: Uneasy Images of Women and Modern Life* (Berkeley and
    London: University of California Press, 1986), pp. 151–164.

11 A third account of these works is provided by Iskin, who interprets them as stagings of
    the female, bourgeois consumer's desire for the commodity. See R. E. Iskin,
    "Impressionism, Women, and the Public Sphere of Modernity," pp. 75–126.

12 In *At the Milliner's* (c. 1882, Museum of Modern Art), the assistant is squeezed into the
    upper-left corner of the image, a gangly silhouette with beribboned hats in each hand;
    in another scene, she is reduced to a squid-like hand, which gingerly fluffs a ribbon or
    flower on a hat she is about to hand to her client (1882–85, Collection of Mr and Mrs
    Paul Mellon).

13 While many commentators have preferred to interpret the scene as depicting two
    women of equal station – see, for example, C. Bailey, *Masterpieces of Impressionism and
    Post-Impressionism: The Annenberg Collection* (Philadelphia: Philadelphia Museum of
    Art, 1989) – the construction of the image suggests otherwise; it may have begun as a
    picture of a milliner arranging a hat on a hatstand, the second figure only added later.

14 Here I diverge from A. Callen, who finds that Degas clearly distinguished the social
    stations of his figures. A. Callen, *The Spectacular Body: Science, Method and Meaning in
    the Work of Degas* (New Haven and London: Yale University Press, 1995), pp. 31–35.

15 For this and the discussion that follows, see M. Brown, *Degas and the Business of Art: A
    Cotton Office in New Orleans* (University Park, Penn.: Penn State University Press,
    1994), and C. Armstrong, *Odd Man Out: Readings of the Work and Reputation of Edgar
    Degas* (Chicago and London: University of Chicago Press, 1991), pp. 21–72.

16 C. Armstrong, *Odd Man Out*, pp. 21–28.

17 M. Brown, *Degas and the Business of Art*, p. 134.

18 In this sense, it is probably no coincidence that he chose to include two of his milliner
    paintings in the 1886 Impressionist show, for that year the question of Impressionism's
    relationship to the commercial dealer system was particularly fraught. See M. Ward,
    "The Rhetoric of Independence and Innovation," in C. S. Moffett, *The New Painting:
    Impressionism 1874–1886* (San Francisco: The Fine Arts Museum, 1986), pp. 421–425.

19 M. B. Miller, *The Bon Marché: Bourgeois Culture and the Department Store, 1869–1920*
    (Princeton, N.J.: Princeton University Press, 1981).

20 See, for example, Bertall's "Revue Comique du Salon de 1875," *L'Illustration* (May 15,
    1875), p. 325. In a vignette titled "L'Exposition pour les dames," two women excitedly
    compare notes on the attractive dresses they have seen in the paintings on display. An
    illustration in *La Vie Parisienne* from May 12, 1877, pp. 258–259, entitled "A l'exposition
    de peinture – modes et confections pour l'année 1877," depicts a number of paintings of
    female subjects (including Manet's *Nana*) as if they were models in a fashion show.

21 See R. E. Iskin, "Selling, Seduction, and Soliciting the Eye."

22 S. Boggs, *Degas* (New York: Metropolitan Museum of Art, and Ottawa: National Gallery of Canada, 1988), p. 396.

23 G. Coquiot, *Degas*, 2nd edn (Paris, 1924), pp. 132–4.

24 Indeed, Impressionist painting generally shows us women in intimate situations, but almost always those situations would have been available to the *flâneur's* gaze: women in brothels, women in the private spaces of the home, women at vulnerable moments in the café, etc. Degas is unusual because he has, in the cases of the bathers and the *modistes*, attempted to depict women in contexts unavailable otherwise to the male gaze.

25 Or almost so. T. Garb imagines the viewer to be a female customer; thus the leering man on the street implies, disturbingly, that she (the viewer) may be stepping into a drama of sexual invitation and exchange as soon as she leaves the shop. See T. Garb, "James Tissot's 'Parisienne' and the Making of the Modern Woman," in *Bodies of Modernity: Figure and Flesh in Fin-de-Siècle France* (London and New York: Thames and Hudson, 1998), pp. 105–8.

Clayson, in an attempt to rationalize this seeming contradiction between the type of shop depicted and the implied gender of the client/viewer, has quite unusually identified the shop as a haberdashery, thereby imagining the customer as quite properly male. See H. Clayson, *Painted Love*, p. 124.

26 M. Ward, "The Rhetoric of Independence."

27 Most commentators have argued that the very fact that they are bathing, considering the suspicion with which the practice was regarded by nineteenth-century hygiene specialists, suggests that we are looking at prostitutes, or at the very least women of uncertain morality, even though they seem to be shown within bourgeois surroundings. See, for example, E. Lipton, *Looking into Degas*, pp. 151–86; H. Dawkins, "Managing Degas," in *Dealing with Degas: Representations of Women and the Politics of Vision*, eds R. Kendall and G. Pollock (New York: Universe Press, 1992), pp. 133–45; and A. Callen, *The Spectacular Body*.

28 G. Geffroy, *La Justice*, May 26, 1886, quoted in C. S. Moffett, *The New Painting*, p. 453 (emphasis added). While for many art historians, this "keyhole view" is understood as a symbolic structure, Dawkins has suggested a more literal source: an illicit practice in nineteenth-century Paris, whereby upper-class, "respectable" men would rent rooms in the public baths that were equipped with small, hidden peepholes, allowing them to watch women bathe. See H. Dawkins, "Managing Degas," p. 143.

29 G. Moore, *Impressions and Opinions* (New York: Brentano's, 1972), p. 230; quoted in R. E. Iskin, "Impressionism, Women, and the Public Sphere of Modernity," p. 95.

30 See, for example, Brettell's entry on *The Millinery Shop* (1879/84) in R. Brettell and S. F. McCullagh, *Degas in the Art Institute of Chicago* (Chicago: The Art Institute of Chicago, and New York: Harry N. Abrams, 1984), p. 131; and R. E. Iskin, "Impressionism, Women, and the Public Sphere of Modernity."

31 G. Pollock, "Modernity and the Spaces of Femininity," in *Vision and Difference: Femininity, Feminism and the Histories of Art* (London and New York: Routledge, 1988).

32 What of the female Impressionists? Cassatt, Morisot, and Gonzalez never tackled the subject of the department store, despite its construction as a so-called "woman's space" in its marketing and popular reputation. Pollock gives us a clue as to the reason: while male Impressionist painters had access to both the public and private worlds of the

flâneur, female Impressionist painters were restricted to painting only *the private world of the flâneur* rather than the worlds (public and private) of the *bourgeoise*. One of the implications of the argument that there was no such entity as the *flâneuse* is that there was no way of conceiving or representing the public life of women within the terms of modern life painting, regardless of the producer's gender.

33 See, for example, two caricatures by Daumier which appeared in *Le Charivari* in 1844; in these, as in many other images of this period, the customer pictured is a top-hatted *bourgeois*.

34 The reading room of the Louvre department store, shown populated almost exclusively by men, was illustrated in *Le Monde illustré* (October 1879). A similar illustration, this time depicting the Bon Marché's *salon de lecture*, appeared in *L'Illustration*, October 10, 1874, p. 237. The paintings gallery at the Bon Marché was pictured in *L'Illustration*, March 6, 1875, p. 164.

35 A number of scholars have recently begun to argue for the department store as a type of "feminine" built space; the work of the feminist architectural historian, Esther de Costa Meyer, is central in this endeavor. While the department store was certainly organized, at least partially, around the model of the female consumer, it was equally (if more subtly) organized around the male consumer: in other words, far from being a space of femininity, it was a space for consumption, and needs to be understood as such.

36 On the solicitation of male consumers by department stores, and male bourgeois participation in the world of fashion in the English context, see C. Breward, *The Hidden Consumer: Masculinities, Fashion, and City Life, 1860–1914* (Manchester and New York: Manchester University Press, 1999). Many of Breward's observations can quite properly be applied to the situation in France.

37 The literature on this question of the complexities of gender vis-à-vis consumerism and the department store in particular is vast. For a good overview, see G. Crossick and S. Jaumain, "The World of the Department Store: Distribution, Culture, and Social Change," in *Cathedrals of Consumption: The European Department Store, 1850–1939*, eds G. Crossick and S. Jaumain (Aldershot and Brookfield, Mass.: Ashgate, 1999). See also R. Bowlby, *Just Looking: Consumer Culture in Dreiser, Gissing, and Zola* (New York: Methuen, 1985); R. Williams, *Dream Worlds: Mass Consumption in Late 19th-Century France* (Berkeley: University of California Press, 1982); and J. Walkowitz, *City of Dreadful Delight: Narratives of Sexual Danger in Late-Victorian London* (Chicago: University of Chicago Press, 1992). For a more recent, excellent account, see L. Tiersten, *Marianne in the Market: Envisioning Consumer Society in Fin-de-Siècle France* (Berkeley and Los Angeles: University of California Press, 2001).

38 "Les Grands Magasins du Printemps," *Le Monde illustré*, April 11, 1874, p. 237.

39 "Les Magasins du Mauvais Marché," *La Vie Parisienne*, March 4, 1876, pp. 131–134. The "Mauvais Marché" department store was the journal's fictional version of the type, and comical stories about it recur throughout the years.

40 An illustrated story that appeared in *La Vie Parisienne* in 1874, for example, entitled "Une première aux Magasins du Printemps: visite aux nouveaux travaux," includes a four-act melodrama about a man who finds his wife getting into an elevator with another man, and ends up having a duel with him to defend his husbandly honor.

41 See S. Sidlauskas, "Contesting Femininity: Vuillard's Family Pictures," *Art Bulletin* 79, no. 1 (March 1997), pp. 85–111.

42 In fact, until well into the twentieth century, the great majority of salesclerks in
    Parisian department stores were men; women, when employed, were mostly doing in-
    house manufacturing or piecework attached to the store, as opposed to more public
    positions. When Zola visited the Bon Marché in the 1880s, only 152 of the nearly two
    thousand employees were female. See M. B. Miller, *The Bon Marché*, p. 78; and Claude
    Lesselier, "Employées de grands magasins à Paris (avant 1914)," *Le Mouvement social*
    no. 105 (October–December 1978), pp. 109–126.

10

City of strangers

Tom McDonough

"A passer-by is someone who looks like everyone else and who cannot be distinguished from anyone. A passer-by resembles nothing so much as another passer-by." So began author P. J. Stahl's physiognomy of that modern urban figure, the *passant*, published in the fall of 1844 in the anthology *Le Diable à Paris*.[1] For Stahl, the passer-by – invariably a male type – was characterized above all by his invisibility, by his perfect similitude to everyone and no one in particular. This condition was, of course, understood as a product of the metropolis's anonymity. Stahl continued:

> Passers-by exist only in Paris. Someone from the provinces has no idea, or only a slight idea, of what a passer-by is. A man you know is certainly not a passer-by. In the provinces you always more or less know a man who passes by and where he is going, but a passer-by is a man whose destination is unknown to you.[2]

Already at this point in the second quarter of the nineteenth century, the primary tropes of a bourgeois myth of metropolitan life had taken the shape they were to retain through their paradigmatic recounting some fifty years later by the burgeoning field of urban sociology. Stahl too would recognize life in the provincial town as defined by affective relationships, by the mutual recognition of acquaintances whose lives repeatedly intersected in myriad everyday interactions; but in the capital, the crowd was composed of individuals whose varied trajectories would never meet, whose goals would remain unknown, unable to be guessed. Within the crowd the *passant* was engulfed in solitude, unaware of the other lives that swirled around him, or aware of them only as obstacles to his progress.

> Passers-by are people who meet, who pass each other, and who – as long as they do not bump into each other – carry on without even noticing that they have met. The passer-by is someone who is alone and who remains alone amidst everyone else, who does not care about you and to whom you yourself are indifferent, wrongly perhaps, for every passer-by is a secret.[3]

The origins of this atomized crowd were needless to say multiply determined. The passer-by as a figure in the bourgeois mythology of the metropolis was inseparable, for example, from the increasing separation of spheres into the private realm of the domestic interior and the public realm of work.[4] Accompanying this development was a retreat of affect from the surface of public life and its apotheosis in the home; that withdrawal found expression in the near-universal adoption in the early nineteenth century of black as the masculine bourgeois uniform, which contrasted with the looser, more expressive clothing worn in the privacy of the home.[5] The indifference, even the faint hostility, which typified interaction between passers-by on the street in Stahl's account was the psychological transcription of this new dispensation. The invention of the passer-by was also related to the perception of overpopulation in the capital. As Philippe Vigier, historian of the July Monarchy, has noted, this was indeed a period of enormous demographic growth: "in fifteen years, between the two quinquennial censuses of 1831 and 1846, the Parisian population grows . . . from 785,862 inhabitants to 1,053,897" – an increase of 36 percent.[6] Yet more significant for Parisian comportment than these raw figures was perhaps the fact that the vast majority of this growth was accounted for not by the natural evolution of the Parisian population, but by migratory movements into the capital from the provinces and abroad.[7] The crowd on the street, then, was more than ever likely to be composed of people unknown to each other, of people who were unable to be located on pre-existent cognitive maps of the city. That indeterminacy was all the more reason to avoid interaction with the crowd and adopt the protective attitude of the *passant*.

The crowd of passers-by described by Stahl would later be reformulated by Georg Simmel as that paradigmatically modern phenomenon, a crowd of strangers – as, that is, one simultaneously embodying nearness and remoteness. Both commentators perceived that, on the street, passers-by might indeed be physically quite close, often uncomfortably so, but that they remained psychically distant from one another, carrying on "without even noticing that they have met," "alone amidst everyone else" – providing they did not knock into each other in the crowd's jostling. Simmel would describe this peculiarly distanced contact as a condition of mobility, whereby "the fundamentally mobile person comes into contact . . . with every individual, but is not organically connected, through established ties of kinship, locality, and occupation, with any single one."[8] If such mobility was at one time the province merely of traders or of certain ritually excluded communities, in a money-based capitalist economy, in a world where "organic" connections were disappearing in favor of the contingent bonds of business, he saw it as a generalized circumstance of urban life, a determinate factor in the fleeting contacts among *passants*.

Stahl depicted the passer-by as a solitary creature, as a stranger to all even among the thronging crowds of Paris's streets, yet this psychic distance might be bridged in the most curious fashion. Stahl concluded his opening section on the *passant* with the somewhat ominous observation that "every passer-by is a secret," a mystery waiting to be elucidated. If Simmel believed that the stranger's very distance and non-involvement allows him often to receive "the most surprising openness – confidences which sometimes have the character of a confessional"[9] – then

Stahl revealed its counterpart, namely that this distance also allowed the passer-by to become not a confessor but a screen on to which individual and collective fantasies could be projected. ("The passer-by is thus merely a relative being, . . . whose particular value is established only after having been met and judged."[10]) The stranger as screen could take on an unlimited number of roles, his very anonymity permitting the most extravagant speculation: "Since on the street nothing distinguishes one man from another, the passer-by may be, according to the onlooker's preference, a government minister or a famous actor, a prince or a member of Parliament, an ambassador or some bourgeois."[11] Yet in one crucial sense Simmel's confessor and Stahl's screen were identical: in both cases the stranger acted as a mirror, reflecting back society's desires as well as its anxieties. "For a guilty man," Stahl wrote, "a passer-by is a threat; for a drunk man, he's a friend. For a jealous man and for an ambitious man, he's a rival. For a miser, he's a thief."[12]

In the late fall and early winter of 1844, not long after Stahl's essay was published, such anxieties appeared well justified, as Paris was gripped by a series of violent night-time attacks on the city's streets. Newspaper stories like the following began to appear with disturbing regularity: "At quarter past seven on the evening of December 7th, a thirty-year-old woman . . . was coming down the Rue Marsollier, where she was going to settle a small debt. She was walking along the sidewalk beside the Théâtre-Italien and made way to allow a man to pass her, which he did."[13] This banal account of common sidewalk civility would soon take a tragic turn, signaled in the story by the substitution of a breathless present for the past tense: "abruptly turning around, he rushes at her, applies a cloth coated with tar to her face, and strikes her in the chest, knocking her against the theater's gate, whereupon he reaches into this unfortunate woman's pocket, takes the 10 francs he finds there, and escapes. All this took only a few seconds."[14] Such an audacious attack caused a great commotion in the neighborhood. Indignant residents complained to reporters that on "days when the theater is closed, these streets are barely lit, and there are certain places where the darkness is total." One inhabitant of the area went so far as to report that "almost every day, cries and calls for help can be heard," and that denizens were "most frightened, locking themselves in after nine o'clock at night." Newspapers responsibly called for the erection of a new police station, to restore order in this dangerous neighborhood ("criminals can easily hide under the shelter of the theater's canopy and escape via the numerous egresses that intersect near the square") through a more conscientious and constant regime of surveillance.[15]

Only five days later, another nocturnal attack warranted a lengthy retelling in the press:

> On the night of December 12th, at around one o'clock in the morning, M. Raymond (an *aide-major* attached to the Val-de-Grâce hospital) was returning from the Quartier Saint-Honoré. Having crossed the Place du Louvre and stepped out on to

the part of the Quai de l'Ecole which ends at the Pont-Neuf, he was suddenly attacked by an individual who, seizing him by the neck, ordered him with threats to hand over his money and his watch.[16]

This time, according to the papers, the victim managed to resist, in a way: "although the attacker had an athletic build and was strong, M. Raymond tried to repulse him, and shouted '*help! thief!*' at the top of his lungs. At the very instant of his shouts," the newspaper reassured its readers, "a patrol of policemen rushed up, but already the criminal, whom the young *aide-major* had had to confront, had time to flee, and not without having left traces of his violent abuse."[17] In contrast to the female victim, whose very vulnerability and helplessness secured the meaning of the crime's terror for a bourgeois readership, the sex and public position of Raymond forced a different telling. The newspaper would appear to be faced with a difficult task here: how to recount a successful attack while not humiliating its relatively eminent prey? Thus we get a story that described resistance to a powerful assailant largely in the form of desperate cries for help and in which, despite these valiant efforts, the thief somehow managed to escape! The account reads as a rather elaborate attempt to save face for Raymond.

An initial search of the area failed to locate the assailant, but Raymond accompanied one of the patrols along with the chief of rounds for the Quartier du Louvre in the hopes of recognizing his attacker. And indeed, by two o'clock that morning "the author of this brazen attack had been arrested while in the company of a woman of ill repute, toward the middle of the Rue Saint-Martin." Her denials of his guilt were of no use – the police were certain they had the right man. Yet despite this quick resolution to the crime, the Prefect of Police announced through the press new measures to augment the night watch: an exceptional call-up of municipal guards, the service of the army of the line, and patrols by the national guard would henceforth supplement the beats currently undertaken. "In sum," the *Journal des Débats* concluded, "the new night watch duty will actively employ 1,031 men, who will comprise . . . nearly 300 patrols." The image offered by the Prefecture was one not merely of increased numbers, but of improved organization; the goal was clearly to render the city absolutely open to observation by "assigning patrols to the same neighborhood, which they will continuously survey in every direction."[18]

Such measures were deemed necessary in order to reassure the city's population "about the exaggerated rumors which have been spreading for some days," remarked the *Journal*. And indeed, rumors were flying throughout town during the month of December. False reports far outnumbered the seemingly veritable crimes, with newspapers attempting to keep track of the shifting situation:

> Several newspapers have reported that . . . an attack took place on the rue des Dames, in Batignolles-Monceaux, by so-called murderous thieves against four people, two of whom were severely wounded. We are authorized by the mayor of the commune . . . to declare that this rumor is pure fiction.[19]

Or, "a newspaper relates that a sieur Gustave X...had been attacked at the corner of the Rue de la Marche by two individuals, who struck him with powerful blows while demanding his money, etc. Nothing justifies this assertion."[20] Or,

> A newspaper, who knows to what end, has announced that after eight o'clock at night, a swarm of bandits goes out onto the Champs-Elysées and directs a system of danger-ously concocted ambushes against passers-by. None of the deeds pointed out by the paper in question have taken place. Never have the Champs-Elysées been better guarded, better surveilled, or better lit, and never have they offered more safety to the population.[21]

This incomplete litany of reports, rumors, and counter-rumors, appearing in the journals of Paris' bourgeoisie over the course of a few weeks, presented the *passant* as a continually threatened and threatening presence. It would only seem to con-firm Louis Chevalier's contention that "'criminal' is the key word for the Paris of the first half of the 19th century," not least, as these accounts demonstrate, "because of the citizens' overwhelming preoccupation with crime as one of their normal daily worries."[22] Chevalier bolsters his account of the panic that gripped citizens of Paris in the winter of 1844–45 with a journal entry of December 21 by Delphine Gay, better known as Mme Emile de Girardin, the great chronicler of Parisian society during the July Monarchy. Her letter of that date is in fact a crucial supplement to the newspaper articles, revealing the full extent of effect of this mys-terious crime wave on the inhabitants of the city:

> For the past month, the sole topic of conversation has been the nightly assaults, hold-ups, and daring robberies. Civilization seems to have had no other result than to render criminals more skilful and crimes more ingenious; this is the true progress, the incontestable perfection.[23]

At the very opening of her chronicle, Mme de Girardin announced this ironic theme of reversal, which would recur throughout, here taking the form of the inversion of "civilization": modern progress and perfection resulted only in crime. But these thieves did not merely mock the century's pretensions to progress, they mocked its pretensions to equality as well:

> What is so terrifying about these nocturnal assaults is the assailants' noble impar-tiality. They attack rich and poor alike; they search through smart and old coats disin-terestedly; whether you have something or nothing at all is merely a more or less happy chance – they kill you first, though they may get the wrong man, but little do they care. This equality in the eyes of murder is a benefit of civilization surpassing all humanitarian dreams.[24]

What was perhaps most frightening to the denizens of Paris was that these crimes did not fit into known patterns. Mme de Girardin's evident consternation was thus exemplary: how did one, after all, explain thieves who targeted both ends of the social spectrum, who insisted on killing first and asking questions later?

After all, by the mid-1840s many city dwellers would have imagined themselves to be in possession of a rather fine-tuned set of classifications of the criminal underworld. Books such as H.-A. Frégier's *Des classes dangereuses . . .* of 1840 provided their readers with an elaborate categorizing of illegal behaviors, ranking the various infractions into a complex hierarchy of crime and insisting on the discreteness of these categories: one might thereby easily distinguish the common pickpocket from the thief, from the assassin or swindler, and so forth. Such taxonomies could become quite intricate, distinguishing the *voleur* by kind but also by preferred method, sex, and so forth.[25] Yet the attacks of December 1844 belied this systematized knowledge of crime; their randomness did not figure on the cognitive maps of Paris with which the city's middle classes were confidently equipped.

The bourgeois response to this crime wave – the only logical response to the seeming irrationality of these attacks – was, as Mme de Girardin noted, to arm itself in preparedness against all contingencies; the city took on the quality of a battlefield, and the home a garrison:

> Every evening party ends like the beginning of the fourth act of the "Huguenots," with the blessing of the daggers. Parents and friends are not allowed to leave without an arms inspection, a terrifying show of daggers, swords hidden in canes, knives, and stilettos; the elegant salon is soon transformed into a gunsmith's shop.[26]

Yet while these arms were meant precisely to reassure the middle classes of their security and their mastery of the city, the effect was precisely the opposite: "what's the good of our living in a place where we pay for the ground, space, water, air, and sunlight, if we cannot even find in it the advantages found in a prison? You may not be free there, but at least you are protected."[27] December's crime wave was thus understood by the city's middle classes as a threat to their presumed control over urban space, as an almost incomprehensible revocation of their right to that city. The ironic nostalgia for the prison's safety was precisely the longing for the more complete imposition of that carceral regime ordered by the Prefect of Police, his promise of continual surveillance of all points in the urban network (although the middle class, of course, would be the agent of this regime, and the urban "other" its subject). But Mme de Girardin did not end her account with this last set of reversals; instead, she concluded with a tale of the endangered *passant*, a story about strangers and projected anxieties which fundamentally changed the stakes of the nocturnal assaults that appeared to plague Paris that winter.

For this "deadly fear and terror," as Chevalier described it, had the curious effect of turning everyone, in the eyes of the middle classes, into a potential thief, creating a situation in which the codes of sidewalk civility could easily break down. As Mme de Girardin explained it: "the danger of being killed by city-dwelling brigands is not the only one threatening you, there is another yet more terrible: that of being killed by your friends. After eight o'clock at night," she continued, "every man who walks behind you is suspect."[28] This was the introduction to a cautionary tale that recounted how, around midnight on a recent evening, a young man was crossing the Rue Royale when he noticed a man crossing the street at the same moment. The young man turned on to the Place Louis XV and walked along the fountains at the center, increasingly nervous about the stranger behind him. In the light of the *réverbères* on the square, he was able to get a better look at the figure trailing him: "the man, who was rather poorly dressed, and was wrapped up in a dark cloak while pretending to shiver, took the same route and seemed to walk in his footsteps and in his shadow."[29] The slightest descriptive details took on an ominous tone in this account: the man's dress suggesting a lower social standing, his voluminous coat hiding his identity yet not adequately protecting him from the cold of a winter's evening along the Seine. The reader could be all but certain that this nocturnal stalker had designs on the youth, hurrying home at this late hour. The disquieted young man increased his pace, reaching the Pont de la Concorde, as the mysterious figure continued to follow him. The two turned down the Quai d'Orsay, and when the former crossed the street along the quai to reach the Rue de Poitiers, the cloaked figure did the same. About to walk down this dark street, he finally turned around and confronted his follower in a desperate attempt to ward off the attack that he was certain approached. Raising his walking stick and speaking in a firm voice, he asked "'why are you following me, Monsieur?'" The response he received, however, was entirely unexpected: "'because I am dying of fright,' answers the unfortunate fellow in a trembling voice. 'I feel quite weak, and I hoped that, if I was attacked, you might well defend me, you, Monsieur, who are so strong.'"[30] His fears dispelled, the terrifying stranger transformed in an instant into a trembling convalescent himself fearful of attack, the young man laughed and agreed to accompany the man safely to his door.

Such urban fears were reflected in the press as well as in private correspondence. Caricaturist Honoré Daumier drew a cartoon for *Le Charivari* – published December 21, 1844, not coincidentally the very day Mme de Girardin recorded her narrative – as the first of his "Paris in Winter" series; entitled "Between eleven o'clock and midnight," it took advantage of the topical concern with crime to examine the mores of the city's bourgeoisie (Figure 34).[31] In it two middle-aged bourgeois men rush down a darkened Parisian street; turning a corner they suddenly come face to face with each other under the harsh light of a *réverbère*. Daumier recorded their thoughts at the bottom of the plate, one man exclaiming to himself "damnation . . . here's quite a fierce-looking fellow . . . he must be a stabber . . . and I don't have even the smallest dagger," while his twin worries "confound it . . . I'm done for . . . this scoundrel is surely a robber and a murderer . . . I'd give ten years of my wife's life for a pistol!" Identically dressed, bespectacled, and altogether quite proper, the night and the current rumors coursing through the capital nonetheless amplified their anxieties until each assumes the other to be a cutthroat. Contrast this image with Daumier's previous vision of Parisian street crime, an image from his "Emotions parisiennes" series published five years previous, in the November 24, 1839 number of *Le Charivari*.[32] Here the young bourgeois

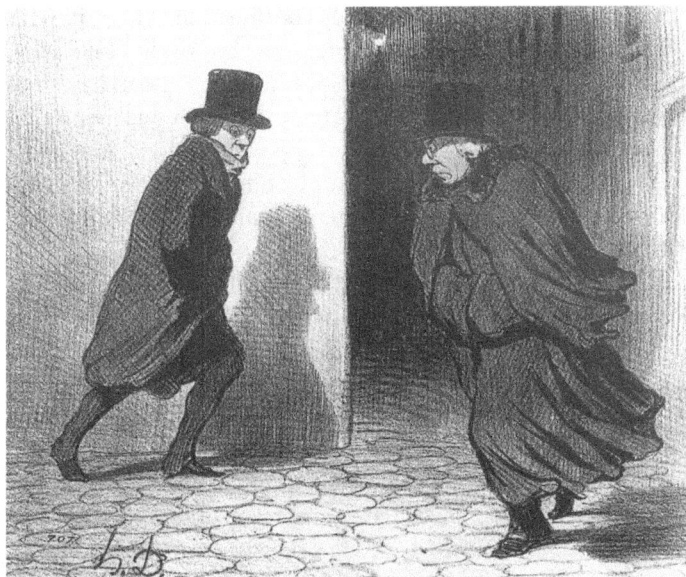

34 Honoré Daumier, "Between eleven o'clock and midnight," 1844

stroller, wandering through the dark and empty city, came unexpectedly upon a very real cut-throat, a ruffian gripping a threatening-looking club, who asked the lone walker "excuse me, do you have the time?" All the menace of this confrontation was contained in the incongruity between the altogether proper question posed to the *passant* and its speaker, the street criminal about to thrash his victim for his wallet. Daumier froze the scene at this moment, just before the enactment of the robbery's violence, thereby only heightening our own sense of anxiety, playing on the middle-class viewers' fear of such random crime. "Between eleven o'clock and midnight" recast this (quite literal) shock-experience, this traumatic encounter, as farce: the misrecognition of two identical passers-by.

This satirical drawing and Mme de Girardin's story both suggest the degree to which "the citizens' overwhelming preoccupation with crime as one of their normal daily worries," to quote Chevalier's characterization, was in fact a specifically bourgeois preoccupation, a fear located among the city's middle classes. Workers actually seldom appeared as victims in the newspaper accounts of the day, despite Mme de Girardin's assertion that the perpetrators of these crimes "attack rich and poor alike." And when they did appear in this role, it would seem that they were merely aping the anxieties of the bourgeoisie. A telling example can be found in a news story of December 16, which related how

the coachman and the footman of M. le comte de Beaumont . . . were returning yesterday around midnight in the direction of the Boulevard Montparnasse, when they noticed three individuals in front of them slacken their pace, seemingly with the intention of waiting for them in the most deserted part of this isolated neighborhood.

Yet the feared attack did not at first materialize: "they continued, however, to walk at the same pace, soon catching up and then overtaking these three individuals who, while observing them with curiosity, refrained from addressing them." Feeling threatened, the two servants hastened their steps, attempting to put as much distance as possible between themselves and the silent group behind them, but "suddenly one of the three men advanced in their direction while running and raising his arm in a threatening manner, as if he had the intention of striking them with a weapon whose steel flashed in the dubious gleam of the *réverbères*." Crying out for help, the coachman and footman were rescued by a police patrol (part of the Prefect's recent reinforcements) which fortunately was monitoring "this remote neighborhood."[33] The individual who chased after the two servants was immediately arrested and brought before the police superintendent, but the declaration he then made only cast its own dubious gleam on what had seemed a straightforward story. From the canton of Tessin, he worked as a painter and glazier, and claimed to be merely playing a joke on the two passers-by, "having noticed, like his companions, the fear that their encounter had inspired in the coachman and his mate." The flashing weapon was nothing but the tools of his trade which he happened to be carrying, and his intentions had been harmless. It would seem that the fears of the noble employer had trickled down to his servants, who in this tense atmosphere might misrecognize working-class play for a serious threat, as if a parody of the propertied classes' fears of the anonymous *passant*. And despite the air of truth around the painter-glazier's words, he was held under arrest. The authorities were little inclined to sympathize with such pranks, certainly not in month of December 1844.

In fact, the Prefecture of Police walked a fine line during these weeks of rampant rumors and widespread reports of nocturnal attacks. On one hand, it was imperative to reassure the public, first that steps were being taken to provide for its safety, and second that there was no need for panic; however, on the other hand, the state of fear gripping Paris offered an ideal opportunity for the police to extend their control over the city's working classes, creating a climate in which the disciplinary mechanisms of the authorities might be welcomed as providing respite from a spreading criminal underworld. The *Gazette des Tribunaux* had set the tone in an article of December 6, in which it asked:

> Is it true that there indeed are, in the center of Paris, sinister associations – some formed to commit thefts, others to commit murder – whose members are each affiliated with the other, who obey the same command, who are subject to a sort of regular discipline, and whose criminal projects night and day threaten the wealth and life of our citizens?

The Prefect of Police attempted to comfort readers that "thanks to God, such an organization does not exist," but even he was forced to admit that "memories of the convict prisons and the jails" create a certain solidarity and promote the formation "of a class of men who can live in crime."[34] Indeed, the specter of the so-called "dangerous classes" weighed heavily over the city during this period. This was a bourgeois vision of a world, which blended rag-pickers and prostitutes, thieves and beggars, vagabonds and workers, all of whom were united in their social marginality, constituting a world apart where labor and crime all too easily shaded into each other. It was a world captured in books like Jules Janin's *Un hiver à Paris*, published in 1845 but certainly largely inspired by the events of the winter of 1844–45; as Janin described it:

> In the hideous lairs which Paris hides away behind its palaces and museums . . . there lurks a swarming and oozing population that beggars comparison. There are crusts and wretched remnants all around. They speak a language spawned in the jails; all their converse is of larceny, murder, prisons and scaffolds. A vile bohemian world, a frightful world, a purulent wart on the face of this great city.[35]

At night this "tribe of the underworld," composed of *chiffonniers*, robbers, and streetwalkers, sets out on its "voracious prowl," stalking prey among the respectable citizenry.

This image of an urban jungle given over to criminal savagery was utilized by the police and the press to justify, beginning late in December 1844, a series of sweeps which rounded up large numbers of Paris's marginal population. On December 20 the *Journal des Débats* announced that "during the evenings and nights of Sunday, Monday, and yesterday, numerous significant arrests were made while executing warrants issued by the public prosecutor's department and the Prefect of Police." These arrests took place

> in places of evil repute at the Barrière des Martyrs and the Quartier des Halles, as well as on the western section of the exterior boulevards, where remnants of the gangs of recently sentenced malefactors and absconders who had up to this moment succeeded in escaping the investigations of the law had transferred the headquarters of their criminal endeavors.[36]

A marginal population, described as "habitual criminals, fugitives, or malefactors of the most dangerous category," was thus linked to a set of marginal locations, either at the literal edge of the city (the *barrières*, the remote outer boulevards) or in its crime-infested inner districts.[37] Some, the *Journal* reported, were arrested "in the middle of the brutish excesses of debauch and of those nameless dances which are performed, accompanied by often bloody brawls, at the *barrières*," while others were caught in the midst of "the nocturnal ambushes that they lay, with the help of their dexterous concubines, for belated passers-by."[38] Even more frightening than the sketch of this criminal geography was the suggestion of a concerted, organized illegality: five of the individuals arrested were linked with the gang of Teppaz and Fourrier, calling to mind a systematic underworld operating within the city, uniting delinquents throughout its neighborhoods. The image being constructed, then, was one of "sinister associations," an army of crime conjured from the lowest ele-

ments of Parisian society. Arrests begot more arrests as the authorities asserted
their determination to recapture the city from this occupying army. A raid the following evening, December 21, on an apartment house on the Rue des Remparts led
to the apprehension of more fugitives associated with known gangs, who themselves implicated further accomplices. As round-ups continued, the net widened to
include not only known criminals, but vagabonds and other figures in the world of
the *petits métiers*: on January 5, 1845, newspapers reported that:

> Arrests, whose numbers have risen to above forty, were made last night in different
> points around Paris, which patrols and the rounds of the municipal service track
> without respite. At La Halle particularly and in its environs, in the district of the
> Place Maubert, and in the Faubourgs Saint-Marceau, de la Courtille, du
> Montparnasse, and de l'Ecole-Militaire . . .

The arrests gathered parole violators ("libérés en état de rupture de ban") as well as
those described as disreputable characters and the homeless.[39]

This cycle of arrests culminated on the night of Saturday, February 9:

> A considerable force, led by three police commissioners and composed of agents from
> the municipal service, brigades of policemen, and a strong detachment of municipal
> guards unexpectedly encircled two establishments on the boulevard du Temple, the
> Café du Puy-de-Dôme and Le Caveau, both owned by a sieur Picard, and in which
> gathered criminals and receivers of stolen goods.[40]

Almost three hundred arrests were made that night in the police trap, an event of
such note that *L'Illustration* published a line engraving of the scene by Valentin
later that month (Figure 35). Here we see a great crowd of men being led out of
Picard's gambling-houses, their social station made clear by the workers' smocks
and soft caps they wear. They are entering the boulevard surrounded by a great
show of force, a forest of bayonets mounted at the end of rifles held at the shoulders
of municipal guards (those bayonets echoing the slender, bare branches of the trees
in the background). At the front of this crowd, one suspect, in a frock coat and top
hat much the worse for wear, seems to be appealing to a member of the guard in a
fruitless attempt to escape what we are certainly meant to see as the implacable
arms of justice. As viewers, we of course stand on the right side of this line, peering
over the shoulders of the guards, like the middle-class *badaud* near the center,
hands stuck deep in the pockets of his coat, proper top hat on his head, getting his
fill of the spectacle. He is the perfect pendant to the agent of the municipal service
standing to his left, sword at his side, hands clasped behind his great coat, his regu-
lation hat, in its martial solemnity, the ideal match to the bourgeois' smart stove-
pipe.

That pairing of policeman and bourgeois *passant* grounds the ideological message of this newspaper illustration, the one guaranteeing the security of the other's
passage. Their two looks, of steely surveillance and of curious, idle gazing, are profoundly linked, and despite the contrast of pose and uniform, I think we are meant

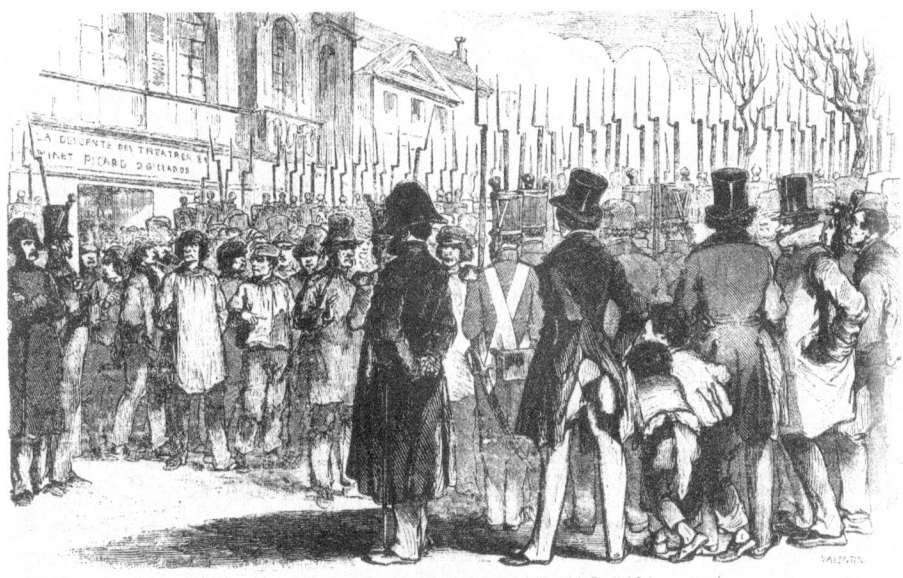

(Arrestation de 297 voleurs, dans les tapis-francs du boulevard du Temple.) 8

35 Valentin, "Arrest of 297 thieves on the boulevard du Temple," 1845

to see the figures as ultimately interchangeable, as composing a united front against the threat made by the crowd of "thieves" out on the boulevard. This image, of the *passant* confronting his classed other across the wary boundary of massed forces of order, is precisely the opposite of Daumier's view of the panic of the winter of 1844–45. In the latter's lithograph "Between eleven o'clock and midnight," same confronts same in a parodic scene of misidentification; without the authority of the law present to establish identities and affix names, all we are left with is uncertainty and the anxiety of surprise encounters on the darkened street, that projection of fantasy which seemed the domain of the anonymous *passant*.

Because fantasy, after all, was precisely at the root of this crime wave. From the moment rumors of vicious attacks began circulating through the city's salons, the responsible press had found it necessary to counter hearsay and, more disturbingly, outright fabrications. By the middle of February 1845, as arrests continued in Paris's working-class districts, many of the attacks which had initiated the panic were being revealed as the inventions of their supposed victims. The story of the woman who had been attacked on December 7 by an unknown assailant who tried to suffocate her with a piece of cloth (sometimes reported as a sheet of paper) covered with tar, for example, soon began to unravel. The judicial inquiry into the case revealed, based on eyewitness interviews, that "it was impossible for the facts to have occurred as the plaintiff described." While she claimed to have been incapacitated on the sidewalk for half an hour, unable to lift the choking cloth off her face, witnesses maintained otherwise, "that she had free use of her hands and pulled

from her pocket a letter which she presented to those who noticed her." Closer
examination found more contradictions: the plaintiff gave inconsistent accounts of
her activities the day in question; a doctor who examined a piece of the tar used in
the crime declared that it could not have been put to that purpose. Finally, "an
inquiry made into the past records of the plaintiff discovered that, following a very
serious hysterical affection, she was subject to nervous incidents which sometimes
threw her faculties into great disorder."[41] With that, this crime which had terror-
ized the capital was put to rest, transformed into the figment of an afflicted mind.
Others had used supposed crimes to advance their own personal agendas, to
aggrandize themselves in a frightened public's eye. On January 8, a sergeant of the
line reported that he had "rescued and saved from certain death a young man . . .
whom malefactors had robbed and thrown into the Seine" near the Pont d'Iéna.
Two workers who happened to be passing by assisted the sergeant in fishing the
young man out of the freezing water, and all three had made a declaration to this
effect at the police station in the Quartier des Invalides. But when the station's
superintendent investigated the story, he found that the sergeant, along with the
victim and the two workers, "had invented the fable with the goal of obtaining a
reward or a promotion."[42] These "mysterious attacks," with which the Prefecture
might mobilize public opinion to justify expanding control over the city's mobile
populations, now began to appear motivated not by shadowy criminal organizations, but by the shadowy motives of private citizens, by their own fantasies of per-
secution or heroism.

Ever the attentive observer, Mme de Girardin remarked on the changed atmosphere of the city:

> One month ago we told you that Paris was in a stupor, one spoke only of assassins, one
> perceived only victims, this woman had fallen, choked by a frightful tar mask, this
> young man had been stabbed ten times with a stiletto, the one had her money stolen,
> the other his fob and watch, and everybody exclaimed, was frightened and indignant.

But only a month later, nothing remained of this panic, and "one after the other,
all these frightful stories that had been given us have been taken back," retracted
voluntarily or disproved after investigation. "The tar mask was an ingenious
invention which hid a love-affair disguised as a victim [here Mme de Girardin
seems privy to some gossip which never reached the newspapers]; the nocturnal
attack against the young dandy was only a tale, the malefactor being merely a
rival." Paris's middle classes could only castigate themselves for their gullibility,
for falling victim not to crime but to rumor, panic, and unwarranted sympathy:
"we were wrong to be afraid, we were wrong to have pity; there are no more assassins, there never were assassins, who then dared to say there were assassins?"[43]
Suddenly, as if overnight, the passer-by against whom one had so resolutely prepared to defend oneself lost his threatening quality, suddenly the stranger
appeared once more for what he was, another bourgeois hurrying home through
the night. All the fantastic projections, the secret associations devoted to crime,

the plots hatched in the city's worst districts, the armies of thieves, retreated from view, dispelled by the banal facts of deception and greed. When the bourgeoisie in these months confronted the fearsome aspect of urban crime, it was actually confronting nothing but itself – a fact grasped by Daumier and even by Mme de Girardin, but not by our own century's urban historians. For Louis Chevalier, the frightening stranger was a demographic fact of the July Monarchy, a fact determined "biologically" by urban population densities which alone transformed part of the laboring classes of Paris into dangerous classes.[44] According to what has been called his "uprooting hypothesis," large-scale social change (of the sort that was driving provincials into Paris in these years) dissolved traditional social ties and inevitably led to desperation and disorder. In this city, crime would no longer be conceived as an individual act, but as a sociological phenomenon, whereby an entire class would be rendered monstrous through demographic pressure – witness the accounts ranging from Frégier's early criminology to the newspaper stories retold here.[45]

But the ambiguities of the panic of the winter of 1844–45 demonstrate that such identifications of laboring classes and dangerous classes were projections of bourgeois fears, not reflections of proletarian realities. As historians like Philippe Vigier have more recently argued, the so-called dangerous classes only ever accounted for a minority of industrial workers, the majority of whom were merely attempting to honestly earn a living at a time when the cost of living was rising and wages stagnating or actually decreasing. Workers responded to such living conditions less by recruitment into criminality than by a return to the corporate actions and demands which had characterized the unrest of 1830–34.[46] Moreover, the anxiety that spread through the salons and streets of middle-class Paris had its roots not in the factual existence of an underclass at the margins of society, but rather in the more diffuse fear of a city made up of passers-by who were essentially ciphers. In the increasingly mobile world of the July Monarchy, where the certainties of birth and rank were giving way to the generalized pursuit of a hierarchy of wealth, the cognitive maps which had formerly guided the bourgeoisie through the city proved less and less accurate. Anxieties about the passer-by, which reached their highest pitch in widespread rumors of random crime, were fundamentally anxieties about this unreadable crowd taking shape on the street. In a city of misers, every *passant* looked like a thief.

Notes

1 P. J. Stahl, "Les Passans à Paris," in *Le Diable à Paris* (Paris: J. Hetzel, 1844), p. 25. (All translations by the author unless an English source is cited.). Stahl was a pseudonym for J. Hetzel himself, the publisher of the volume. The critical literature on the nineteenth-century physiognomic genre is extensive; two of the most valuable are M. Cohen, "Panoramic Literature and the Invention of Everyday Genres," in *Cinema and the Invention of Modern Life*, eds L. Charney and V. R. Schwartz (Berkeley: University

of California Press, 1995), pp. 227–252; and R. Sieburth, "Une idéologie du lisible: le phénomène des 'Physiologies'," *Romantisme: revue du dix-neuvième siècle* 15, no. 47 (1985), pp. 39–60.

2 P. J. Stahl, "Les Passans à Paris," p. 25.

3 P. J. Stahl, "Les Passans à Paris," p. 25.

4 W. Benjamin in fact located this separation of spheres as a defining characteristic of the July Monarchy; see his section on "Louis-Philippe, or the Interior," from "Paris, Capital of the 19th Century," in W. Benjamin, *Reflections: Essays, Aphorisms, Autobiographical Writings*, ed. P. Demetz, trans. E. Jephcott (New York: Schocken Books, 1986), pp. 154–156.

5 R. Sennett discusses the bourgeois regime of fashion in *The Fall of Public Man* (New York and London: W. W. Norton, 1976), pp. 161–174.

6 See P. Vigier, *Nouvelle Histoire de Paris: Paris pendant la Monarchie de Juillet (1830–1848)* (Paris: Bibliothèque historique de la Ville de Paris, 1991), pp. 230–1.

7 See P. Vigier, *Nouvelle Histoire de Paris*, pp. 244–261.

8 G. Simmel, "The Stranger," in *The Sociology of Georg Simmel*, ed. and trans. K. H. Wolff (New York: Free Press, 1950), p. 404.

9 G. Simmel, "The Stranger," p. 404.

10 P. J. Stahl, "Les Passans à Paris," p. 27. Note how, in a capitalist economy, it is implied that strangers are individuated only through the assignment of worth ("*valeur particulière*").

11 P. J. Stahl, "Les Passans à Paris," p. 27.

12 P. J. Stahl, "Les Passans à Paris," p. 27.

13 *Journal des Débats*, December 9, 1844, p. 2.

14 *Journal des Débats*, December 9, 1844, p. 2.

15 *Journal des Débats*, December 9, 1844, p. 2.

16 *Journal des Débats*, December 14, 1844, p. 2.

17 *Journal des Débats*, December 14, 1844, p. 2.

18 *Journal des Débats*, December 14, 1844, p. 2.

19 *Journal des Débats*, December 8, 1844, p. 3.

20 *Journal des Débats*, December 13, 1844, p. 2.

21 *Journal des Débats*, December 19, 1844, p. 2.

22 L. Chevalier, *Laboring Classes and Dangerous Classes*, trans. F. Jellinek (Princeton, N.J.: Princeton University Press, 1973), pp. 2–3.

23 Mme E. de Girardin, *Oeuvres complètes*, vol. 5 ("Lettres parisiennes, 1840–1848") (Paris: Henri Plon, 1860), p. 364.

24 E. de Girardin, *Oeuvres complètes*, p. 364.

25 See H.-A. Frégier, *Des classes dangereuses de la population dans les grandes villes…*, vol. 1 (Paris: J.-B. Baillière, 1840), pp. 213–253, for such a taxonomy of the various categories of thievery.

26 E. de Girardin, *Oeuvres complètes*, pp. 364–365.

27 E. de Girardin, *Oeuvres complètes*, pp. 364–365.

28 E. de Girardin, *Oeuvres complètes*, p. 365.

29 E. de Girardin, *Oeuvres complètes*, p. 366.

30 E. de Girardin, *Oeuvres complètes*, p. 366.

31 H. Daumier, "Entre onze heures et minuit," 1844 (L. D. 1329, H. D. 2202).

32 H. Daumier, "Quelle heure est-il?," 1839 (L. D. 695, H. D. 1640).

33 *Journal des Débats*, December 16, 1844, p. 2.

34 *Gazette des Tribunaux*, December 6, 1844, quoted in J. Tulard, *La Préfecture de police sous la Monarchie de Juillet* (Paris: Commission des Travaux Historiques, Ville de Paris, 1964), p. 87, n. 10.

35 J. Janin, quoted in L. Chevalier, *Laboring Classes*, p. 67.

36 *Journal des Débats*, December 20, 1844, p. 3.

37 On this dynamic of the city margins in the nineteenth century, see J. M. Merriman, *The Margins of City Life: Explorations on the French Urban Frontier, 1815–1851* (New York and Oxford: Oxford University Press, 1991), especially pp. 3–30.

38 *Journal des Débats*, December 20, 1844, p. 3.

39 *Journal des Débats*, January 5, 1845, p. 2.

40 *Journal des Débats*, February 10, 1845, p. 2; see also the *Journal* of February 14, 1845, p. 3 for an update on these arrests.

41 *Journal des Débats*, February 14, 1845, p. 3. This ascription of "hysteria" must itself be seen as overdetermined; on the little evidence provided, the veracity of this woman's claims must remain unknown.

42 *Journal des Débats*, January 19, 1845, p. 3.

43 E. de Girardin, *Oeuvres* complètes, pp. 368–369.

44 See L. Chevalier, *Laboring Classes*, pp. 293–309 notably.

45 Chevalier's thesis had long been met with challenges in the historical literature; in fact, the rebels of Paris's nineteenth-century revolutions were not drawn from the uprooted, "dangerous" classes, nor were they the most poor. They were, rather, skilled artisans defending their way of life against large-scale economic changes over which they had no control. Craft solidarities and organizations led people to the barricades, not their belonging to a criminal underworld. See, notably, G. Rudé, *The Crowd in History* (New York: Wiley, 1964); D. H. Pinkney, *The French Revolution of 1830* (Princeton, N.J.: Princeton University Press, 1972); and C. Tilly and L. Lees, "The People of June 1848," in *Revolution and Reaction: 1848 and the Second French Republic*, ed. R. Price (London: Croome Helm, 1975).

46 See P. Vigier, *La Monarchie de Juillet*, 3rd ed. (Paris: Presses Universitaires de France, Coll. "Que sais-je?," 1969), pp. 52–55.

11

The contemporary *flâneuse*

Helen Scalway

The ordinary practitioners of the city . . . are walkers . . . whose bodies follow the thicks and thins of an urban "text" they write without being able to read it. These practitioners make use of spaces that cannot be seen; their knowledge of them is as blind as that of lovers in each other's arms. (Michel de Certeau, *The Practice of Everyday Life*)[1]

It's about a constant struggle to find a place, a place which is not marked by the longitude/latitude of power/knowledge. (Steve Pile, *The Body and the City*)[2]

Can there be such a person as a *flâneuse*? Is it not an absolute contradiction in terms? The nature of that fraught contradiction is my subject in this essay and in every walk I take, or make – a significant distinction. What am I looking for? Why do I go on these walks, as a woman who walks the street but is not a "streetwalker?" No one reason and many knotty ones. This is so different from the easy enjoyment of going out with friends or family. I am trying to find, or perhaps more accurately to build, something: a space, a path. I am looking for the possibility of new meanings in the very awkwardness of the situation, of being the solitary woman walking – for the woman who strolls alone is still either a streetwalker or a stupidly naive victim who is just asking to be robbed. There's desire in this walking, of course.

It is an apparently purposeless activity, this walking, or it has a number of purposes which are hard to specify; easier to say what it is not, than what it is. *I want to see what I can see. But I also want to see what, in the city, acknowledges me.* So I am looking for a place in the city.

The journey starts with clothes, because the first thing is to decide what to wear. It is always tricky because there will be moments when I shall want to be invisible, moments when I will be invisible whether I want it or not, and moments when I might want to be, never conspicuous, but at least present. For my purposes today that means to be a chameleon ... interchangeable layers of garments, disguises. I even pause over the possibilities of bags that fold inside each other and can be popped round to encase each other. Duffel, plastic carrier, glossy leather. It's already quite a performance, and I'm not even out of the door.

If this were Naples or New York the narrative would be very different. In Los Angeles, they say, no one walks. In Venice, everyone must. But every walk is a particular one. I happen to live in north-west London between Paddington and Kilburn, on the 6th floor of a council block. *Flânerie* takes place in city centers, however. In trying to create my counter-version of it, I often set out towards the center, which for me somehow means within Zone One, within the gold of the yellow Circle Line. The pleasure center, cinemas, parks, cafes, shops, markets, museums, *monuments*.

Getting into the center on foot is part of the experience, however, and presents obstacles which are themselves revealing. I step out alone on to the street and turn south. It is a mile to Marble Arch and the West End, and I can go straight down the Edgeware Road. Or, as I don't like Oxford Street, I may wander through quieter streets to get to Notting Hill. Before I get there I must negotiate the street much closer to home. Aggressively fast boy cyclists on the pavements – and all the *stopped* people: unemployed youths claiming space by their demeanor, probably because they have no space anywhere, really; all the homeless, the beggars, the drugged, drunk, deranged, predatory; other victims of care in the community. In my turn I avert my eyes from our familiar local beggar – to see him would be to allow a very complex obstacle to form in my mental path – and set off down Lanark Road. To stop, even here, would be to invite risky attentions, but it could also make me appear one of the outsiders I've just been talking about. I ponder this position.

Outsider/insider is a border the *flâneuse* must skirmish on constantly, if only with herself. Could I make use of the disguise of beggary to increase my understanding, to see more? Or is it at bottom a kind of exploitation of the position of those genuinely on the street who, unlike me, cannot go home? The position of the vagrant is in any case one of unequivocal exclusion and it's actually too extreme for what I am after, which is a threading between the ill-defined edges of more ambivalent territories of belonging and not belonging. Being critical of what belonging entails, yet needing to belong and being unable fully to do so. In any case standing still when the street is crowded is really hard to do. To become an obstacle in a path designed for circulation, to hang around not even looking as though you are waiting for someone . . . I can never keep it up for long. Some invisible mental muscle feels just too much stress. Without having a reason to be stationary, one becomes a *loiterer* (what a word), so I have to have a watch to look at or a map to unfold: *acting props*. For me it is an effect of embarrassment. I am sure this crosses the boundaries of gender. Embarrassment is interesting: to stand still in the street is, among other things, to risk looking mad. It is relevant to my attempt to analyze my experience of trying to *create a flânerie in the feminine* to note that I am still, after a lot of London walking, sensitive about appearances. Inconspicuousness is safety, it still carries a real charge for me; it still means belonging at home among the clean and neat – that is, among the respectable, those who are of fixed abode. That brings with it overtones of mores I know I tend not to question: *decency*, *hard work* and *honesty*, a complex of attitudes that perhaps I do not want to escape, underpinning and guaranteeing so much of my unconscious life. To take refuge in appearances of either *eccentricity* or *cool*, or becoming a *character*, is irrelevant, dishonest, just not useful. I must path-build for the more inward people I am.

These sensitivities go right to the heart of the matter, they are central to the difficulties inherent in my already impossible role of *flâneuse*. The experience is relevant: it touches some of the difficulties many women might feel at some level once they cast themselves as idle strollers in the city. The edgy path of sensitivities and potential for embarrassment in the street, lying as it does between the psychological territories of acceptable and unacceptable behaviors and appearances, is one of the most revealing of all the paths I am talking about. I could spend a long time trying to map the street in an A–Z of potential embarrassment, my own and other peoples', on the pavements. For women, as anyone may observe (and theoreticians of the city often do), do not usually walk in an obviously purposeless way. They are everywhere, going about their business; their badge of respectability (that is actually vital to their safety) is that they are nearly always either carrying something or pushing something. This pushchair, bag, case, or letter may aid the necessary self-permission for the idle, pleasurable intention of going for a walk. To stop safely, I have to buy space (in a café or cinema) or look as though I am at least a potential purchaser in a shop, or possess a pass to gain admission to a library, museum, club, etc.

Before I can gain access to the most exciting of the city center's amenities, before I ever reach the space of *flânerie*, I have to pass under Westway – one of the great roads into London, the city end of the M40 (Figure 36).

Here are the twee houseboats of Little Venice and three seconds away is the first glimpse of the great barrier of Westway bisecting the world, the 1960s roaring

36 Helen Scalway, "Joining Westway," 1999

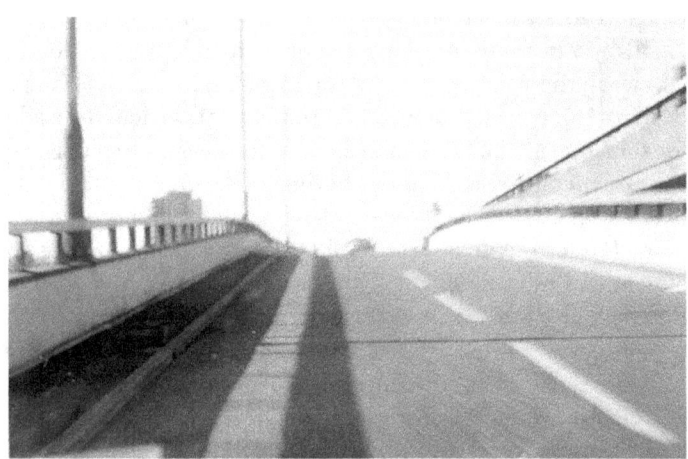

concrete flyover with the nineteenth-century railway line into Paddington beyond – all structures created by engineers and technicians in times marked by extreme macho confidence in construction. Every north–south road in this part of London must go under Westway. On maps these great traffic trajectories are straight, linear geometries of unimpeded perspectives, embodying apparently "rational," actually brutal logic in concrete. In them, power is invested. Up above on the concrete road you can see nothing of the under-surface. The upper space forces one to share its view that is both dominating but also very incomplete. I connect this to an inflexible and domineering stance in its planners. Westway is an intensely gendered space. Its underneath is more interesting than its top. But I want to pass under Westway because my walk takes me to the other side. I am immediately offered a subway, a hell-mouth which I would never voluntarily enter. So I walk round the long way instead. This involves doubling back on myself, the first of a number of weavings my route must take if I am to thread through to the other side, in contrast to the straight hurtling trajectory above.

Like all hells or Hades this one has its fascination. Of course you have to walk or weave really fast through it. Whereas up above the drivers' eyes must be fixed as drivers' eyes are, ahead, on the road, down here the view is more complex, involving for a start the view from the eyes in the back of the head, peripheral vision, the view immediately around within bag-snatching radius, and a constant and more distant reckoning of possible escape routes. Also along this stretch is the enormous Westminster police car pound; I have heard tell of a caravan store further on, and tennis courts under the roar. These spaces too evidently represent no one. Their officially assigned uses are unconvincing; there's something half-hearted about all of them, like the occasions when, not having a decent excuse, one makes too many excuses. Like many spaces that are still open and ambiguous, they have been colonized by young men, often those marginalized themselves. I must negotiate this also.

Where the Portobello Road has to pass beneath Westway, that chichi tourist street of antique dealers transmutes itself into a squalid alter ego, the Portobello Green Arcade. There's a second-hand clothes shop there owned by a middle-aged woman who wears a series of unplaceable, vaguely period disguises from her shop, shifting identities within one outfit and between outfits along a gamut of looks from old leather to old lace. She is the most convincing inhabitant of this ambivalent space just because she's a shape-shifter. I come to the railway bridge whose corrugated iron sides have been bashed out every two steps. I check who else is on it – for the bridge is caged in under thick wire mesh (imprisoning? protecting?) – and start across it, the worst part of this walk for there are no escapes; once on the bridge there's no way but a narrow fast forward. Ah, the barriers between myself and the spaces of *flânerie* . . . .

I emerge on the far side, the Notting Hill Gate side inside the Circle Line. We all know how fashionable it has become; it used to be a suburb, but then everywhere in London used to be a suburb. I'm looking for a place, places, where the city will speak for me – speak me, indeed. *Utter me*. The walk eventually brings me out in a busy shopping street: Queensway, abuzz in the evening, past Whiteley's, an old and august department store. In the nineteenth century, such a place would have been one of the few territories designed for the pleasure of the woman browser (drifter, walker). Her pleasure, that is, as a consumer, and in a fashion store, she consumes her own image. Perhaps all desire seeks its own image across a space; the narcissism of fashion, however, collapses that space to the few curtained inches around the woman and her reflection in the mirrored trying-on cubicle. This cubicle is not big enough, that is, interesting enough. It is too reductive.

I am still looking for the place in the city that lets me take up a wider range of positions beyond the dyad of threatened walker/seduced shopper. A place that embodies a fuller *citizenship*. But for me, to walk down Queensway, or other streets – whether their character is shopping or business or whatever – is like inhabiting someone else's dream. I'm reduced to someone else's idea of what I should be – clothes shopper, target for advertisements (Figure 37). Once I refuse Whiteley's retail "therapy," with its endless offer to compensate an unassuageable lack, I become an unauthorized, transgressive, profoundly displaced person. Other kinds of London buildings give meanings to other streets. Restaurants you do not enter alone. Banks, financial institutions, museums, monuments. These embody dreams – overwhelmingly in the masculine – uttering in brick, stone, and glass the ideas, desires, meanings of successive generations of clients who could command or negotiate built expressions of their power and desire. This produces for me a disconcerting sensation. Looking to find the complexity of my being represented – looking for a symbol with which to identify – I find none. It might be like looking in a mirror and finding that I cast no reflection. Indeed, too long in some parts of London can leave me feeling ghost-like; not just disembodied, but actually, more dangerously, not entitled to a body.

My question then as a walker is not how can I possess the city as an occupying force, but *how can I be in it at all?* What would it really mean to be *at home* in this city where I was born and where I work, full of private memories, yet lacking public meanings for me? The experience of a woman who was, for example, a fund-manager in the City's financial square mile, might be different – but such a woman might have a great many other questions about her occupation of that particular intensely gendered space.

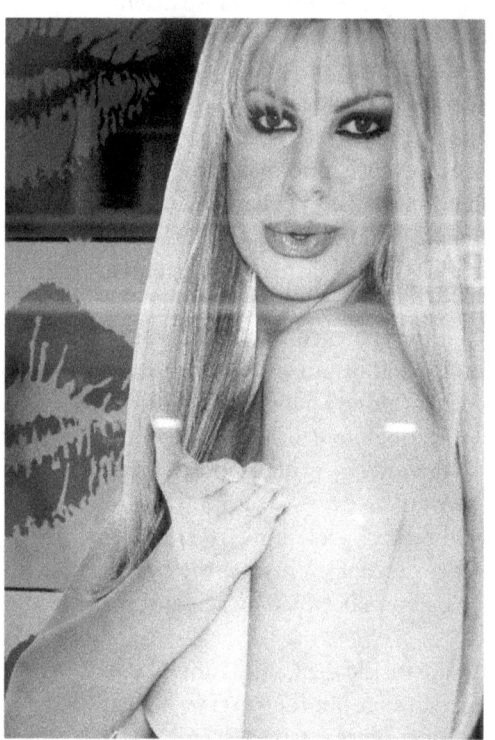

37 Helen Scalway, "The Window," 1999

The question endlessly reiterated – *how can I be here?* – is what this walking is about. The fact that there are no easy answers to these questions is why the walks – miming the insistent return of the question – are again and again repeated. But in trying to construct a city within the city that is full of meaning and significance for myself, something else often happens. My gaze, like everyone's, is full of fantasy and of denial; I find myself pausing over the nature of my own looking.

Unable to hold the large scene in a controlling view, not identifying with large dominating perspectives and vistas, my gaze often seems to collapse in space into a touching with the eyes, and with more than the eyes; a visual caress of fragments that interest me. Indeed I am convinced that if I could see the vista, the large perspective, then I would not actually be able to perceive anything else. In fact my exclusion as a subject from the controlling perspective both impels me *and* enables me to seek into a much more bodily and complex relationship with my surroundings. My perception is really coming from a different place. It has – necessarily – to do with tacit knowledge. The experience of walking is chaotic and fragmentary. Fragments for me often resolve into the bodily sense of dancing steps changing pace, sense of direction and skillful change of direction, the estimate of a gap to slip through; and then, the details of texture, color, potential touchability, temperature and smell, foul or fresh. Suddenly, serendipitously, the street slows down and the space which is for ever squeezing me out, lets me back in – just for an instant. These sensuous moments, still taken guardedly in the melee of the street, are characterized for me by a slow and pleasurable tactility and physicality involving more senses than sight alone; moments in which I am neither solely invader nor solely invaded but fluidly occupy both positions simultaneously and points between. My version of counter-*flânerie* is occasionally about trying, just for a second, and of course in vain, to slow down the acceleration whereby the time and space of the modern city environment are compressed into less and less. The slowed-down walking, the slow tactility, and a kind of non-privileging of sight may just occasionally resonate in a brief instant of bodily, tacit, complex awareness of the presences of the city before I am caught up again in the dance steps of its pavements.

I associate these sensuous moments with something I mentioned earlier, the attempt to construct paths of significance through places where there are no pre-existing ones for me to follow. Paths made out of scraps, sensory rubble of all sorts, pointers and markers for private negotiation. But the scraps and details, though they come from the public space of the street, denote still only a private and guarded existence within it. They are all small and incomplete, private pleasures that exist away from the public meanings of what contained them, often in spite of those public meanings. For myself as "contemporary *flâneuse*" they cannot – yet – build into symbols with shared meanings. The idea that a street such as Queensway, that is currently bruisingly hard for the woman who is a seeing subject to negotiate, the idea that this street could be a site for *positive shared meanings* for walkers in the feminine remains largely a dream. It's interesting to me that the scraps and details, the visual rubble, are the opposite of *monuments*, with all that word implies. Still,

Queensway offers other possibilities: its dynamism in the evening, its pavement dance. I think about the manner of my walking. So, then, how, actually, do I walk? It's a *looking for spaces to slip through and round, weaving and threading a path through that opens and closes, darting, dodging and dancing, two-stepping, giving way, persistently returning.*

The words that come to my mind to describe my movement through the street imply that it's a much more difficult negotiation. Yet even in the heart of that difficult negotiation, is there possibly a space for resistance on the part of a contemporary *flâneuse*? It depends where; it is not self-evident. I sometimes feel as though as a walker I am squeezed into a narrow path opening and closing between solid bodies and lethal traffic – squeezed into what draughtsmen call *negative space*. Yet I can struggle to turn the phrase "negative space" around, so that it is no longer *negative* but *provisional*, still open; to find the path linking a constellation of such provisional spaces whose meanings are still unfixed and where there is still a fluid potential. Down Queensway, it has to be said, there is precious little space of any kind.

Sometimes I find myself no longer looking at the pavement before my feet, but seeking this unfixed space in odd elsewhere places: streets in the sky . . . the inside of a tourist "snowdome" bought in one of Queensway's many tourist shops . . . the strange nowhere yet somewhere of reflected space . . . *flânerie* through the city's dreamspaces and nospaces.

Yet still there is pleasure in the street. Pleasure that even unpromising Queensway, like any crowded street, has a life beyond me. The sense of other people weaving their Londons around me. Because I'm always curious about these I talk to anyone when I think it's reasonably safe to do so, first securing my line of retreat, of course. In this way I have the most extraordinary conversations and people share with me things I later feel privileged to have received. For once I open up to the city's people, they return my openness with such wealth, such generosity, I receive back so much more than I thought possible. I am not looking to cast the city as another of my selves or to see it as an index of lives I might have led. For me its fascination is its power of letting me in on occasion to the realization of the myriad other ways that there are of seeing the world and of being in the world. As an artist I want to privilege that. So the truth is that I find walking difficult and fascinating. The dance of the pavement, its textures and temperatures; the sudden opening out into proffered insight. I think also that there is a richly satisfying relationship for me between the tactility of walking and the tactility of drawing where to create a line or a tone on paper involves such bodily alertness. This is so much to do with sensuality going far beyond the purely visual. It brings me to two issues I must briefly touch on, concerning my role as someone who is concerned with the representation of urban space: representation through map-making and through photography – large subjects. From time to time I have found it expedient to experiment with them. Yet my experience with both leads me to question the extent of their usefulness for my purposes.

My photographs often show the back, retreating view of passers-by because to take a photo without permission is an aggressive act. I am afraid of the consequences if I snap someone close up and head on. The voyeuristic power involved here works absolutely against my motives for doing what I do. To photograph something is to alter it, and to go out to take photographs changes the nature of the walk. So the existence of these photographs goes against the grain. I am well aware also that in taking some of them I was actually exploiting my female identity – two different men have said that they would have been "punched in the face" if they had tried to take these shots openly. So clearly each gender experiences different freedoms and difficulties in the street.

Secondly, cartography. There is a real difference between what can be mapped and what cannot. Maps are fascinating and often very visually seductive. They are also rightly objects of suspicion, being so much to do with the aerial view, the edited view from above, powerful, controlling. Maps like photographs are for telling lies with. The famous phrase "botanizing on the asphalt," with its suggestion of Linnaean classification, has much to do with cartography and control. Private maps are intriguing because of the glimpse they offer into other peoples' private navigation systems. But when it comes to the real complexity of tacit knowledges, then cartographic techniques break down because their devices can never be more than crude codes for what is both transient and experienced as infinitely nuanced.

My project as an artist has been to produce an atlas: an A–Z of the sensations of walking through London, an A–Z of slippage that would confound the classifications implied within the notion of the atlas. But I have had to realize that it needs *more* than even the expressive, fragmented cartography that I thought I was trying to produce. My work in progress is to seek – perhaps to invent – means of moving away from cartography's dependence on the powerful controlling aerial view and cartography's elision of all the processes of journeying by which maps come into being in the first place, and of which they exist as mere traces. Perhaps *the tour* as a representational mode offers some possibilities; but verbal language itself with its loadedness and its limitations also crumbles.

On these kinds of edges both my practices, my practice of the city and my practice as an artist, teeter . . .

Notes

1 M. de Certeau, *The Practice of Everyday Life*, trans. S. Rendall (Berkeley: University of California Press, 1984), p. 93.

2 S. Pile, *The Body and the City* (London: Routledge, 1996), p. 249.

12

Afterword

Linda Nochlin

Women and public space have had a problematic relationship since the beginning of modern times. The very asymmetry of our idiomatic speech tells us as much. A "public man," as in Richard Sennett's *The Fall of Public Man*, is an admirable person: politically active, socially engaged, known and respected. A "public woman," on the other hand, is a phrase used traditionally for the lowest form of prostitute. In the case of the term "streetwalker," moreover, even though no gender is indicated by the term in English, it is understood to be female in its negative connotations, and is by no means identical with the French *flâneur* or sophisticated male stroller through the city – a man at home in the urban crowd, and a canny observer of the worldly scene.

In art history, the texts of Janet Wolff and Griselda Pollock have vividly contrasted the confined domestic space of femininity, in the nineteenth century at least, with the confident occupation of public space understood to be the masculine sphere. Yet the papers collected in this anthology have definitively problematized and nuanced that clear-cut opposition between a feminine private space and a masculine public one. Even if no man was ever represented as human decoration in a suffocating décor, as is the case in Alfred Stevens's *Porcelain Collector* (1868), and no woman was ever in the nineteenth century represented striding so confidently through Paris as Vicomte Lépic in Degas's *Place de la Concorde* (1875), nevertheless the "woman in public space" topos is, in Caillebotte's *Pont de l'Europe* (1876) for example, filled with ambiguity and contradiction. And as Ting Chang has demonstrated, the stride of the *flâneur* becomes considerably less arrogant in the face of an unknown culture, of a very different urban experience in Asia from that of Paris. Still, even the man enfolded in the domestic space – usually understood to be "feminine" – is not totally, or truly, feminized by this position. In Caillebotte's painting *Man at the Window* (1875), the subject's pose is confident, his gaze directed outward to the street, focusing perhaps on the tiny, isolated figure of an anonymous woman below his controlling vantage point. And Degas's *Women on a Café Terrace, Evening* (1877), women out in the city, are immediately recognizable through signs of physiognomy and gesture as prostitutes, thus potentially available to the solicitation of the men, adumbrated as shadowy silhouettes, striding *flâneur*-like on the boulevard behind them.

Now, it is certainly true that the dichotomy of female/private space and male/public space is broken down in the nineteenth century by the existence of works like Morisot's *A Summer's Day* (1879), set on the lake at the Bois de Boulogne, and Cassatt's *Woman in Black at the Opera* (1880). Certain in-between areas of the modern city, areas differentiated from the male-controlled and -dominated street, café, plaza, or political arena, certainly existed. As Greg Thomas has pointed out, these in-between areas of the modern city of Paris – the parks and the loges of the theater, a sort of sexual *terrain vague*, as it were – offered an ambiguous welcome to women at certain times of day, under certain circumstances, if chaperoned. The matinee in particular, then as now, was feminine territory to which proper women might go in pairs. The department store, a mid-nineteenth- century Parisian invention, welcomed women into its sheltered feminine purlieus, and the museum or salon might be visited, although as Berthe Morisot indicates in an important letter, "art is better enjoyed on the arm of a male companion than all by oneself."[1] And of course, despite Mary Cassatt's inscription of the well-bred woman in the loge as part of the public space of the opera house, one could certainly not envision the well-bred woman as a performer on the public space of the stage. Ballet dancers like Pauline and Virginie, pictured by Degas in one of his series of *La Famille Cardinal, Pauline and Virginie Conversing with Admirers*, were understood to be instantly available to wealthy admirers, and the backstage of Garnier's Opera House was designed with that idea in mind. The dancers, the public performers, were considered "public women" in the traditional sense of the word.

On the whole then, it is hard to imagine a well-bred woman striding through the Place de la Concorde with the insouciant air of authority that marks the passage of Degas's Vicomte Lépic through that prototypical Parisian public space, accompanied by his pure-bred dog and his two little daughters. The respectable woman's place in public space was, then, highly circumscribed by custom, by the rules of propriety, by the sexual danger that lurked in the streets and the civic arena if she should venture into it unprotected. In visual art, this circumscription is brilliantly indicated by distance, in the case of Morisot's *On the Balcony* (1872), or by creating a private cocoon of domesticity within the bosom of the great city, as is the case of Mary Cassatt's *Woman and Child Driving* (1881), where the topic of the family – to an even greater extent than in Daumier's *Third Class Carriage* (1863–65) – dominates over the anomie of the metropolis and its public transportation. The female equivalent of the *flâneur* (itself a representational construction rather than a social actuality), the *flâneuse* – an urban woman, free, confident, in charge of her life, striding or strolling down the avenues, an observer and constructor of public life – was more or less invisible in the nineteenth century, if she existed at all.

Now, things certainly changed in the twentieth century, especially with the advent of the "new woman" (so called), the working woman, and the suffrage movement with its organized marches in public space, and the entry of women (in limited numbers to be sure) into the public world of business and the professions. Yet this change, interestingly enough, is reflected much more in literature than in the visual arts. Novels like Dorothy Richardson's *Pilgrimage* or Virginia Woolf's *Night and Day* or *The Years*, for instance, as Deborah Parsons has demonstrated in her important study of the phenomenon, represented women engaging with the city in newer, freer ways: as walkers, watchers, workers, denizens of cafés and women's clubs, apartment dwellers, observers and negotiators of the public space of the city – breaking new ground without the help of tradition, literary or otherwise. As Parsons has so eloquently put it in the conclusion of her study:

> The "heroic" women of modern London and Paris . . . do not act out a pretence at heroic ancient myth [like T. S. Eliot or James Joyce] as they have none to follow. Rather they create their own heroism, stepping out on their own pilgrimages. For . . . Richardson, and Woolf, the city of London was a stimulating lover; for [Elizabeth] Bowen a visionary ruin. For [Jean] Rhys, Paris became an intoxicating narcotic; for [Janet] Flanner, a haven for the exiled. All these women wrote as *flâneuses*, for whom the city was irresistible.[2]

Yet despite this new freedom of women in the urban milieu, things changed in some ways less than we think. Growing up in New York City, Brooklyn specifically, in the 1930s, '40s, and '50s of the last century, I experienced some of the ambiguities facing a woman – particularly a young woman – in the space of a great city. On the one hand, we were offered an unprecedented degree of freedom: roller skates, going to the park by ourselves, going to museums, to theaters, the unrestricted use of public transportation. Yet, sexual harassment and even more, the threat of aberrant sexuality, was an ever-present, hovering specter, restricting our access to the public life of the city or at least making us wary in public spaces. We adolescent girls, as a protective ploy, organized or categorized a whole range of what we called "sex fiends." There were a whole range of these so-called "sex fiends" that made our lives a little more restricted, our dreams a little darker. There were subway fiends, roof fiends, park fiends, and even the occasional museum fiend, often found at opening time when the museum was less crowded and tactile access to nude statuary unimpeded. There was also the library fiend, who delighted in reading visible pornography when seated next to a well-brought-up teenager. And most certainly the dreaded movie fiend, who groped his innocent young victim in the dark under protection of the ever-present raincoat.

About the lone young woman negotiating the streets of Rome or Florence or Madrid in the 1950s and '60s, the less said the better. But it was in the 1960s that women as a group, as activists rather than *flâneuses*, really took over public space for themselves, asserting their agency by marching for woman's right to control her own body, as our grandmothers had marched to gain the vote. And not coincidentally, as Luc Nadal points out in his recent Columbia dissertation, the term "public space" itself begins to be used with greater and greater frequency by architects, urban designers, historians, and theoreticians at just this time; says Nadal, "the rise of public space in the 1960s corresponded to a shift at the center of the discourse of planning and design."[3] Nadal connects this project with "the vast movement of liberatory culture and politics of the 1960s and early '70s." It is within this context of liberatory culture and politics that I would like to consider the once-invisible *flâneuse* in her most recent avatar: not merely as a visible presence in public space, but in her practice as a highly visible and original shaper and constructor of it, a woman with agency. For women today have become agents in relation to public space, in playing a major role in the construction of the most original public sculpture and urban monuments in existence today. And these monuments are of a new and different sort, unassimilable to those of the past, often centers of controversy. Some, of course, have called these "anti-monuments."

Rachel Whiteread, for example, recreated a condemned house on a bleak plot in London, turning the architecture inside out and creating a storm of reaction and public opinion. A temporary anti-monument, it was later destroyed amid equal controversy; it was a public issue, existing in a public space and fought over by public discourse. Her recent Holocaust memorial in Vienna, at the Judenplatz, also turns both subject and form inside out, forcing the viewer not only to contemplate the fate of the Jews, but to rethink the meaning of the monumental itself by memorializing it in the heart of Vienna, one of the major sites of their extermination (Figure 38). Jenny Holzer, too, using both words and tradi-

tional and untraditional materials, created scandals in Munich and also Leipzig with her provocative public intrusion into space. Her memorial to the poet Oskar Maria Graf in Munich exists as a functional café at that city's Literaturhaus (Figure 39). This is, to borrow the words of my student Leah Sweet, a conceptual memorial that refuses to present its subject through a likeness or a biographic account of his life and work. Rather, Graf is represented through excerpts of his writing, selected by Holzer and scattered through the café, and, interestingly enough, shorter excerpts appear on dishes, place mats and coasters, so that the bits of inscription appear only when you eat your dinner, emerging as the food is consumed – an ironic use of what one might call "the domestic abject mode" of memorialization.

Maya Lin is probably the foremost and best-known of these women inventors of new monuments with new meanings, and above all with new, untried ways

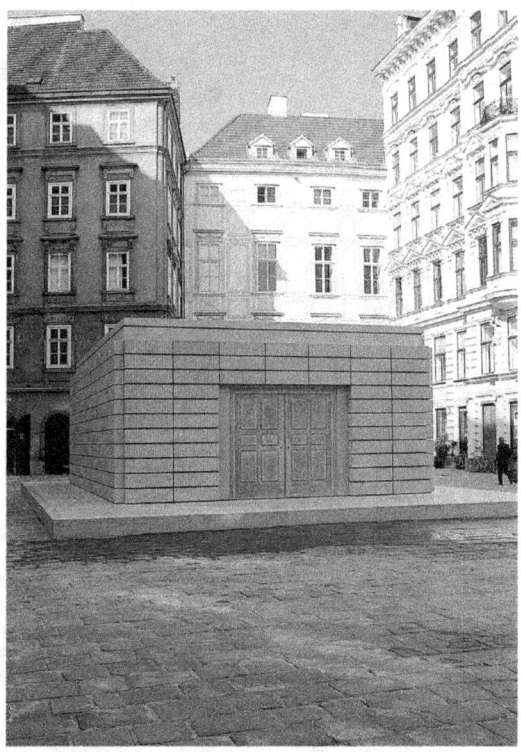

38 Rachel Whiteread, *Holocaust Memorial*, 2000, Judenplatz, Vienna

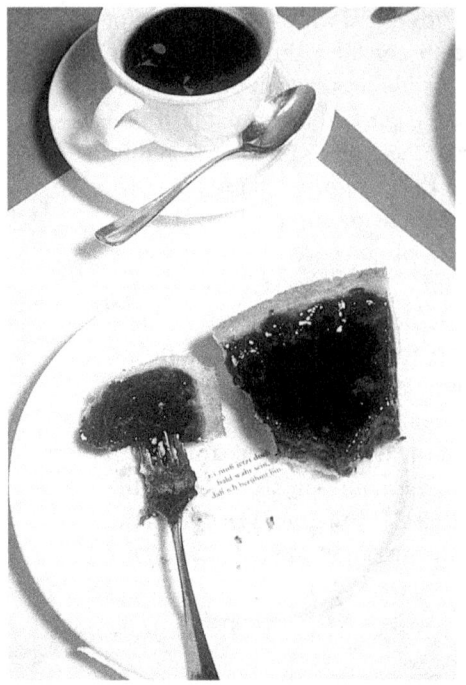

of conveying meaning and feeling in public places. Lin's own words best convey her unconventional intentions and her anti-monumental achievement in this most public of memorials, the Vietnam Memorial in Washington:

> I imagine taking a knife and cutting into the earth, opening it up, an initial violence and pain that in time would heal. The grass would grow back, but the initial cut would remain a pure flat surface in the earth, with a polished, mirrored surface. There was no need to embellish the design further. The people and their names would allow everyone to respond and remember.

Still another unconventional public memorial is Lin's *Women's Table*, a water table created in the heart of Yale's urban campus in 1993, commemorating with words, stone, and water the admission of women to Yale in 1969 (Figure 40). It is a strong but gentle monument, asserting women's increasing presence at Yale itself, but also, to use Maya Lin's words, "marking more generally the emergence of women in modern society."[4]

39 Jenny Holzer, *Oskar Maria Graf Memorial*, 1997, Literaturhaus München, Munich

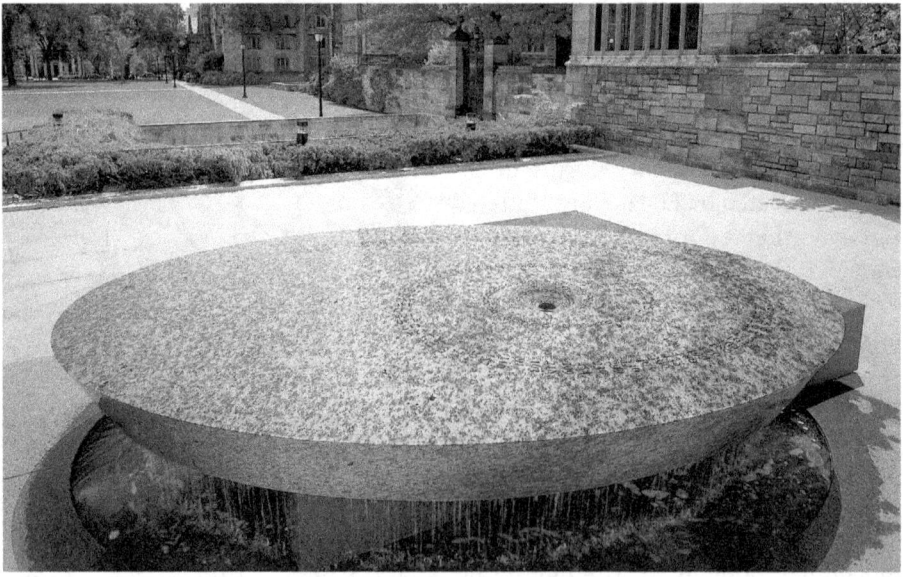

40 Maya Lin, *Women's Table*, 1993, Yale University, New Haven, Conn

Yet despite its assertive message, inscribed in facts and figures on the surface, the *Women's Table* is at one with its surroundings; despite the fact that it constitutes a critical intervention into public space, its effect vis-à-vis that space is very different from that of Richard Serra's *Tilted Arc* of 1981, in Federal Plaza. Lin's *Women's Table*, like the Vietnam Memorial, establishes a very different relationship to the environment and the meaning and function of the public monument than does Serra in his no less original and controversial *Tilted Arc*. I am not coming out for a feminine versus a masculine style of public memorial with this comparison, I am merely returning to the theme of this session and suggesting that woman's long history of a certain kind of engagement and relationship to public space has caused women to create and wish to construct a very different experience of that public space and the monuments which occupied it, than do their male counterparts.

Notes

1 Denis Rouart, *The Correspondence of Berthe Morisot*, intro. and ed. Tamar Garb and Kathleen Adler (London, 1986).

2 Deborah L. Parsons, *Streetwalking the Metropolis: Women, the City and Modernity* (Oxford: Oxford University Press, 2000), pp. 222–3.

3 Luc Nadal, "Discourses of urban public space, United State of America, 1960–65: An historical critique," Ph.D. diss., Columbia University, 2000, p. 12.

4 Quoted in Public Affairs Television, "Becoming American," interview with Maya Lin, available at www.pbs.org/becomingamerican/ap_pjourneys_transcript5_print.html (accessed April 2005).

Select bibliography

Adler, K. "The Suburban, the Modern, and 'une Dame de Passy.'" *Oxford Art Journal* 12, no. 1 (1989): 3–13.

Baudelaire, C. *The Painter of Modern Life and Other Essays*. Trans. and ed. J. Mayne. London: Phaidon Press, 1964.

Benjamin, W. *Charles Baudelaire: A Lyric Poet in the Era of High Capitalism*. London: New Left Books, 1973.

Benjamin, W. "Paris, Capital of the 19th Century." In *Reflections: Essays, Aphorisms, Autobiographical Writings*. Trans. E. Jephcott. New York: Schocken Books, 1986.

Benjamin, W. *The Arcades Project*. Trans. H. Eiland and K. McLaughlin. Cambridge, Mass.: Belknap Press of Harvard University Press, 1999.

Bowlby, R. *Just Looking: Consumer Culture in Dreiser, Gissing, and Zola*. New York: Methuen, 1985.

Breward, C. *The Hidden Consumer: Masculinites, Fashion, and City Life, 1860–1914*. Manchester and New York: Manchester University Press, 1999.

Bruno, G. *Streetwalking on a Ruined Map: Cultural Theory and the City Films of Elvira Notari*. Princeton, N.J.: Princeton University Press, 1993.

Buck-Morss, S. *The Dialectics of Seeing: Walter Benjamin and the Arcades Project*. Cambridge, Mass.: MIT Press, 1989.

Chang, T. "Collecting Asia: Théodore Duret's *Voyage en Asie* and Henri Cernuschi's Museum." *Oxford Art Journal* 25, no. 1 (March 2002): 17–34.

Chevalier, L. *Laboring Classes and Dangerous Classes*. Trans. F. Jellinek. Princeton, N.J.: Princeton University Press, 1973.

Choay, F. "Haussmann et le système des espaces verts parisiens." *Revue de l'art* 29 (1975): 83–99.

Clark, T. J. *The Painting of Modern Life: Paris in the Art of Manet and his Followers*. Princeton, N.J.: Princeton University Press, 1984.

Clayson, H. *Painted Love: Prostitution in French Art of the Impressionist Era*. New Haven and London: Yale University Press, 1991.

Cohen, M. "Panoramic Literature and the Invention of Everyday Genres." In *Cinema and the Invention of Modern Life*. Eds L. Charney and V. R. Schwartz. Berkeley: University of California Press, 1995.

Colette. *Claudine in Paris*. Trans. Antonia White. New York: Farrar, Straus, 1958.

Collins, B. R. *Twelve Views of Manet's Bar*. Princeton, N.J.: Princeton University Press, 1991.

Corbin, A. *Women for Hire: Prostitution and Sexuality in France After 1852*. Trans. A. Sheridan. Cambridge, Mass.: Harvard University Press, 1990.

Crossick, G. and S. Jaumain. *Cathedrals of Consumption: The European Department Store, 1850–1939*. Aldershot and Brookfield, Mass.: Ashgate, 1999.

Davidoff, L. and C. Hall. "The Architecture of Public and Private Life: English Middle-Class Society in a Provincial Town, 1780 to 1850." In *The Pursuit of Urban History*. Eds D. Fraser and A. Sutcliffe. London: Edward Arnold, 1983.

de Certeau, M. *The Practice of Everyday Life*. Trans. S. Rendall. Berkeley: University of California Press, 1984.

Deutsche, R. *Evictions: Art and Spatial Politics*. Cambridge, Mass. and London: The MIT Press, and Chicago: Graham Foundation for Advanced Studies in the Fine Arts, 1996.

Ferguson, P. Parkhurst. *Paris as Revolution: Writing the 19th-Century City*. Berkeley and London: University of California Press, 1994.

Foucault, M. "Of Other Spaces." *Diacritics* 16, no. 1 (1986): 22–27.

Friedberg, A. *Window Shopping: Cinema and the Postmodern*. Berkeley: University of California Press, 1993.

Garb, T. "Berthe Morisot and the Feminizing of Impressionism." In *Perspectives on Morisot*. Ed. T. J. Edelstein. New York: Hudson Hills Press, 1990.

Garb, T. "James Tissot's 'Parisienne' and the Making of the Modern Woman." In *Bodies of Modernity: Figure and Flesh in Fin-de-Siècle France*. London and New York: Thames and Hudson, 1998.

Gleber, A. *The Art of Taking a Walk: Flânerie, Literature, and Film in Weimar Culture*. Princeton, N.J.: Princeton University Press, 1999.

Herbert, R. L. *Impressionism: Art, Leisure, and Parisian Society*. New Haven and London: Yale University Press, 1988.

Iskin, R. E. "Selling, Seduction, and Soliciting the Eye: Manet's *Bar at the Folies-Bergère*." *Art Bulletin* 77, no. 1 (March 1995): 25–44.

Kerber, L. K. "Separate Spheres, Female Worlds, Woman's Place: The Rhetoric of Women's History." *Journal of American History* 75, no. 1 (June 1988): 9–39.

Kunzle, D. "*L'Illustration*, journal universel, premier magazine illustré en France, affirmation du pouvoir de la bourgeoisie." *Nouvelles de l'éstampe* 43 (January–February 1979): 8–19.

Le Men, S., L. Abélès, and N. Preiss-Basset. *Les Français peints par eux-mêmes*. Paris: Réunion des musées nationaux, 1993.

Lears, J. "Beyond Veblen: Rethinking Consumer Culture in America." In *Consuming Visions: Accumulation and Display of Goods in America, 1880–1920*. Ed. S. J. Bronner. New York and London: W. W. Norton, 1989.

Lesselier, C. "Employées de grands magasins à Paris (avant 1914)." *Le Movement social* 105 (October–December 1978): 109–126.

Lipton, E. *Looking into Degas: Uneasy Images of Women and Modern Life*. Berkeley and London: University of California Press, 1986.

Marcus, S. *Apartment Stories: City and Home in 19th-Century Paris and London*. Berkeley and London: University of California Press, 1999.

Massey Schenker, H. "Parks and Politics During the Second Empire in Paris." *Landscape Journal* 14, no. 2 (Fall 1995): 201–219.

Merriman, J. M. *The Margins of City Life: Explorations on the French Urban Frontier, 1815–1851*. New York and Oxford: Oxford University Press, 1991.

Miller, M. B. *The Bon Marché: Bourgeois Culture and the Department Store, 1869–1920*. Princeton, N.J.: Princeton University Press, 1981.

Moffett, C. S. *The New Painting: Impressionism 1874–1886*. San Francisco: The Fine Arts Museum, 1986.

Nead, L. *Victorian Babylon: People, Streets and Images in Nineteenth-Century London*. New Haven and London: Yale University Press, 2000.

Nord, D. E. "The Urban Peripatetic: Spectator, Streetwalker, Woman Writer." *19th-Century Literature* 46, no. 3 (1991): 351–375.

Nord, D. E. *Walking the Victorian Streets: Women, Representation, and the City*. Ithaca, N.Y.: Cornell University Press, 1995.

Parsons, D. *Streetwalking the Metropolis: Women, the City, and Modernity*. Oxford and New York: Oxford University Press, 2000.

Pollock, G. "Modernity and the Spaces of Femininity." In *Vision and Difference: Femininity, Feminism and the Histories of Art*. London and New York: Routledge, 1988.

Pollock, G. *Mary Cassatt: Painter of Modern Women*. London: Thames and Hudson, 1998.

Pollock, G. and C. Arscott (with J. Wolff). "The Partial View: The Visual Representation of the Early 19th-Century Industrial City." In *The Culture of Capital: Art, Power and the Nineteenth-Century Middle Class*. Eds J. Wolff and J. Seed. Manchester: Manchester University Press, 1988.

Poster, M. "Culture and History: The Cases of Leisure, Art, and Technology." *French Historical Studies* 18, no. 1 (Spring 1993): 131–135.

Rappaport, E. D. *Shopping for Pleasure: Women in the Making of London's West End*. Princeton, N.J.: Princeton University Press, 2000.

Sennett, R. *The Fall of Public Man*. New York and London: W. W. Norton, 1976.

Sheon, A. "Parisian Social Statistics: Gavarni, *Le Diable à Paris*, and Early Realism." *Art Journal* 44, no.2 (Summer 1984): 139–148.

Sieburth, R. "Une ideologie du lisible: le phénomène des 'Physiologies'." *Romantisme: revue du dix-neuvième siècle* 15, no. 47 (1985): 39–60.

Simmel, G. "The Stranger." In *The Sociology of Georg Simmel*. Ed. and trans. K. H. Wolff. New York: Free Press, 1950.

Simon, M. *Mode et peinture: le Second Empire et l'Impressionisme*. Paris: Hazan, 1995.

Tagg, J. "The Discontinuous City: Picturing and the Discursive Field." In *Grounds of Dispute: Art History, Cultural Politics and the Discursive Field*. Minneapolis: University of Minnesota Press, 1992.

Tester, K., ed. *The Flâneur*. London: Routledge, 1994.

Tiersten, L. *Marianne in the Market: Envisioning Consumer Society in Fin-de-Siècle France*. Berkeley and Los Angeles: University of California Press, 2001.

Van Zanten, D. *Building Paris: Architectural Institutions and the Tranformation of the French Capital, 1830–1870*. Cambridge: Cambridge University Press, 1994.

Veblen, T. *The Theory of the Leisure Class: An Economic Study in the Evolution of Institutions*. New York and London: The Macmillan Company, 1899.

Walkowitz, J. *City of Dreadful Delight: Narratives of Sexual Danger in Late Victorian London*. Chicago: University of Chicago Press, 1992.

Weschler, J. *A Human Comedy: Physiognomy and Caricature in 19th-Century Paris*. London: Thames and Hudson, 1982.

Williams, R. *Dream Worlds: Mass Consumption in Late 19th-Century France*. Berkeley and Los Angeles: University of California Press, 1982.

Williamson, J. *Decoding Advertisements: Ideology and Meaning in Advertising*. London: Marion Boyards, 1978.

Wilson, E. *The Sphinx in the City: Urban Life, the Control of Disorder, and Women*. Berkeley and Los Angeles: University of California Press, 1991.

Wolff, J. "The Culture of Separate Spheres: The Role of Culture in 19th-Century Public and Private Life." In *The Culture of Capital: Art, Power and the Nineteenth-Century Middle Class*. Eds J. Wolff and J. Seed. Manchester: Manchester University Press, 1988.

Wolff, J. "The Invisible *Flâneuse*: Women and the Literature of Modernity." *Theory, Culture & Society*, 2, no. 3 (1985): 37–46.

Zola, E. *The Ladies' Paradise*. Intro. and trans. Kristin Ross. Berkeley and London: University of California Press, 1992.

Index

Note: Page numbers in *italics* refer to illustrations in the text.

EU authorised representative for GPSR:
Easy Access System Europe, Mustamäe tee 50,
10621 Tallinn, Estonia
gpsr.requests@easproject.com

www.ingramcontent.com/pod-product-compliance
Lightning Source LLC
Chambersburg PA
CBHW080910170526
45158CB00008B/2065